CRUSADE CHARTERS
1138–1270

Medieval and Renaissance Texts and Studies

Volume 197

CRUSADE CHARTERS
1138–1270

Corliss Konwiser Slack

with English translations by
Hugh Bernard Feiss

Arizona Center for Medieval and Renaissance Studies
Tempe, Arizona
2001

*The publication of this volume has been supported by
a grant from Whitworth College, Washington.*

© Copyright 2001
Arizona Board of Regents for Arizona State University

Library of Congress Cataloging-in-Publication Data

Crusade charters, 1138–1270 / edited and translated by Corliss Konwiser Slack.
    p. cm. — (Medieval & Renaissance Texts & Studies ; v. 197)
Introd. in English; the charters are in Latin, with English translations.
Includes bibliographical references and index.
ISBN 0-86698-239-6 (alk. paper)
    1. Crusades—Sources. 2. Charters. I. Slack, Corliss Konwiser, 1955– II. Medieval & Renaissance Texts & Studies (Series) ; v. 197.
D151.C77 2000
909.07—dc21   99-055554

∞
This book is made to last.
It is set in Garamond Antiqua typeface,
smythe-sewn and printed on acid-free paper
to library specifications.

Printed in the United States of America

TABLE OF CONTENTS

Acknowledgements   vii

Abbreviations   viii

INTRODUCTION

On this Edition   ix
Background Information   xi
The Crusades   xii
Charters   xiii
Church Reform and Crusade Idealism   xvi
The Coucys: Thomas de Marle   xviii
The Coucys and Church Reform   xix
Financial Arrangements as a Key to Motivation   xxix

CHARTERS

1.	1138, Enguerran II de Coucy	2
2.	1142, Radulph Canis	12
3.	1146, Thierry, Count of Flanders	18
4.	1147, Robert I de Boves	24
5.	1147/1151, Alelmus de Flichecourt	34
6.	1147, Burchard de Guise	42
7.	1157, Thierry, Count of Flanders	48
8.	1164, King Louis VII of France	54
9.	1168, Raoul I de Coucy	60
10.	1178, Raoul I de Coucy	66
11.	c.1178, Ives de Nesles, Count of Soissons	72
12.	1178, Henry, Count of Troyes	78
13.	1180, Radulph de Duri	84
14.	1184, Osto de Trazegnies, with the confirmation document of 1188	88

15.	1188, Simon de Thiméon, and confirmation document	100
16.	1189, Three Crusade Charters for Basse-Fontaine	106
17.	1190, Raoul I de Coucy	116
18.	1190, Gerard, chancellor of Flanders	122
19.	1193, Lambert, bishop of Thérouanne	126
20.	1201, Viard de Prés	132
21.	1202, Baldwin, Count of Flanders	136
22.	1202, Simon de Malesnes	140
23.	1204, Thomas, soldier of Leez	144
24.	1209, Guy de Arblincourt	148
25.	1210, Simon de Chavigny	152
26.	1212, Gervase, Abbot of Prémontré	156
27.	1216, Godescalc de Morialmé	168
28.	1218, Gerard, merchant of Veurne	178
29.	1219, Guy de Monceau	184
30.	1232, Jean de Verneuil	188
31.	1270, Eustace de Trazegnies	194

Appendix: Charter Documents 199

Bibliography 207

Index 227

ACKNOWLEDGEMENTS

I am in debt to a great many people, first to my family, and then to Whitworth College, the Pew trust, and the Graves Foundation, who supported this work in various ways, not least financially. The idea for the collection of the charters came from the late Karl Leyser. Much of the energy for pushing this project forward came from Douglas Sugano. I am grateful to both Robert Patterson and Rudolf Hiestand for much-needed guidance on the use and interpretation of charters. Neither is in any way responsible for any errors here.

My greatest debt is to Hugh Bernard Feiss, who generously translated those portions of the charters I was able to transcribe. He helped a great deal in correcting my Latin and completing the transcriptions. He was generous with his advice, and he, also, should be absolved of all blame. Jean Pond did much of the original proof-reading. Without their help this book would never have been completed. I am grateful to Laura Gross, associate editor at the Arizona Center for Medieval and Renaissance Studies, for proof-reading and good advice, and to Dr. Leslie S. B. MacCoull, for the benefit of her translations, proofing, and editorial suggestions.

ABBREVIATIONS

BN — Bibliothèque nationale, Paris

CERP — Centre d'études et de recherches Prémontrées (director of publication: Martine Plouvier), 3 rue Abélard, F-02000 Laon. *Actes officiels* are published annually.

DHGE — *Dictionnaire d'histoire et de géographie ecclésiastique.* Ed. A. Baudrillart et al. Vols. 1– . Paris, 1912– .

GC — *Gallia Christiana*, ed. Congregation of St. Maur. 16 vols. Paris, 1751; repr., Farnborough, Hants, 1970. I have used this primarily as a source of printed charters.

Migne, *PL* — J. P. Migne, *Patrologiae cursus completus. Series Latina.* Paris, 1844–1865.

MGH SS — *Monumenta Germaniae Historica, Scriptores*, edited by George Henry Pertz. 30 vols. Hanover, 1826–1896; repr. Stuttgart, 1963–1965.

RHC — *Recueil des historiens des croisades*, ed. Académie des Inscriptions et Belles Lettres. 15 vols. Paris, 1841–1906.

RHGF — *Recueil des Historiens des Gaules et de la France*, ed. M. Bouquet et al. 24 vols. Paris, 1737–1904.

La vita comune — Essays published in two vols. under the title *La vita comune del Clero nei secoli Xe–XIIe*, in *Miscellanea del Centro di Studi Medioevali* 3 (1962).

INTRODUCTION

ON THIS EDITION

The common thread of this charter collection is imminent departure on crusade. The reader will notice that twenty-four of the thirty-one charters record gifts to Premonstratensian abbeys. The first houses of this order were founded after 1121 in northern France, and so none of the charters deals with the First Crusade (1095). The donors form a loose geographic unit: they are "new men," from recently formed lordships in what was then a sort of no-man's land between the areas effectively controlled by the kings of France and by the counts of Flanders. Close reading of the charters and notes will reveal a network of family and political connections among the donors. There are some commoners and some leaders of expeditions, but the men represented are mostly members of the lower nobility, many of whose families grew in wealth and status during the twelfth century. It is my contention that the crusades helped them to achieve financial and political success.

Historians attribute the crusade movement to a wide variety of causes, from population surplus to the militarization of Europe. In the last twenty years or so it has become a common-place to discuss crusade motivation in the context of religious conviction, and particularly to discuss it in terms of the impact of the ideals of the apostolic life movement.[1] Originally these charters were collected in an attempt to prove that the preaching of the Premonstratensian order in particular motivated many people to take crusade vows out of religious conviction. St. Norbert of Xanten, who founded the order, was an itinerant preacher, and his original foundation became popular immediately. Between 1121 and 1150 more than a hundred

---

[1] Marcus Bull, "Origins," in *The Oxford Illustrated History of the Crusades* (Oxford, 1995), 23, ed. Jonathan Riley-Smith, sums up many recent studies on this issue; François Petit, *La Spiritualité des Prémontrés aux XIIe et XIIIe siècles* (Paris, 1947) puts the case for the influence of the Premonstratensians in particular. Both offer bibliography. For a different view see C. J. Tyerman, "Were there any Crusades in the Twelfth Century?," *English Historical Review* 110 (1995): 553-77.

houses of Premonstratensian canons were founded all over Europe. One of the primary goals of the order was the revival of preaching, and its canons were chosen by the papacy to help promote the crusades.[2] It made sense that their message of imitation of the apostles would lead to the kind of interest in the Holy Land that the crusades illustrate, and that their insistence on the penitential value of poverty would fit with the sacrifice required in undertaking and paying for a crusade. These expeditions could take from one to three years, and the charters left by people preparing for them read like wills. Crusaders took very seriously the possibility that they would die in Palestine. Only piety, perhaps inspired by the preachers of apostolic poverty, would explain vows that resulted in exile from home and family, with the doubtful outcome of liberating the Holy Land or even collecting a material reward as a consequence of the journey. This collection is only a beginning of what should be a lengthy investigation of charter evidence for various orders, but its scope represents an attempt to begin to collect information about the lay response to preaching by the first Norbertines.

What this small collection of charters suggests is that piety is too simple an explanation. Of course many other factors came into play—piety alone has never been suggested as a complete explanation for why people went on crusade. But in this investigation of what sort of religious ideas inspired crusade vows, the ideas discovered are not exactly religious. The reader will find that these crusaders had various reasons for going, but that the general tenor of their vows, although expressed in the context of their relationship to the church and clearly with the intention of displaying piety, is not devotion. It is rather a sort of pious practicality: the need to placate the local church after attacking its property, for instance, or the desire to acquire the prestige of having joined a royal expedition to Jerusalem. Religious devotion is demonstrated in some of the stories attached to the charters, but it is expressed, for example, by an individual honoring the church founded by his family, or establishing his own reputation by imitating an ancestor who went on crusade. In short, these crusaders seem to have been motivated not by a sudden outburst of religious fervor, which might be explained by their response to a new religious order, but by the more prosaic concerns common to medieval people. In the case of these particular charters, there is a web of family relationships that does more to explain why individuals went than any ideology.[3]

Note on this edition: This collection differs from most others in that a

---

[2] See the notes to charter 26, below, for Premonstratensians as crusade procurators.

[3] On the role of the family connections in crusade motivation, see Jonathan Riley-Smith, *The First Crusaders, 1095-1131* (Cambridge, 1997).

range of documents from various sources has been brought together to illuminate a topic. Given the eclectic nature of the collection, combined with the effort to provide more infomration about the families mentioned than is usual in editions of charters, the emphasis is on the translations and notes rather than on the issues of Latin style and other topics normally central to the editor's task. The most annoying omissions for experts will be connected to the technicalities of the presentation of the documents from various sources, the interpretation of dates and calendar information, specialized Latin vocabulary, and spelling. Names are given in Latin, French, or English, according to which spelling was most useful in researching the subject. It is expected that experts on documents will want to return to the originals, whether printed or manuscript. Some photographs of original manuscripts have been included to make that task easier. An additional challenge was presented by indexing the book, which is essentially a list of names and places organized according to region and chronology. No attempt has been made to reorganize all of the information alphabetically. The alphabetical index offers only the most prominent families and places.

The intent of this book is to make these thirty charters available to teachers and researchers to use as they wish, in the hope that a conversation may be opened about the meaning of the evidence. In that spirit the Latin texts are presented as they appear in the editions used and photographs of the manuscripts are provided. Names of persons and places have not been translated into any consistent form, but are presented as they are found in the reference works appropriate to each family. The bibliography is not meant to be comprehensive, but it includes all the references used in preparing this edition. However, basic sources with extensive bibliographies have been included for each major topic. Notes have been kept to a minimum, but the first on each topic refers to a work where bibliography may be found.

The main issues of concern to the scholar are laid out briefly above, but non-specialists using the text may want basic information on the crusades, on the Premonstratensians, on the charters themselves, or on the families represented by the documents. Information on these topics is offered below in labeled sections, with an emphasis on bibliography in English available in the United States. To assist scholars who may want to use the charters for teaching, English translations of the documents have been provided.

BACKGROUND INFORMATION

The slight connections among the people represented by these charters make a sketchy narrative. The story takes place largely in northern France, with

excursions to the south, to eastern Europe, and to the Holy Land. The characters are mostly members of the lower nobility of France and of Flanders, whose stated purpose is the service of Christ. What that kind of statement means is defined partially by contemporary church teaching, and partly by the situations in which the individual crusaders found themselves.

THE CRUSADES

In 1095 Pope Urban II preached a sermon during a church council held in the city of Clermont, France. There was a large enough audience so that he spoke in a field, rather than in the cathedral. The people listening were not only clergy, but also lay persons who had come either to participate in the council or simply to see and hear the pope. Every bishop, abbess, and nobleman was attended by canons, nuns, or vassals, so that a good cross-section of the upper levels of medieval society was represented.[4] There are several versions extant of what the pope said, but they agree on some essentials. He spoke of the Muslims as enemies of Christ who had conquered and desecrated Jerusalem and were persecuting Christians there. He called on his audience, particularly the knights, to go to the rescue. In this context he mentioned their continual fighting among themselves and suggested war against Muslims as a more suitable outlet for their valor. He promised them plunder, but more importantly the gratitude of Christ and the church, which they would receive as forgiveness for their sins. He reminded them that even if they died on the journey, they would enjoy all the spiritual benefits of martyrs.

The pope got a far greater response to this sermon than he expected. The chief difficulty of the First Crusade was restraining unsuitable people from going. The poor, the sick, all non-combatants who would slow down an army, were discouraged from setting out. In spite of these attempts, thousands of people died during the next two years on the way to Jerusalem. No subsequent crusade matched the enthusiasm of 1095/6, and none was as successful. However, Europeans continued to go on crusade for over a hundred years. The question is, why? What caused the excitement, what motivated an attack on a sovereign people who lived a year's journey from France, and whose activities were therefore obviously not a threat to Europe in 1095? The answer suggested by Pope Urban's speech is religious

---

[4] The most recent general discussion of the crusades, which includes an article on historiography and a bibliography, is Jonathan Riley-Smith, ed., *The Oxford Illustrated History of the Crusades* (Oxford and New York, 1995). Quite a bit has been written about Urban's sermon; to start, see Edward Peters, ed., *The First Crusade*, 2nd ed. (Philadelphia, 1998); and H. E. J. Cowdrey, "The Papacy and the Origins of Crusading," *Medieval History* 1 (1991): 48–60.

enthusiasm, yet these expeditions, accompanied as they were by the massacres of Jews in 1096, and of the non-combatants in the conquered cities, are morally repugnant to a modern sensibility. In what context could Christian belief lend itself to this kind of violence?[5]

The issue of human motivation is one of endless complexity, and no historian is satisfied with a single answer to this kind of question. Much has been written about why people took crusade vows, but two main threads of interpretation go back to two main points in Urban's sermon: the way the medieval church defined service to Christ, and what the individual crusader understood could be gained from that service.[6] Those two issues bring together at least two fields of study, each with huge literatures and numerous fascinating offshoots. The first is the church reform movement of the eleventh and twelfth centuries, which shaped the spiritual idealism behind Urban's sermon. The second is the medieval context, the everyday realities which shaped both Urban's ideas and the lives of the people who listened to him, the things they took for granted that made crusading attractive to them. Part of that context was the military structure built into medieval society, with its own ideology and the family relationships which underlay it.[7]

CHARTERS

Individuals had various reasons for undertaking a crusade, so even at the time it was difficult for chroniclers to categorize the movement as a whole.[8] One method of getting close to individual motivation is charter evidence. The chronicles, letters, and other documents in print were written by, for, and largely about the medieval elite. These leaders of the movement had various goals for their patronage or production of chronicles, which make their accounts valuable, but of limited use for the analy-

---

[5] See Penny J. Cole, "Christians, Muslims, and the 'Liberation' of the Holy Land," *Catholic Historical Review* 84 (1998): 1–10, for violence as religious activity.

[6] Again, the references in note 1 will be helpful for recent thoughts and bibliography, along with the more detailed: K. M. Setton, gen. ed., *A History of the Crusades*, 2nd ed., 6 vols. (Madison, Wis., 1969–1989); and H. E. Mayer, *The Crusades*, 2nd ed., translated by J. Gillingham (Oxford, 1988).

[7] For recent works on chivalry and culture see Maurice Keen, *Nobles, Knights and Men-at-Arms in the Middle Ages* (London and Rio Grande, Ohio, 1996); and on the importance of households/retinues in forming military contingents, Michael Prestwich, *Armies and Warfare in the Middle Ages. The English Experience* (New Haven, 1996).

[8] For two contemporary opinions, see William of Tyre, *Chronique*, ed. R. B. C. Huygens, 2 vols. (Turnhout, 1986), 1: 182–83; Geoffroy de Villehardouin, *The Conquest of Constantinople*, trans. M. R. B. Shaw (London and New York, 1963): 29.

sis of the motivation of the majority of people who followed them. A partial response to this gap in the evidence is the use of charters.

The charters collected here are documents issued by crusaders just before departure from northern France between 1138 and 1270. Many of them read like wills: the knight details what should be done with his property if he does not return. Others record gifts made to religious institutions in order to have prayers said for the success of the expedition. Most were written not by the crusader, but by a monk from a local monastery, since lay people were typically either illiterate, or at least unable to write the Latin considered appropriate for an official document. Charters were originally important more as records of an event than as legal contracts, more like a snapshot of a wedding than like the marriage license. Sometimes they record a solemn assembly before an altar, witnessed by a crowd of people related to the crusader and/or belonging to the religious institution. The witnesses' names are written by the scribe, and the participants may be represented by an "X" they have drawn at the bottom. The most important person present may signify his approval and authority by having his wax seal attached to the animal skin or parchment, as a guarantee of the charter's authenticity, since it could be drawn up after the event.[9]

Whereas chronicles are written by an eyewitness or an historian looking back, sometimes over many years, charters are often immediate. They are usually written at or soon after the event they record. A chronicle is an expensive undertaking, financed by an important person, and often reflecting that person's or community's response to the events described. Charters reflect the same kinds of bias on the part of the people who produce them, but because they are so brief there is much less at stake.[10] A cleric at the castle of a less important noble, or the canon of a

---

[9] The great works on charter interpretation are in French. Some are listed in the bibliography, among them Giry's manual, and Avril's article on spirituality expressed in the preambles of charters. Good starting places in English would be Giles Constable, "Medieval Charters as a Source for the History of the Crusades," in *Crusade and Settlement*, ed. Peter Edbury (Cardiff, 1985), 73–89; and Leonard E. Boyle, *Medieval Latin Palaeography: A Bibliographical Introduction* (Toronto, 1984).

[10] The question of interpreting charter collections from religious houses or families is complex. Each institution had a purpose in gathering and presenting the material, and the analysis of that record can be the work of many years. Recent works in this field are: Amy G. Remensnyder, *Remembering Kings Past: Monastic Foundation Legends in Medieval Southern France* (London and Ithaca, N.Y., 1995); Patrick J. Geary, *Living With the Dead in the Middle Ages* (Ithaca, 1994); Constance Brittain Bouchard, *Holy Entrepreneurs. Cistercians, Knights, and Economic Exchange in Twelfth-Century Burgundy* (London and Ithaca, 1991); Ghislain Brunel, "Les activités économiques des Prémontrées en Soissonnais aux XIIe et XIIIe siècles: politique original ou adaptation au milieu?" *Actes officiels du centre d'études et de recherches prémontrées* (Amiens, 1989): 67–79; Constance Hoffman Berman, *Medieval Agri-*

small religious establishment produces a page, witnessed by the clergy and family members who are most concerned with the arrangements recorded in the document. Two sets of interests are typically recorded, instead of just the chronicler's: those of the donor and those of his heirs or other recipients. Sometimes the two parties are resolving a quarrel, and the charter records their settlement. Both the immediacy of the document and the varied interests represented bring the events sharply into focus, and the opportunity to collect many charters of the same type (which is obviously not an option with chronicles) gives a more detailed and complex picture of the topic than any chronicle can. Researchers may return to the same charters repeatedly, each time posing different questions, and gleaning different kinds of information. For instance, many charters record the names of the donor's family, and so may be used to create genealogies. A list of the properties disposed of by the donor can be used to establish the size and importance of the family's land-holdings. The charters in this collection lend themselves to all kinds of research, but for a study of crusade motivation, the two main issues are the religious institution chosen by the crusader, and the financial arrangements which made the expedition possible.

The charters here deal with crusades to the Holy Land, or in two cases to southern France. They were chosen because each mentions the crusade specifically, so that there is at least a phrase about the expedition to look at as a clue to the individual's motivation. Again, their interpretation goes back to the two themes of Pope Urban's speech. Since the document is penned by a member of a religious community, not the crusader, the wording reflects the church's teaching about the crusades. In most of the charters in this collection the brief phrase expressing motivation refers specifically to penitence, which was certainly one of the themes preached by the church. However, there are at least two ways in which the charter also reveals something about the lay response to that teaching. The crusader selected a particular church over another as a source of prayers or as a recipient of his gift, and recorded the financial arrangement in the document. Presumably those choices reflect enthusiasm for that religious community and show whether the crusade expedition represented a sacrifice or an advantage to the crusader's family. In the case of most of the charters collected here, an investigation into the relationship between the crusader and the church chosen reveals a quarrel over land which is being resolved by an exchange of property and a crusade vow.[11]

---

culture, the Southern French Countryside, and the Early Cistercians: a Study of Forty-three Monasteries (Philadelphia, 1986).
[11] Marcus Bull, *Knightly Piety and the Lay Response to the First Crusade: The Limousin*

CHURCH REFORM AND CRUSADE IDEALISM

All of the charters here mention a crusade. Beyond that, all of them benefit a particular kind of religious community: houses of what were known as "Augustinian" or "regular" canons. This is significant because these canons were a new development in the church from about 1050. Crusaders were donating money to a new group of clerics; one explanation for that might be that these new orders of canons were particularly effective crusade preachers.

Most of the families of the crusaders represented had previously supported houses of Benedictine monks. In some cases the family had founded the Benedictine monastery, continued to donate land to it, and relied on the monks for a number of services, including burial of family members at the abbey. The most numerous and familiar monastic orders for men and women used the rule of St. Benedict of Nursia, written in the sixth century, and offering guidance on communal life. Variations on the rule advised members of the monastic community on daily schedules for prayer, manual labor, meals, and so on. These communities were valuable to medieval people as institutions where prayers would be offered for individuals and families, and where the liturgy was celebrated regularly. Monasteries varied in their service to the outside world, but offered such services as schools, care for the sick, alms and/or food for the poor, lodging for travelers, and burial in the monastic church. They were the "regular" church, because they lived by a rule (*regula*). In some cases they replaced or competed with what was called the "secular" church: the local bishop operating out of his cathedral and directing the activities of the parish priests. Members of the secular church most often were ordained, but they did not live in a community guided by the Benedictine or any other rule of monastic life.[12] Typically they had individual incomes and houses. In the 1050s, there was

---

and Gascony, *c.970–c.1130* (Oxford, 1993) offers a definitive statement on medieval piety and crusade motivation based on a detailed study of a particular area. It is not my purpose to use thirty-one charters to challenge that view. Rather, I would like to suggest a slightly different interpretation and to continue a conversation on those topics after a larger body of charters has been investigated.

[12] The literature on the Benedictines is vast and intimately connected with the rise of medieval European civilization. Perhaps the best place to begin for general information and bibliography on many topics including church organization and reform is Brian Tierney and Sidney Painter, *Western Europe in the Middle Ages, 300–1475*, 5th ed. (New York, 1992). A wonderful short volume on church reform (unfortunately out of print) is Brenda Bolton, *The Medieval Reformation* (London, 1983). For the Augustinian rule start with the article on Augustine of Hippo in the *Dictionary of the Middle Ages*, ed. Joseph Strayer, 13 vols. (New York, 1982-1989); George Lawless, *Augustine of Hippo and His Monastic Rule* (Oxford, 1987); T. J. Van Bavel and R. Canning, ed., trans., *The Rule of St. Augustine* (London, 1984). On canons, see the articles listed in the bibliography under Charles Dereine.

a movement within the church to "reform" the secular church by requiring that its members live in communities, according to a rule. The reform particularly addressed cathedral canons, who were responsible for the episcopal functions in terms of both liturgy and administration. Houses of canons independent of cathedrals were also affected. Since the function of canons was supposed to differ from that of monks, the Benedictine rule did not seem appropriate. The rule most often chosen instead by reformers was called the Augustinian rule, since it was supposedly written by St. Augustine of Hippo (354–430). The crusade charters in this collection show knights beginning to support the reform movement by making donations to these reformed or "regular" canons, who followed the Augustinian rule, rather than to the Benedictine monks.[13]

There are any number of reasons why a departing crusader should choose to make a donation to a house of canons. The first thing to remember is that these gifts were not isolated acts of charity. A gift to a religious community initiated a lasting relationship between the donor's family and the canons.[14] On one side the lay donor offered economic support and sometimes military protection, while on the other the monks or canons offered continued prayer for the family. Thus the family received a sort of spiritual benefit or protection in return for gifts of land or income. There could be more concrete benefits offered by the abbey: it might be that members of the family would enter the religious house to be educated and then to make their careers in the order, or that the connection to a famous religious house would enhance the prestige of the family.

These particular charters show, in almost every case, that an original donation which had opened a relationship between a "new" lordship and a local religious house later was contested by an heir. After a quarrel and test of strength with the house, whose claim was often upheld by the bishop, the situation was resolved by a written agreement, sometimes simply restoring the original gift, but usually adding to it in the church's favor. The lay disputant sealed the arrangement with a crusade vow, expressing contrition for his attack on the church. Perhaps the best way to see the importance of these relationships is to look at a family such as the Coucys, famous both for crusading and also as the founders of a successful

---

[13] Again, the literature on the church in the middle ages and the reform movement is vast. See the bibliography under Caroline Walker Bynum, Giles Constable, Uta-Renate Blumenthal, Colin Morris, and E. D. Hehl.

[14] Lay patronage of religious institutions is another large topic. Two suggestions for recent works which offer an overview and bibliography: Rosemary Morris, *Monks and Laymen in Byzantium, 843–1118* (Cambridge and New York, 1995) lays out the basics and makes comparisons to the west; Gerd Tellenbach, *The Church in Western Europe from the Tenth to the Early Twelfth Century*, trans. Timothy Reuter (Cambridge, 1993) does the same for Europe, especially in chapters four and seven.

Augustinian community. The charters in this collection were issued by members of the Coucy family, their vassals, neighbors and rivals, and most benefit the canons of Prémontré who used the Augustinian rule.[15]

THE COUCYS: THOMAS DE MARLE

The first Coucys were ferocious brigands of unknown origin who began to terrorize northern France in the late 900s. Originally the success of the family was based on land acquisition by force or by shrewd marital alliance. Their first holding seems to have been a fief granted to them by the archbishop of Reims. In theory the archbishop held land from the king of France, as an agent of the church, and knights like the Coucys in turn held pieces of the church land in return for their military service. They were vassals of the archbishop, bound to support him in war at his call, or to surrender their fief if they failed to obey him. The castle at Coucy was said to have been built by the archbishop as a base from which to defend his territory about eighty miles north of Paris, along the Oise River. Only the ruins of the castle remain, but it is still an impressive sight, perched on a hilltop and undergirded with caves once used for storage and defense. It was one of the largest castles in Europe after its reconstruction in the early 1200s, and an important tourist destination until 1918, when it was used and then destroyed by the Germans. In the 1050s only the beginnings of this great fortification had been built, and the castle stood in a largely uncultivated area bounded by the cathedral cities of Laon, Soissons, and Amiens. At about this time the Coucys broke with their overlord and began to use the castle as a base from which to attack local churches and lords and seize land. The story of the Coucys has been retold frequently, but nothing matches the original medieval accounts, one by Suger, abbot of St.-Denis near Paris, and the other by Abbot Guibert of Nogent. St.-Denis was a royal abbey, and Suger was a close associate of King Louis VI (1108–1137). He recounts the stories of several royal expeditions made to punish the Coucys for their attacks on churches, and records Thomas de Marle's attempt to ambush the king. Thomas was lord of Coucy, and the famous description of his activities is Guibert's. Nogent was the Coucy family's own foundation, a Benedictine house in the village below the

---

[15] In the first chapter of *A Distant Mirror* (New York, 1978), Barbara Tuchman offers a brief history of the Coucy family, with a wonderful description of their now-ruined castle. Bibliography for the family can be found under charter 1 (Enguerran II de Coucy, 1138), including Dominique Barthélemy's study of the lordship. I have accepted Barthélemy's view of Thomas rather than the one expressed by Marcus Bull in "Origins," n. 1, above. For Prémontré the recent comprehensive bibliography is Bernard Ardura, *Abbayes, prieurés et monastères de l'ordre de Prémontré*... (Nancy, 1993).

castle fortifications. Its abbot reveled in descriptions of Thomas's brutality, and immortalized him for cruelty "unheard of in our times."[16] Thomas was also one of the great heroes of the First Crusade and the founder of one of the most important Augustinian abbeys of the twelfth century. It is tempting to credit Thomas's crusade vow and his foundation gifts to the power of the preaching of the canons at Prémontré. He left no charter behind, but his successors continued to support both the Augustinian canons and the crusade movement. So here is a place to start looking at crusade motivation to see lay response to the church's teaching. At first sight it did seem that Thomas was one of the quarrelsome knights Pope Urban mentioned, who took his enthusiasm for battle to Palestine and eventually was won over as a supporter of the church reform.

The kings of France could not control Thomas and his descendants, much less oust them from their stronghold. Both Paris and Reims were too far away to lend regular assistance to the local church. The closest authority was the bishop in Laon, only fifteen miles from Coucy. Laon had been the site of a cathedral, the center of an episcopal diocese since 500, and through the twelfth century was one of the most important cities of France. A famous school developed there over the course of the Middle Ages, based at the cathedral, which also became a pilgrimage center and hospice. The medieval portions of the city have been largely destroyed, but the site itself continues to inspire awe. This region of northern France, called Picardy, is mostly flat, so that the hill on which Coucy stands, for instance, easily commands the countryside. The cathedral and city of Laon are 330 feet above the surrounding plain. The story of the building of the cathedral focuses on the difficulty of getting stone up to the plateau, and the life-size stone oxen which decorate the towers commemorate a miraculous pair of animals who made the construction possible.

THE COUCYS AND CHURCH REFORM

The bishop who built the cathedral also became responsible for dealing with Thomas. He was Barthélemy de Joux, who was in office between 1113 and 1151.[17] Barthélemy was very well-connected, related to estab-

---

[16] Suger, *The Deeds of Louis the Fat*, translated with introduction and notes by Richard Cusimano and John Moorhead (Washington, D.C., 1992); *Self and Society in Medieval France, the Memoirs of Abbot Guibert of Nogent*, ed. with an introduction by John F. Benton (Toronto, 1984).

[17] All of the sources on Barthélemy are in French or Latin. Since he is credited with being one of the principal founders of Prémontré, all accounts of the origins of the order mention him, but see especially the bibliography under Ardura, Canivez, Kaiser, Labrusse, Martinet, Max. Melleville, *Notice historique sur ... Laon*, and Wyss. The last deals with Premonstratensian houses in Switzerland, established through the bishop's family. The

lished local nobility and to the kings of France, whereas the Coucys were upstarts. The bishop seems also to have been distantly related to Pope Calixtus II (1119-1124), and possibly to the most influential cleric of the twelfth century, St. Bernard of Clairvaux (1090-1153). It was probably partly due to Barthélemy's influence that Louis VI and his heir came to Coucy to deal first with Thomas, and then with his son Enguerran. Although the bishop's aristocratic status and powerful office, if not his piety, should have made more of an impact on Thomas, there is evidence that they made some difference. Through Barthélemy's mediation, Thomas was induced to give property to the church. Granted, it appears to have been wasteland, an uncultivated forest between the holdings of the Coucys and of the bishops. Thomas probably consolidated a shaky claim to the area by involving the bishop. Also the Coucys continued to exercise control over the property. But Thomas did allow Barthélemy's protégé, St. Norbert of Xanten, to establish first a small hermitage for a few companions, and eventually a double monastery for men and women in the forest. The place was called Prémontré.[18] The place gave its name not only to Norbert's first foundation, but to over one hundred other Premonstratensian abbeys all over Europe within the next thirty years. St. Norbert had been inspired by the New Testament Acts of the Apostles to hope that cathedral and parish priests would imitate the communal life he found recorded there. He had dedicated his own life to absolute poverty, living by preaching and then accepting alms. He walked barefoot from town to town preaching the gospel with several companions, at least one of whom died from exposure. As one of the church reformers mentioned above, he tried to persuade the canons at Barthélemy's cathedral to live in poverty, sharing their living quarters and pooling their individual incomes, using the Augustinian rule in its strictest form. The canons at Laon resisted the reform, but the bishop had invited Norbert to his diocese and was determined to settle him there somehow. In fact, the religious house at Prémontré became one of the centers of the Augustinian reform which did convert many cathedral chapters in twelfth-century Europe.[19] Beginning in the 1050s this reform movement affected the church as a whole,

---

bishop's family connections have been debated. I have accepted Marcel Pacaut, *Louis VII et les élections épiscopales dans le Royaume de France* (Paris, 1957), 111.

[18] Hugo, *Sacri et canonici ordinis praemonstratensis Annales*, 51.

[19] Again, the best sources on these events are in French and Latin. See the bibliography, below, for Ardura's *Dictionnaire*, which includes an article on Prémontré with a comprehensive bibliography; Petit, in both *Norbert*, and *Spiritualité*, on the founding and influence of the order; Chaurand on Thomas; and Dominique Barthélemy on the Coucys, especially in the article "Fondateurs." There are short articles with English bibliography on the "Premonstratensians" in Strayer's *Dictionary of the Middle Ages* and the *New Catholic Encyclopedia*.

including the papacy, the regular monastic orders, and the secular church. In this larger context it is called the "apostolic life" movement, because it was based on an imitation of the life of Christ and the apostles.[20] The most effective crusade preachers, from the hermit Peter who recruited independently for the First Crusade, to St. Bernard of Clairvaux and others who preached at the request of the papacy, focused on the imitation of Christ and personal devotion to him. Whether this emphasis expressed itself as a demand for spiritual service or as vassalage to Christ as ultimate feudal overlord, it was a call to the laity to participate in the "apostolic life" of the church. The most ferocious knight could enter the service of Christ, and perhaps earn martyrdom, as a crusader. The hope of reaching heaven after an unedifying life presumably motivated crusaders and also lay founders of monasteries. They hoped that their sins would be forgiven because of their good deeds and approval by the church.

Here we see Thomas involved in both movements. He made and kept a crusade vow. He was reportedly one of the first Europeans to enter Jerusalem after the siege of 1099, and presumably he participated in the resulting massacre, when "... men waded in blood up to their ankles" in the Temple of Solomon.[21] His behavior after his return home was not edifying, but after 1114 he participated in the Augustinian reform movement by donating land to St. Norbert through Bishop Barthélemy, a notable reformer in his own right. Norbert, the bishop's protégé, became famous as the founder of an Augustinian order, as bishop of Magdeburg, and as "Apostle to the Slavs." The saint reportedly wished to go to Jerusalem and preach to the Muslims. Although he did not go, canons from houses he founded did establish themselves in the Holy Land.[22] Doesn't Thomas's response to the crusade message and to the reformers show the laity embracing apostolic idealism as it was preached by the church?

Thomas had caused quite a bit of trouble on the way to the Holy Land, taking the land route through eastern Europe and eventually being chased out of Hungary. Albert of Aix, who referred to Thomas in his chronicle of the First Crusade, attributed his ignominious flight to moral failure. This was evidenced not so much by the attacks on Jews in Christian cities as by the inordinate number of prostitutes he brought with him.[23] Thomas was, if anything, even more brutal and uncontrollable after his return, which was the era of the royal expeditions. But it was during this period,

---

[20] See notes 12 and 13, above, as well as Henrietta Leyser, in English; in French, the articles listed by Charles Dereine; and M. H. Vicaire.

[21] *Gesta francorum*, translated in Peters, *First Crusade*, 209.

[22] Andrew Jotischky, *The Perfection of Solitude: Hermits and Monks in the Crusader States* (University Park, Pa., 1995).

[23] Albert of Aix, *Historia Hierosolymitania*, RHC, vol. 4: 293-95, 315.

in about 1120, that he agreed to the establishment of Prémontré, and attended the consecration of the new church with his young son Enguerran. It is tempting to think of Thomas, swayed by his bishop and the sanctity of Norbert, following up the earlier inspiration that had prompted his crusade vow by contributing to the reform movement. Unfortunately there is really no evidence to support this interpretation of his actions. The crusade set a precedent that others in his family followed, one that ended in their constructing a great hall decorated with statues of legendary heroes, including those of 1099.

It is arguable that the prestige of crusading helped the family to legitimize their standing in France. Thomas's behavior in 1096 on the way to Jerusalem seems to have been prompted by his notorious companion, Emich of Flonheim, who pursued Jews against the express orders of the church, in order to rob them.[24] This would seem to indicate that it was plunder, rather than forgiveness, that attracted Thomas. His behavior on his return does not indicate an interest in church reform. He turned his ferocity from his father, his chief target before his departure, to his neighbors. Thomas was excommunicated in 1114 for his attacks on church property, and the king burnt one of his castles.[25] He ambushed Louis VI in 1130 when the king was again moved to punish him, and was mortally wounded in the resulting battle. In a memorable chapter, Abbot Suger uses the story of Thomas miraculously kept from receiving the Eucharist during Last Rites to illustrate the fact that the urging of his wife and the local clergy did not bring him to repentance on his deathbed. Even the evidence for Thomas's relationship with St. Norbert is ambiguous. The story of Radulf Canis, in charter two, leaves the reader in some doubt that Norbert's intervention did Radulf any good. Thomas's presence at the consecration of Prémontré, which would seem to indicate real interest in the saint's new foundation, is complicated by shadowy hints that there was some kind of commotion at the first gathering, so that part of the building was damaged and the ceremony had to be performed again.[26] The most recent history of the Coucys has attributed the foundation of Prémontré to three motives: Thomas's desire to end his excommunication of 1114 by

---

[24] Riley-Smith, *The First Crusaders*, 157, 204 for specifics on Thomas and Emich, but also in general, "The First Crusade and the Persecution of the Jews," *Studies in Church History* 21 (1984): 51–72; and Robert Chazan, *European Jewry and the First Crusade* (Berkeley, Los Angeles, and London, 1987).

[25] There is a suggestion that those who agreed to act against Thomas were offered the same indulgence as crusaders. See Labande's version of Guibert, 410 (and note 4)–12; Tyerman, "Crusades," 561.

[26] Charles Taiée, *Prémontré. Étude sur l'abbaye de ce nom, sur l'ordre qui y a pris naissance, ses progrès, ses épreuves et sa décadence* (Laon, 1872–1873), 4.

conciliating the bishop; the efforts of the family to punish the Benedictines at Nogent for their independent attitude toward their lay patrons; and a desire to legitimize the family possessions by getting the local clergy to accept grants from them.[27] To sum up, piety was not the explanation that contemporaries gave for Thomas's actions, and there is nothing in Thomas's history which can be used to contradict their accounts. Both his crusade vow and his assistance in the foundation of an Augustinian house can be explained without positing religious fervor on his part. Thomas seems not even to have deliberately used the crusades and reform for his own advantage, but to have benefited from both in spite of himself. He went on crusade at a moment when his own career at home was stymied by his father, and supported Bishop Barthélemy only when pressured by the excommunication and royal expedition of 1114. In his case the message of the church is clear, but it is difficult to categorize his behavior as a response to it.

There was a response to the church's message from within Thomas's family. His third wife Melisende founded one of the first Premonstratensian abbeys for women. The early history of this house is hard to trace, but it looks as if Norbert established a hospital as part of the foundation at Prémontré, run by "sisters" of the order. For reasons which are not clear, the sisters moved to several sites in succession: to Fontenille in 1138/40, to Rozières by 1142, and then to Bonneuil in 1170. Thomas apparently gave land at Rozières, which was very close to Coucy, to the Premonstratensians as part of his original donation. In 1141, Melisende made a further donation, which enabled the women to move there.[28] What her motive was for founding the house is unknown. She gave it her dowry land, which might indicate that she intended to retire there, but nothing further is known about her. She appears briefly, unnamed, in Suger's account of Thomas's death, where he is permitted by the king to have her present during his final futile negotiations with the church.

If it is difficult to credit Thomas with a pious motive for his donations,

---

[27] See the article by Barthélemy on the Coucys as "Fondateurs".
[28] Melisende was the daughter of Guy of Crécy. There are entries under the names of the women's houses in Ardura, *Dictionnaire*, and Backmund, *Monasticon*, which include extensive bibliographies. Dominique Barthélemy, *Coucy*, 412 and note 192, gives some details and references for the donation; others can be found in Vernier's *Coucy*, 184-85; the *Obituaire* (ed. Waefelghem), 131; and Florival, *Barthélemy*, 376-77, no. 101. All of these references conflict at various points. The standard explanation for the move is a desire to separate the early double monasteries, and then to exclude women from the order. For instance, Caroline Walker Bynum has commented on this in *Holy Feast and Holy Fast* (Berkeley, 1982), 19-22; and Martine Plouvier, "Les soeurs de l'abbaye de Prémontré", CERP, 1991. There is a charter in BN, Collection de Picardie 267, folio 106 for "Fontenelle" in 1141, issued by Barthélemy of Laon.

there does not seem to be any other for his wife's. The Coucys continued their relationship with Prémontré under Thomas's heir, but her donation is separate from any of his. The family eventually claimed to be "advocates" or protectors of the house, with lasting rights over it, but again, her donation is not a necessary part of that development. If it was simply a gift, it was a generous one. If Melisende retired to the abbey, she participated in a rigorous form of the religious life. While retirement to a Benedictine convent could mean a quiet retreat among other noble women, attended by servants and surrounded by familiar luxuries, Norbert's foundations were strict. Women were silent, slept in dormitories, ate sparingly, and devoted themselves to manual labor.[29]

In any case, the Coucys continued to make donations to Prémontré, over the protests of the Benedictines at Nogent. They also continued to go on crusade and attack their neighbors. Where they made donations or fulfilled vows, the motive seems to be the same as Thomas's: to escape excommunication or royal punishment, to get the recognition of the bishop for disputed land, and to advance the standing and legitimacy of the family. These motives seem to hold true for the vassals and neighbors who joined them on crusade.

Thomas had precipitated the quarrel with Louis VI in 1130 by refusing to allow two merchants to pass through his land without paying him a fee which would guarantee their safety. He imprisoned them, defying the king, who had already received payment for safe conduct from them and demanded their release. Thomas may have been absolved by his bishop for crimes committed against local churches, and he may have been reconciled with the monks of Nogent, because he was buried at the abbey.[30] He never acknowledged the king's claim. His two sons inherited his holdings: Enguerran II at Coucy, and Robert I at Boves. Enguerran was unwilling or unable to make the full restitution for his father's crimes demanded by the king in 1130. He was excommunicated by 1132, when King Louis VI again attacked the Coucy holdings. Once again the king was unable to defeat the family, and in fact the expedition boosted their fortunes. In the course of the negotiations it was decided that Enguerran should marry a cousin of the king's. This seems to have been the turning point for the family in establishing their legitimacy. Enguerran II went to Palestine in 1138, after making numerous gifts to the local church and having his son baptized by Bishop Barthélemy. This pilgrimage can be seen from two perspectives. It was a seal to the bargain that had been struck between the Coucys, the

---

[29] On the severity of the early foundations see F. Petit, "L'Ordre de Prémontré de Saint Norbert à Anselm de Havelberg," in *La vita comune*.

[30] Auguste Janvier, *Boves et ses seigneurs* (Amiens, 1877), 50-54.

king, and the local church. Also, Enguerran made one of the numbers of people who went to the Holy Land not as part of an organized expedition, but in the small groups which left Europe on a regular basis, providing a steady stream of armed visitors who fought for a season and returned home.[31] Enguerran then made a second voyage when he joined the Second Crusade of 1147, which was led by King Louis VII (1137–1180). This crusade was not a success and Enguerran died in Palestine, but the family fortune was made. The Coucys had made their leap from brigands to royal companions. They were able to go on to create trouble between Louis VII and the counts of Flanders to their own advantage. Again, piety is not the keynote of this story. Enguerran II was pushed into compliance with the local church's demands by a royal army. The family gained badly needed legitimacy and prestige by allying itself with the monarchy and the church through the crusades. The Premonstratensian order was growing quickly. St. Norbert was almost as famous in France as St. Bernard of Clairvaux, who preached the Second Crusade. King Louis himself made several donations to Prémontré, as did some of the Coucys' neighbors, including Radulf Canis and Burchard de Guise, whose charters can be found in this collection.[32]

Bishop Barthélemy continued to promote the interests of the canons after Norbert's original foundation. He expelled a group of secular canons at the house of St. Martin, outside the walls of his city, because they refused to be reformed. Instead, the bishop installed twelve Premonstratensian canons there, along with a hospice served by women. There is still a hospital on the grounds, although the abbey now houses the municipal library. The bishop also established another new house of Augustinian canons in Laon, the Templars, who fought the Muslims in Palestine and protected pilgrims instead of performing a more acceptable monastic task such as manual labor or manuscript copying.[33] Their chapel also survives, on the grounds of Laon's museum. When Barthélemy eventually retired in 1150, he was replaced by a Premonstratensian, Gautier de St. Maurice, the

---

[31] For more detail on Enguerran, see charter 1 below. Dominique Barthélemy, in "Fondateurs," casts some doubt on Thomas's involvement in Prémontré's foundation, crediting Enguerran instead: 190–93.

[32] For royal donations see BN, Collection de Picardie 267, 107, 214, 235; Matton, *Archives*, 120; Hugo, *Annales*, 163, and "probationes," xiv–xvii. Compare Luchaire, *Actes*, nos. 22, 153, 178, 247, 250, with Barthélemy, *Coucy*, 101 and note 199.

[33] The Templars and other "military" orders are a fascinating product of the crusade movement. Any of the basic works on the Middle Ages mentioned above will give some information about them: see especially the *Oxford Illustrated History of the Crusades*, ed. Jonathan Riley-Smith. See also Malcolm Barber, Marion Melleville, and Anthony Luttrell for further information and bibliography.

abbot of St. Martin's.[34] At some point in the twelfth century a monument was set up at one of gates of Laon to commemorate all those who had made the pilgrimage to the Holy Land. An antiphon or chant on Jerusalem and the crusades was performed regularly as part of the liturgy in the cathedral.[35]

The Coucys were careful to continue to emphasize their connections to the crusades and to Prémontré. Given their proximity to Laon and recent troubles with the monarchy, it would have been impolitic not to do so. Dominique Barthélemy, who wrote the history of the family, commented that Thomas was the last Coucy in the original line, the ones who created the lordship by violence. His son was the first of the "new" Coucys, those who worked to legitimize the lordship by connecting it to the monarchy and to the local church.[36] Marrying into the king's family, accompanying him on crusade, winning a place in the list of donors to a prestigious new religious order, being recognized by the local bishop—these were all ways for a "brigand" to become respectable. There is a charter in the collection for Enguerran's brother Robert which helps to bring into focus a career very reminiscent of their father's, especially in the uneasy relationship with the local church. The charters and stories of Coucy vassals and neighbors, Radulf Canis, Burchard de Guise, Allelmus de Flichecourt, Ives de Nesle, Radulph of Duri, Guy of Arblincourt, Simon of Chavigny, Guy of Monceau, Jean of Verneuil, display the same pattern, the same motives, on a smaller scale. The men who held land from or near the Coucys used the same methods to establish their own families in the district.

Raoul I of Coucy (1160–1190) issued a charter in 1168 which emphasized all of these elements in the family history. The charter detailed gifts by the family to the Augustinian canons at Nazareth, where his father Enguerran II was buried. Raoul added a rent, or regular income, which would ensure that the family would be remembered by the canons, a gift that was to be delivered through the Templars. The purpose of the Templar foundations in France, like the one at Laon, was to channel recruits and funds to Palestine. The charter was issued at Noyon in the presence of King Louis VII.[37] Raoul continued to issue charters which established the

---

[34] Again, see Bur, Kaiser, Martinet, and Melleville on Laon, and Ardura, *Dictionnaire*, on St. Martin's. Ardura says that Gautier received a piece of the true cross from the emperor of Constantinople, which added to Laon's prestige as a pilgrimage site (also see François Petit, *Norbert et l'origin des Prémontrés* [Paris, 1981], 161). The icon of Christ given to the cathedral by Pope Urban IV remains on display for pilgrims.

[35] Jacques Chaurand, *Thomas de Marle, Sire de Coucy* (Marle, 1963), 46, 48.

[36] Barthélemy, "Fondateurs," 190–92. See also Barthélemy, "Monachisme."

[37] Jules Tardif, ed., *Monuments historiques. Cartons des rois* (Paris, 1866; repr. Nendeln, Liechtenstein, 1977), 308–9, no. 613; and see below, charter 9.

legitimacy of his ancestors as lords of Coucy, and he emphasized the family's "special devotion" to Prémontré, which had continued to grow in importance. The most important for the latter purpose was the charter of 1178, which put forward Raoul's claim to be "advocate" of the house. Raoul was the second son of Enguerran II, whose namesake died before 1160. Raoul's first wife, Agnes de Hainaut, died in 1173, after which he married Alix de Dreux, the king's niece. Their five children were Enguerran III who inherited Coucy, Thomas who inherited the family property at Vervins, Robert of Pinon, Raoul the clerk, and Agnes. Previous charters were issued by the bishop for the Coucys, but this one is issued by Raoul and witnessed by his men. He credits his grandfather and father with the foundation of Prémontré, without mentioning Bishop Barthélemy or the fact that the original hermitage was purchased by the bishop from the monks at St. Vincent of Laon. All of the family's gifts to the order, of land, income, or exemption, are mentioned and tied firmly to the patronage of Thomas and Enguerran II. Rozières for instance is listed, but not Melisende. Founders of religious houses frequently did become advocates, lay patrons and protectors of those institutions. Given the prestige of the order by 1178, the office of advocate for all or part of Prémontré's holdings would add status to the Coucy family. This charter sanitizes the uneasy relationship between the Coucys and the order; for instance, Enguerran almost certainly attacked the property of the canons before his public repentance in 1138. It erases the pressure originally put on Thomas by the bishop, and it creates a new image. Raoul now appears as the scion of a long and legitimate line, which had founded one of the most important new orders of the twelfth century.[38] In his will, written before he left on crusade in 1190, Raoul continued to emphasize these connections, putting the canons at Prémontré in charge of the income he left to his daughter. The wording makes very little of the impending expedition or of devotion to any of the religious houses mentioned. The emphasis is on the division of property and the avoidance of any future controversy. However, the orders specifically mentioned with Prémontré are the Hospitallers and the Templars. Both were identified with crusading, and especially with their mother houses in Jerusalem. Prémontré also had two houses in the Holy Land by 1150, and had lost both to the Muslims by 1187.[39]

Thomas had participated in the surprisingly successful First Crusade, of

---

[38] For Barthélemy's comments on this charter and on Raoul, see *Coucy*, 56–57; "Fondateurs," 192, and the charters issued by Raoul below, nos. 9, 10, and 17.

[39] See the text with references under charter 17, below; and Barthélemy, *Coucy*, 405–11, and the notes on 217. For the Norbertines in the Holy Land, see Corliss Konwiser Slack, "The Premonstratensians in the Crusader Kingdoms in the Twelfth and Thirteenth Centuries," *Analecta Praemonstratensia* 67/68 (1991/1992).

1096–1099, when Jerusalem was captured by a mixed European force. His son Enguerran died in the course of the Second Crusade, which failed to offer any concrete assistance to the Europeans who had stayed on to found a kingdom at the Holy City. Raoul died in Palestine on the Third Crusade, in 1191. This is the famous crusade of Richard the Lion-heart, the king of England who was captured and held for ransom on his way home through Germany, and whose return is combined in popular legends with Robin Hood. The history of the family is connected with so many good stories from the Middle Ages that Barbara Tuchman used it as a focus for her work on the fourteenth century. However, the Coucys were equally colorful in the eleventh and twelfth. Raoul's son Enguerran III was even more closely associated than his predecessors with some of the best adventure stories of medieval Europe. Like the rest of his family, he gives every sign of being politically astute and conventionally pious, rather than particularly affected by the spiritual idealism the church preached as a motivation for the crusades.

His story is told in pieces by charters in this collection, and summarized in the notes to the charter for Abbot Gervase of Prémontré. He was involved not only in the Albigensian Crusade, which eventually extended the control of the king of France over the southern provinces, but also in the struggle between France and Flanders. King Philip Augustus of France (1180–1223) was one of the most effective medieval monarchs, adept at recognizing and exploiting his opportunities to consolidate and extend his holdings. His opponents in the effort at expansion were the king of England, who controlled French territory, the counts of Flanders on his northern borders, and the provinces to the south, which did not recognize his authority. Philip was able to launch an attack on England, initially with the pope's encouragement, which eventually resulted in his control of most of England's territory on the continent. The Crown's control of Poitou and Toulouse was consolidated by Philip's heir due to the crusade against the Albigensian heretics. Philip's attack on Flanders was more subtle and less successful. His attempts to encroach on the territory were resisted by the counts, whose wealth came from their mercantile cities, and whose prestige was high in Europe. Philip returned without notable accomplishment from the Third Crusade of 1191, but Baldwin IX of Flanders became the first Latin Emperor of Constantinople when the Fourth Crusade took that city in 1204. Baldwin and other counts of Flanders are represented by several charters below, including some for their vassals and neighbors in Namur and Hainaut who would have joined them on crusade: Gerard chancellor of Flanders, Osto of Trazegnies, Simon of Thiméon, Arnulf of Thérouanne, Thomas of Leez, Godescalc of Morialmé, and of course the Coucys themselves who were both neighbors and enemies. Enguerran III supported Philip Augustus in Albi, at Bouvines, in England in the struggle against King John, and in any conflict

with Flanders, whose counts occasionally laid claim to Coucy land. Again, a close look at Enguerran's activities reveals the ally of the king much more than the pious patron of any religious order.

FINANCIAL ARRANGEMENTS AS A KEY TO MOTIVATION

It will be remembered that there were two ways charters could be used to comment on crusade motivation: through the choice of religious house and through the financial arrangements made to pay for the crusade. More work needs to be done on the people who issued these charters to make a firm decision on whether the expeditions can be said to have been a real sacrifice for them. The only family for whom there is an answer is the Coucys, because of the investigation made by Dominique Barthélemy into the lordship in general and its relationship with the local church in particular. For them a reading of the charters leaves a fairly clear picture of financial and political advantage from participation in the crusades. Going to Jerusalem or Albi helped to establish legitimacy for lands and rights essential to the lordship. The motive for taking the cross was reconciliation with the local church, which was both rival for land and source of legitimacy; and the prestige to be gained from participation in royal or comital expeditions.

For the counts of Flanders, Brienne and Champagne, the great crusading families, the answer is more difficult to reach. Their case is analogous to that of the kings of France. Donations made to churches before or after the expedition fit with a general pattern of church patronage, rather than representing a sacrifice by the donor. The finances of these great powers have been and will continue to be the subject of numerous studies. It would be well beyond the scope of this essay to say whether the crusades represented a net gain or debit for them. Certainly the French monarchy did well out of Albi in the long run, and Count Baldwin IX of Flanders thought the empire based at Constantinople worth defending once he obtained it. But the point here is that the few charters for these great men do not seem to have much to do with financial loss or gain. They fit a long-standing pattern of patronage for a variety of religious institutions, including new ones, where the famous patron could establish a "fashion" of donation to a particular house or order. The financial arrangements recorded in these few charters offer as few clues to crusade motivation for Flanders, Brienne, or Champagne as they do for France.

For the vassals of Flanders and France the evidence is much more sketchy than it is for the Coucys. Sometimes even the identification of the crusader is missing. However what evidence is available, for instance for Trazegnies, shows a pattern similar to the one for the Coucys and their vassals. New lordships, which had often been established at the price of conflict with local religious houses, were legitimized and reconciled to the

church through a donation sealed with a crusade vow. The donation often seems to represent a settlement of competing claims, rather than a sacrificial gift. It could be argued that the agreement to settle up was a sacrifice, and should be honored as an expression of piety. While that may be true, it is not necessary to posit piety to explain the vows. Where information exists about the crusader, the political and financial advantage of the expedition is sufficient to warrant the journey.

This is not a definitive statement on crusade motivation, but a comment offered at the very beginning of an investigation. One factor that may be definitive for the unsettled area of northern France where Prémontré was founded is the room, both literally and figuratively, for both new orders and new lordships. The picture of lay patronage is very different in more settled areas, both for churches which were not involved in opening new territory and for lordships that had long histories. The motivation for a crusade vow taken in this unstable region may be specific to that situation, rather than a key to understanding general European involvement in the crusades.

Another factor which comes through very clearly as a motivator and is difficult to chart is the web of family and political alliances that underlie the charters in this collection. Witnesses are shared not only within the Coucy and Flanders contingents, but between them; intermarriage connects the two groups, as well as the friendships among several reforming bishops.[40] These charters have been collected with an eye to the connection between the founding of new orders and the families who patronized them, rather than to compiling a record of an individual house or family. The method of selection opens new questions about crusade motivation rather than providing a definitive statement. Doubtless experts on particular houses and families will be able to add more information to the charters already collected, which may affect their interpretation. This is an attempt to take the charters out of the context of their issuing institutions, where they are lost in specialist monographs, in order to highlight both the pattern of reconciliation with the church and the network of relationships among reformers, families, and contingents of crusaders.

There are not enough charters here to warrant conclusions, and not enough information about the documents presented. Charters should continue to be collected, edited, and investigated, so that eventually enough information will appear in print to allow for an informed conclusion to be reached.

---

[40] See, for example, the intermarriage between Hainaut and Nesle, no. 11; the connections of Béthune to both Coucy and Flanders, no. 22; and the bishops Milo of Thérouanne, Jean of Warneton, and Lambert of Arras, no. 19.

CRUSADE CHARTERS
1138–1270

1
1138, ENGUERRAN II DE COUCY

Archives de la Société archéologique, historique et scientifique de Soissons 1, pièce 5. A photograph of this document has been printed in CERP (1989): 104. Another copy of the charter exists in the Bibliothèque municipale at Soissons, 7, folio 1.

In nomine sancte et individue Trinitatis. Ego Bartholomeus Dei gratia Laudunensis episcopus. Notum fieri volo tam futuris quam praesentibus, quod Ingelrannus filius Thome de Coci ob remedium animae sue et patris et matris sue et predecessorum suorum Premonstratae ecclesiae perpetuo remisit winagium et naulum in omni loco terre sue ubi ab alienis accipiebatur nisi de re que ematur ut iterum venalis exponenda deferatur.

Facta est autem ista concessio anno Incarnati Verbi M° C° XXX° VIII°, Epacta VII, Indictione I, Concurrente V. in choro eiusdem Premonstrate ecclesie ea die qua ad peregrinandum exiit Iherusalem, astante fratre suo Roberto, et matre sua Milissende et sorore eiusdem nominis Milissende, quorum voluntate etiam assensu hoc donum factum est.

Astantibus etiam multis hominibus et de suis nobilioribus de quibus quosdam annotave curavimus, quorum ista sunt nomina: Wido castellanus, Ado de Guni et Iterus frater eius, Robertus Iitulus, Joffridus et frater eius Sarrazenus, Gerardus Auris.

Quod ut ratum et inconvulsum permaneat sigilli nostri impressione corroboravimus et tam nostram quam domini pape excomunicationem praedicto Ingelranno favente apposuimus ut scilicet quicumque contra hoc venire temptaverit secundo tercio ve commonitus, nisi resipuerit reum se divino judicio existere de perpetrata iniquitate cognoscat, et a sacratissimo corpore et sanguine Dei et Redentoris nostri Jhesu Christi alienus fiat atque in extremo examine districte ultioni subjaceat. Conservatoribus autem sit pax Domini nostri Jhesu Christi quatenus et hic fructum bonae actionis percipiant et apud districtum judicem premia eternae pacis inveniant. Amen.

[Note: the scribe is inconsistent in the use of a/ae endings and the text printed here reflects that.]

In the name of the holy and undivided Trinity. I, Barthélemy, by God's grace bishop of Laon, wish it to be known to those to come and to those present that Enguerran, son of Thomas de Coucy, for the salvation of his soul and for those of his father, his mother, and of their ancestors, gives perpetually to the church of Prémontré exemption from the taxes (*wionage* and *naule*) levied on the transport of wine by road and water in all of his land where they are collected from non-residents, except on that which is bought so that it may again be transported and sold.

This concession was made in the year of the Incarnate Word 1138, epact 7, indiction 1, concurrent 5, in the choir of that same church of Prémontré on the day on which Enguerran left on pilgrimage for Jerusalem. His brother Robert, his mother Melisende, and his sister, also called Melisende, were present to give their approval and consent to this donation.

Many men were also present, and we have recorded the names of certain of them who are his nobles: Guy, the castellan, Ado de Guines and Iterus his brother, Robert Vitulus, Geoffrey and his brother Sarracin, Gerard d'Oreille.

So that this donation may remain uncontested we corroborate it with our seal. In addition, and with the approval of the aforesaid Enguerran, we impose our excommunication and that of the Lord Pope on whoever attempts to challenge this agreement. If he refuses to repent after the second or third warning, he will know himself to be under divine judgment as a perpetrator of iniquity, and alienated from the most blessed body and blood of our God and redeemer Jesus Christ, as well as subject to strict punishment at the Last Judgment. Let the peace of our Lord Jesus Christ be to those who preserve it, and may they receive the reward of their good deed here as well as find the rewards of eternal peace with the just judge. Amen.

SUMMARY OF THE CHARTER

This is a donation made by Enguerran II de Coucy (d. 1147) to the abbey of Prémontré, on the day he left for Jerusalem in 1138. The charter was issued on the knight's behalf by the local bishop, who was also one of the founders of the abbey, Barthélemy of Laon (1113-1151). The gift to the abbey is not land, but exemption from a tax Enguerran could otherwise have charged the canons. The canons of Prémontré had vineyards and were increasingly involved in the making of wine; and in transporting it either to market or to other houses of the order. Enguerran would normally have collected tolls ("wionage" and "naule") from anyone transporting goods on his roads or across his bridges, on the theory that he would offer them safe conduct in his territory, and would hear any complaint in his court. This charter represents an early example of this type of exemption, which became more complex as lords tried to retain control over, and make a profit from, their roads. Eventually, exemption from wionage and naule would be given only for a certain amount of wine, what could reasonably be claimed as for consumption by the order. Even here, Enguerran reserves the right to collect tolls on wine the canons sold.

The charter is witnessed by Enguerran's "men": Guy the castellan of Coucy, Ado of Guny and his brother Iterus, Robert Vitulus, Jeoffrey and his brother Sarracin, and Gerard l'Orielle (Auris). All of these men held fiefs from Enguerran, and formed what was called his entourage, or court. For further security, Bishop Barthélemy attached his seal to the document. The combination of witnesses and seal would assure the legal force of the exemption.

The bishop needed to be cautious on Prémontré's behalf because the Coucy family were both founders and despoilers of local monasteries. Enguerran and his mother Melisende, who controlled the fief until her son came of age, had been under threat of excommunication for thefts of land from various abbeys since 1131. In some cases these "thefts" were an attempt to reclaim land previously donated by the family. This gift was one of a series made by Enguerran in 1138, when he came of age, to make peace with the bishop and local abbots. The charter records a ceremonial presentation that was made formally in the abbey church of Prémontré, in the presence of Enguerran's mother and sister, both named Melisende, and his younger brother Robert, who inherited the family property at Boves. Enguerran, in the presence of the canons, the bishop, the Coucy family and vassals, promised to respect the integrity of his gifts to the canons. His pilgrimage to Jerusalem, 1138-1139, was a further proof of his repentance for his attacks on Prémontré and on other churches in the diocese. It may also have been a way to terminate the excommunication which he was certainly under in 1136, and which seems to have been in

force when he made his crusade vow (see below on Enguerran). Release from excommunication was a crusader privilege which developed over the course of the twelfth century, essentially because the crusade was accepted as penance.[1]

In the following charter, one of Enguerran's vassals, Radulph Canis, also makes a penitential pilgrimage after attacks on the property of Prémontré. Both Enguerran and his brother Robert of Boves, along with several of their men, participated in the Second Crusade in 1147. The third charter in this collection records Robert's gift to another house of regular canons just before his departure. Enguerran died after reaching the Holy Land for the second time in 1147, and was buried at the shrine served by regular canons in Nazareth.

NOTES ON THE CHARTER

Excommunication latae sententiae

This charter is interesting not only because of the crusade vow, but because of the exemption (see below), and because it is an example of a particular type of excommunication, developed in the early twelfth century. The Second Lateran Council, held in 1139, established the precedent for the excommunication *latae sententiae*, a sentence that took effect immediately as the crime was committed. With the exception of the crime of heresy, crimes normally had to be judged in the proper court, with a sentence of excommunication as the possible result of that process. This charter anticipates the council, in the sense that Bishop Barthélemy threatens automatic excommunication to anyone who disturbs the arrangements detailed in the charter.[2]

Enguerran II

For general information and bibliography on the Coucy family, the bishop of Laon, and the Premonstratensians, see the introduction.

Enguerran's life, unlike that of his famous father, is known chiefly through charter evidence. He issued eleven between 1139 and 1147, and there are twenty-four issued by Bishop Barthélemy of Laon which offer information about him. What can be known from these and other sources is detailed in Dominique Barthélemy's *Les deux âges de la seigneurie banale. Pouvoir et société dans la terre des sires de Coucy (mil.XIe–mil. XIIIe siècle)*

---

[1] On the development of crusader legal privileges, see James Brundage, *Medieval Canon Law and the Crusader* (Madison, Wis., 1969). On the medieval theory and practice of penance, and its relationship to crusade motivation, see the articles by H. E. J. Cowdrey listed in the bibliography.

[2] Elisabeth Vodola, *Excommunication in the Middle Ages* (Berkeley, 1986).

(Paris, 1984). According to Barthélemy, Enguerran was the eldest son of Thomas de Marle and his third wife, Melisende, and was named after Thomas's father. Enguerran II was three years old when his father took him to the consecration of the new church at Prémontré in 1121. He was twelve when Thomas died in 1130. His father's death left Melisende as guardian of the fief for her son, and they are both mentioned in charters dealing with their property in 1130-1138. Thomas died defending his lordship from King Louis VI (1108-1137). The king left Coucy in Melisende's hands on the condition that she make restitution for Thomas's attacks on local abbeys. In 1131, Anselm, abbot of the Benedictine house of St. Vincent at Laon, complained of the behavior of the Coucys to the newly elected Pope Innocent II, who was visiting Laon. The pope was unable to settle the quarrel during this visit, but followed up by writing to the bishop of Laon. The bishop threatened the Coucys with excommunication and interdict if they did not make reparation within forty days. Anselm's complaint was that while restitution of the abbey's property had been made in 1130, the death of the previous abbot during that year had given the Coucys a pretext for reclaiming the property. Melisende and Enguerran made partial restitution in 1131, but obtained permission to delay the rest for four years.

There were other complaints. King Louis' attack on Coucy had been made in response to appeals by the bishop of Laon and other local landholders including the counts of Vermandois. Raoul of Vermandois had killed Thomas in 1130, and was again assisting the king in an attack on the Coucys in 1132. A siege of the castle of La Fère by the king's forces lasted two months (6 May-8 July), and led to negotiations which were settled by the marriage of Enguerran to Raoul's niece, who was also related to Louis VI. Enguerran was forced to acknowledge that he held Marle and Vervins from Raoul, and to accept Bishop Barthélemy, who was Raoul's uncle, as overlord for La Fère. As a result of the marriage, the Coucys became important members of the court. Enguerran gained at least as much as his overlords from the new arrangement. The lordship acquired by violence was regularized; as Dominique Barthélemy has said, Louis VI never really conquered the Coucys. Enguerran was in effect simply promoted from "brigand" to "baron."[3]

---

[3] All of the information on Enguerran II comes from Barthélemy, *Coucy*, 71, 84-86, 87, 115. On Anselm, abbot of St. Vincent, see A. Dubrulle, (no. 19) "Anselme," DHGE. The Coucys were proud of their independence. Their motto ran: "Rois ne suis; ne prince, ne duc ne comte aussi. Je suis le sire de Coucy." According to Emile Coët and Charles Lefèbvre, *Histoire de la ville de Marle et des environs* (Compiègne, 1897), 75, Enguerran married Agnes, daughter of Raoul de Beaugency, cousin-german of King Philip I (1060-1108), and niece of Count Raoul V of Vermandois.

Enguerran and his brother inherited Coucy and Boves in 1132/1133, when Enguerran's marriage was arranged. The wedding did not take place until 1138. Between 1132 and 1136 local abbeys continued to complain of Enguerran. He was excommunicated in 1136, along with his prévôt Gerard l'Oreille, and again he made partial restitution. The charters of 1138 represent a permanent settlement with the local church. Dominique Barthélemy has categorized the pilgrimage of that year as "penitential," and the exemption as a gift, rather than as a thinly-disguised sale to raise money for the journey.[4]

There seems to be a record of Enguerran's presence in the Holy Land. On 5 February, 1138, the king of Jerusalem issued a foundation charter for the abbey of Saint-Lazare. Under "pilgrims" the witness list includes Ives de Nesle, Arnulf advocate of Thérouanne, and Enguerran "de Bova."[5] Enguerran was back in France by the winter of 1140/41, since he witnessed the charter recording Yves de Nesle's succession as count of Soissons.[6] There was a continuous stream of Europeans who went to Palestine in small groups between major expeditions; Enguerran was apparently part of one formed as penance and as part of the resolution of his disputes with the church.

The settlement which legitimized Enguerran's lordship was solidified through his status as a crusader and as a patron of the bishop's foundation at Prémontré. In 1142, Enguerran III was baptized in the abbey church at a ceremony that included the penitential crusade vow of Radulph Canis (see charter 2, below). Melisende built a Premonstratensian nunnery at Rosières between 1137 and 1142.[7] The change in the family's relationship to the Crown, from adversaries to courtiers, is illustrated by the fact that Enguerran was with Louis VII when the king and court took the cross in 1146. The Coucys built on their new connection to both the king and the

---

[4] Barthélemy, *Coucy*, 85–87; cf. Ghislain Brunel, "Les activités économiques des Prémontrés en Soissonnais aux XIIe et XIIIe siècles: politique originale ou adaptation au milieu?" CERP (1989): 67–79. See also Jacquemin, *Soissons* (61, no. 97), for Enguerran's restitutions to the abbey of Nogent in 1138, and for the crusade in the same year of "Pierre, son of Gervin ... seized by the fear of God on the point of departure for Jerusalem" (59, no. 94).

[5] Bresc-Bautier, *Cartulaire*, no. 34. Professor Rudolf Hiestand has pointed out a discrepancy in the dates here, since it would have been impossible for Enguerran to be in Jerusalem in February. The possibilities are that there is another Enguerran of Boves or that the witness list is wrong or one or more of the documents is inaccurately dated. I am unable to resolve this difficulty.

[6] William Mendel Newman, *Les seigneurs de Nesle en Picardie (XIIe–XIIIe siècles): leurs chartes et leur histoire*, 2 vols. (Philadelphia-Paris, 1971), vol. 1: 25, vol. 2: 29–33.

[7] M. Plouvier, "Les soeurs de l'abbaye de Prémontré," CERP (1991): 20–27; Ardura, *Dictionnaire*: s.vv. "Bonneuil," "Fontenille," and "Rosières."

bishop by making gifts to local religious houses on the eve of their participation in a royal expedition.[8]

Exemption from Wionage and Naule

Dominique Barthélemy sees the charter of 1138 as part of a struggle played out in the twelfth century between the nobility and the church. Thomas de Marle had made donations out of what he saw as his inalienable territory. They were not gifts so much as fiefs, granted in return for prayers and other benefits, and revocable at his convenience. The holder of the fief had rights as well, however, and the clergy considered the donations to be irrevocable, at least so long as they performed the services required. Barthélemy of Laon became bishop at a time when the churches of his diocese had been "ruined" by the usurpation of land and income by local lords. During his episcopate, 1113–1158, he had to rebuild the cathedral and restore almost all of the abbeys in the diocese. The acts issued by the bishop in the 1130s, including this one, "introduced the idea that gifts to churches were irrevocable."[9]

In addition to the quarrel over the status of gifts made to the church, there was the question of the tolls this exemption mentions. The Coucys' castles were the foundation of their power, and they provided bases from which to control the traffic on the Roman roads from Champagne to Flanders, as well as on the Oise, the Serre, and the Ailette Rivers. The Coucys objected to the building of new roads on their territory, and considered that merchants ought to pay for protection and justice in their domains. "Wionage" was the toll on the roads, "naule" the tax on the rivers. The problem during the 1120s and 30s, known chiefly from the cartularies of churches, was that the Coucys wanted to charge tolls simply for local use of the roads, rather than just for commercial traffic on them. The bishop was anxious to establish a general exemption for "domestic" use (carrying goods intended for use by the canons). In the absence of a law code, every local church wanted its own charter of exemption to guarantee its rights. Enguerran II granted thirteen exemptions between 1139 and 1147, mostly to churches. In general, these exemptions were granted as a prelude to a crusade, and Barthélemy has seen them as "gestures of piety," offered as a concession to the church's desire to "regulate"

---

[8] Barthélemy, *Coucy*, 99–100, Chesne, *Coucy*, 208–9, and "preuves," 339–40. One of Chesne's charters (*Coucy*, 340), issued by Enguerran for the Benedictines at St. Vincent, reads: "... quod Ingelranno de Fare Hierosolymam ituro cum Francorum Rege ..." Louis VII (1137–1180) was interested enough in Prémontré to make a gift to the order before his departure on crusade; see the introduction.

[9] Barthélemy, *Coucy*, 97–98; and see the bishop's letter defending his episcopate in Migne, *PL* 82, col. 696.

the tolls "in writing."[10] Premonstratensian houses tended to specialize in a particular agricultural product, as the order grew, and for those houses in the Coucy domain the product was wine. The canons wanted to protect their right to distribute wine they had produced to the various houses of the order without paying a tax on it.

Both of these issues, the status of gifts to the church and the question of tolls, form part of the more basic question of the existence of the Coucy lordship. The family simply had taken by force castles, land, and feudal rights that belonged in theory to royal domain, and in fact to several parties willing to defend themselves: the counts of Vermandois and the bishops of Laon, to name only the most vigorous. King Louis VI's negotiations with Thomas and Enguerran II were the result of his inability to dislodge them. For Dominique Barthélemy, the career of Enguerran II represents the conclusion of a conquest by "brigandage" and "rape," a conquest that was regularized through negotiation and legitimized by donations like the one we are studying. By accepting the gift of the exemption the church recognized the legitimacy of the Coucy lordship. When he gave land or revenue to the church, Enguerran II exchanged income for acknowledgement of his lawful authority over his domain. His gifts to various houses just before the Second Crusade cemented his position as lord of Coucy, recognized by church and king: "Enguerran of La Fère, upon leaving for Jerusalem with the King of the Franks," as one of the charters begins. His crusade vow, which he took while at court, helped to enroll him among the "barons" of France.[11]

THE WITNESSES

Ado (Adon) de Guny and his brother Iter (Itier): Guny was a *villa* close to Coucy, on the Ailette River. Ado and Iter were sons of Guy, who, from 1116, is listed first among the knights of Coucy. The brothers were regular witnesses for Enguerran II after 1130. They were nephews of the castellan of Coucy, and Ado married the sister of another of the knights listed in this charter, Sarracin.[12]

---

[10] Barthélemy, *Coucy*, 380–87. Nine of the eleven charters issued by Enguerran himself are exemptions from wionage. Stephen White, in his *Custom, Kinship, and Gifts to Saints* (Chapel Hill and London, 1988), 242, n. 5, has suggested that "grants of this kind were often made after at least some of the customs in question had been the subject of a dispute." It would make sense that tolls would be one of the issues in the disagreements between the Coucys and the bishop of Laon.

[11] Barthélemy, *Coucy*, 381, 115; and see note 6, above. For the crusade vow of the court see Suger, ed. by A. Molinier, *L'Histoire du Roi Louis VII* (Paris, 1887), 159.

[12] For these witnesses and their families, see Newman, *Picardie*, vol. 2: 96; Barthélemy, *Coucy*, 150–55.

Bishop Barthélemy of Laon: see the introduction.

Gerard Auri/l'Oreille: was a frequent witness for the Coucys 1138–1162. He belongs to the family of the lords of Housset.[13]

Guy: castellan of Coucy and Noyon, witnessed six charters for Enguerran II before leaving for Jerusalem in 1143. The castellans were a powerful family, who took the name "of Coucy."[14]

Robert It/Vitulus/le Veau: is known only from attestation as part of the Coucy court.[15]

Sarracin and J/Geoffroy, brothers: Sarracin was castellan of La Fère (1133–1177) and also of Laon (1166–1177), holding offices of the Coucys and the bishop, respectively. The castellan had three brothers, Geoffroy de Condren, Hugues le Captif de Vendeuil, and Raoul Bouchart, all of whom can be found as Coucy witnesses 1130–1170.[16]

---

[13] Barthélemy, *Coucy*, 521.

[14] Barthélemy, *Coucy*, 507–10; Maximilien Melleville, *Notice historique et généalogique sur les châtelains de Coucy* (Laon, n.d.); and A. Rondeau, *Chansons attribuées au chastelain de Coucy* (Paris, 1964). Both Melleville and Barthélemy agree that Guy went on pilgrimage with his three sons in the entourage of King Louis VII to Compostella in 1156 (see 17–18 and 508, respectively). Maxime de Sars, in *Laonnois*, vol. 1: 270, said that Guy took vows as a Premonstratensian in 1140, but gave a reference which seems to be erroneous.

[15] Barthélemy, *Coucy*, 155.

[16] Barthélemy, *Coucy*, 147, 389 and note 94, which says that as castellan Sarracin "had his part in the *winagium* of Lord Enguerran"; Newman, *Picardie*, vol. 2: 94–100, 203.

2
1142, RADULPH CANIS

Bibliothèque nationale, Collection de Picardie 290: Originaux de Prémontré, folio 3. Fragment in: Chesne, *Coucy*, "preuves," 338.

In nomine sancte et individue Trinitatis. Ego Bartholomeus, Dei gratia Laudunensis episcopus. Notum fieri volo tam futuris quam praesentibus, quod domino Norberto viro spectabilis religionis qui primo in Praemonstrato loco ad commanendum se contulit et fratribus suis proximas valles eidem loco circumiacentes episcopali auctoritate tam a decimis quam a ceteris consuetudinibus emancipavi ab omnibus qui iure hereditario aliquid ibi possidere videbantur eo ordine quo a me ipso in ipsorum privilegiis sanccitum est: Post longum vero temporis curriculum surrexit quidam Radulphus Canis cognominatus filius Walteri de la Turnela qui inquietare voluit quod factum fuerat pro quadam particula decime que est in parrochia de Broincurt quam de feodo suo esse dicebat. Quam inquietationem .lx. solidos donando ipsi Radulfo sedavi ea die qua ad baptizandum Ingelrannum domini Ingelranni de Coci filium veneram et quod inde abbati et ecclesiae forisfecerat Iherosolymam iturus veniam petiit et accepit et ut ecclesia predicta in perpetuum libere possideret ob remedium animae sue ibique attinentium concessit me presente & aliis legittimis testibus Roberto capellano, Radulfo presbitero Droci, Widone de l'Oisi, Walone milite, Fulcino cellerario, Drogone & Nicasio famulis episcopi, Petro filio Arnulfi.

Ut autem hec nostre confirmationis pagina inviolatum robur obtineat sigilli nostri impressione subsignavimus et inperturbatoribus nisi resipiscant anathematis innodatione inperpetuum apponere curavimus. Actum est hoc anno Incarnationis Dominice M. C. XL. II., Indictione IIII, epacta III, concurrente III. Signum Bartholomei archidiaconi, S. Widonis decani, S. Hoet vicedominici, S. Arnulfi clerici, S. Petri, S. Willelmi a Gasonis, S. Nicolai clerici, S. Harberti de Broincurti, S. Odonis, S. Fulko.

In the name of the holy and undivided Trinity. I, Barthélemy, by God's grace Bishop of Laon, wish it to be known to those to come and to those present that for the Lord Norbert—a man of outstanding religious life who was the first to go to Prémontré to settle there—and for his brethren, I by my episcopal authority freed the nearby valleys surrounding that place both from tithes and from other customary duties from all who seemed to possess such rights there by hereditary right, just as it was ratified by me in their privileges. After a long space of time a certain Radulph, with the cognomen Canis, the son of Walter de la Tournelle, arose and wished to disturb what had been done regarding a certain division of the tithes in the parish of Brancourt, which he said was of his fief. This challenge I put to rest by giving 60 solidi to this same Radulph on the day on which I came to baptize Enguerran, son of the Lord Enguerran of Coucy. He was about to set out for Jerusalem, so he sought and received pardon; and what he had forfeited from there to the abbot and church, he granted that the aforesaid church could freely possess in perpetuity for the remedy of his soul and the souls of those attending him there. This occurred in my presence and that of other lawful witnesses: Robert, the chaplain; Radulph the priest of Droci; Gui of l'Oisi; Walo, knight; Fulcuin, the cellarer; Drogo and Nicasius, the servants of the bishop; Peter, the son of Arnulf.

So that this page containing our confirmation may secure inviolable force, we sign it with the impression of our seal and we take care to place forever in the tangles of anathema any who seek to overthrow this, unless they repent. This is in this year of the Lord's Incarnation 1142, epact 3, concurrent 3. The sign of Bartholomew, archdeacon; the sign of Gui, dean; the sign of Hoet, vicar; the sign of Arnulf, cleric; the sign of Peter; the sign of William de Gasonis; the sign of Nicholas the cleric; the sign of Herbert de Brancourt; the sign of Odo; the sign of Fulk.

SUMMARY OF THE CHARTER

The charter was issued by Bishop Barthélemy of Laon on the day when Enguerran II had his son and namesake baptized. The baptism took place in the church at Prémontré, and a great number of witnesses were present, both from the abbey and from Enguerran's court. The charter was issued to settle a long-standing quarrel between Radulph Canis and the canons of Prémontré over part of the tithe of the parish of Brancourt, which had been given to the canons by Radulph's father, Walter (Gautier) de la Tournelle. To show his repentance for trying to recall this gift Radulph was leaving that same day for Jerusalem. The bishop of Laon, who had been the principal protector and founder of the monastery, offered 60 *solidi* to Radulph as a countergift (see below, note 2) in exchange for his claim on the property. The bishop appended his seal and threatened with excommunication anyone who attempted to violate the agreement.

This charter offers information which is difficult to find in other types of evidence, namely the crusade motivation of the lesser nobility. It is another example (see the previous document) of the legal form excommunication *latae sententiae*.

This gift was confirmed by Radulph's heirs in a charter issued by Roger, bishop of Laon, in 1192. Radulph's son and namesake confirmed and augmented his father's gift in Roger's presence (see below).

NOTES ON THE CHARTER

The Quarrel

In 1126, when this quarrel began, St. Norbert of Xanten, who had founded Prémonté in 1121, was still at the new abbey. Radulph's father, Gautier, was one of Thomas de Marle's vassals, and held the fief of Brancourt from the Coucys. Thomas deseized Gautier, for reasons unknown, and refused to return the fief to Gautier's widow, Agnes, when she requested it. Agnes asked for St. Norbert to intervene on behalf of her son, Radulph Canis. St. Norbert was able to arrange for the fief to go to Agnes during her lifetime, but upon her death, the fief was to go to Prémontré. It is unclear, from the few details that are known, whether the Premonstratensians, whose early history is one of avoiding this kind of dispute, wanted to retain the fief, or if Thomas was the instigator, feeling that it would remain more accessible to his control if it was part of the holdings of the abbey. In any case, as soon as he came of age, Radulph Canis attacked the abbey to recover the fief. St. Norbert's role as peacemaker seems a bit dubious here, since the quarrel was not resolved for sixteen years, and the canons kept the fief. The final agreement seems to have been negotiated by Bishop Barthélemy, who was able to gain Radulph's ac-

knowledgement of the abbey's rights, and a penitential pilgrimage.[1]

The witnesses would appear to be members of the episcopal court, and canons of the house of Prémontré.

On the Identity of Radulph Canis

Radulph was apparently a small fief-holder and a vassal of the Coucys, but neither of the recent histories dealing with this area mention him, beyond stating the information above, which comes from an unpublished charter of 1140. Various men with the cognomen "Canis" witnessed charters issued by lords in the area centered on Coucy and Laon from the 1120s through the 1170s.[2] There are fiefs called le Chêne and la Tournelle within six miles of Coucy, and a sketchy genealogy can be worked out for Radulph's family from the charter of 1140, another issued by his son in 1192, and the *Obituaire de l'abbaye de Prémontré*.[3]

---

[1] The few available details of the story come from BM Soissons 7, fols. 24–25; discussed by Barthélemy, *Coucy*, 159–61, who categorized this as a penitential pilgrimage, 87 n. 145. There is some question as to Ralph's identity and the derivation of the name "Canis": see Newman, *Picardie*, vol. 1: 199; vol. 2: 117, 150–51; and cf. Melleville, *Dictionnaire*, "Le Chêne," with de Sars, *Laonnois*, vol. 1: 247 (La Tour and Chanvallon), and 547 (Brancourt). Ardura, in *Dictionnaire* (389), lists Brancourt as a church incorporated with Mont-Saint-Martin. The latter was an Augustinian house affiliated with Prémontré by 1134, located near Saint-Quentin, in the diocese of Cambrai (now Soissons). To further complicate the evidence for Radulf's identity, there is a charter for the abbey of Eename (Belgium), which mentions a Rodulfus Canis holding a fief at Alost: Charles Piot, *Cartulaire de l'abbaye d'Eename* (Bruges, 1881), 363, no. 388. The charter runs as follows: "Sciant tam posteri quam moderni quod Rodulfus Canis et Udelinus de Hasselt, qui filiam predicti Rodulfi habuit, terram quandam, que jacet in parrochia de Elst, quam tenuerant in feodo de domino Ywaino de Alost, ipsi reddiderant, et eandem terram nobis dedit ad opus elemosine nostre predictus Ywainus. Hujus rei testes sunt: Hugo de Kemeseca, Erardus de Berdamera, Wiricus de Dackenham, Jordanus et Theodericus de Beverne, Reinerus Scara." I was not able to see E. Beaucarne, *Notice historique sur la commune d'Eename*, 2 vols. (Gand, 1893–1895).

[2] Newman, *Picardie*, vol. 2: 77–80, no. 27 (Robert Canis, 1157–1161, and cf. nos. 71, 74); Newman, *Charters of Saint-Fursy of Péronne* (Cambridge, Mass., 1977), nos. 12, 18, 48; BM Soissons 7, fols. 20–21. The charter of 1192 was issued by Roger, bishop of Laon, and says that for the salvation of his soul and of his wife Cecilia, Radulf Canis had given whatever he held of the tithe of Brancourt to Prémontré. After Radulf's death his son Jean confirmed the gift and added other tithes with the consent of his wife, asking that charter be made so that the arrangement between the family and the abbey would be perpetually affirmed. There are no witnesses except for the chancellor William, who wrote the document (Bibliothèque nationale, Collection de Picardie 290, fol. 18). Compare the evidence for Radulf, Cecilia, and their son Jean with the family of la Chaînée, whose charters can be found in Jacquemin, *Soissons*, 82–87, 125, nos. 134, 142, 143, 215.

[3] Arthur Vernier, *Histoire du canton de Coucy-le-Château* (Paris, 1876), 193, 370; Charles Taiée, *Prémontré...*, 2 vols. (Laon, 1872), vol. 1: 43, 71, 77. The charter of 1140 mentions the foundation by Norbert, and continues: "partem decime que est in parrochia de Broientia Walterus de la Tornele a domino Thoma de Coci in feodo tenuerat. Sed quoniam forefecerat predictum feodum eodem tempore dominus Thomas in manu sua receperat. Post mortem ... Walteri Thomas feodum reddere uxori eius Agneti et filio eorum Radulpho qui Canis

Countergifts

Constance Brittain Bouchard, in her study of Cistercian charters, has discussed the practice of countergifts.[4] Although the money Radulph received from the bishop probably assisted him in fulfilling his crusade vow, the document seems to record the resolution of a quarrel rather than a sale. It was a common practice for the house which received a gift from a lay donor to respond not only with the expected spiritual benefits (see the introduction), but with tokens given as gifts to relatives who would be affected by the alienation of property to a religious house. Most often the countergift was money, and Bouchard gives several examples of this kind. The purpose of the countergift, according to her, was to recognize the ongoing relationship between the abbey and the family of its lay patron, as well as serving as "a concrete sign that a relative had indeed agreed to the original gift."[5] This was especially true where there had been a dispute, and here the bishop specifies that the 60 *solidi* were given to "quiet" the disturbance made by the heir.

---

cognominatur nullo modo voluit, donec pro eis Norbertus vir deo plenus interveniens rogavit. Cuius predictus Thomas ut dignum fuerat satisfaciens predicte Agneti feodum tali conditione redditit quod ipsa Premonstrate ecclesie decimam liberam in perpetuum remisit. Fratre suo R/Goberto cum ceteris parentibus suis concedente et assensum prebente. Radulfus autem filius Agnetis puer adhuc erat." (The story continues as explained above.) See the *Obituaire*, Waefelghem, 134, 135 and n. 1; and cf. Barthélemy, *Coucy*, 394, 521, where Raduph is identified as a fief-holder who died in 1190. Warlop, *Flemish Nobility*, vol. 2: no. 43, lists two men using the name Canis: Eustace (1197) and Thomas (1230), the latter with an equestrian seal. Léonard, *Temple*, lists a Eustace Canis as "Magister Franciae" (1163–1171), 113. Eustace's name also appears in Victor Carrière's *Histoire et Cartulaire des Templiers de Provins* (Paris, 1919), no. 89.

[4] Constance Brittain Bouchard, *Holy Entrepreneurs. Cistercians, Knights, and Economic Exchange in Twelfth-Century Burgundy* (Ithaca and London, 1991).

[5] Bouchard, *Holy Entrepreneurs*, 89.

3
1146, THIERRY, COUNT OF FLANDERS

Thérèse de Hemptinne and Adriaan Verhulst, eds., *De Oorkonden den Graven van Vlaanderen (Juli 1128-September 1191)*, II. Uitgave-Band I: *Regering van Diederik van de Elzas (Juli 1128-17 Januari 1168)* (Brussels, 1988), 151, no. 91.

Quoniam generationum decessione ac successione rerum gestarum memoria interit, litterarum apicibus, quibus nil memorie fidelius servit, tam presentibus quam futuris memorandum relinquere congruum duximus, quia ego Theodericus, divina permissione Flandrensium comes, cum glorioso Francorum rege Lodevico Iherosolimam profecturus, Helmaro, Yprensis ecclesie venerabili preposito, quecumque predecessores eius a predecessoribus meis iura sive consuetudines, tam in *scabinatu* quam in ceteris, omni exactione exclusa tenuerunt, ob remedium anime mee et uxoris mee Sibilie concessi.

Signum domini Milonis Morinorum episcopi. S. Bernardi Clarevallensis abbatis. S. Walteri Gonella. S. Gilleberti Bergensis. S. Walteri Audomarensis castellani.

Because with the passing and succession of generations, the memory of human actions is lost, we make provision to leave behind a written charter, which will serve more faithfully than any recollection as a suitable reminder for present and future generations. I, Thierry, by divine permission count of Flanders, about to set out for Jerusalem with Louis, the glorious king of the Franks, grant to Helmar, venerable provost of Ypres, that they may hold without any fees, whatever rights or customs were granted his predecessors by my predecessors, both in *echevinage* and others. This I grant as a remedy for my soul and that of my wife Sybil.

Sign of Lord Milo, bishop of Thérouanne; sign of Bernard, abbot of Clairvaux; sign of Walter Gonella; sign of Gilbert Bergensis; sign of Walter, castellan of St. Omer.

SUMMARY OF THE CHARTER

Thierry of Alsace, count of Flanders (1128-1167), issued this charter in 1146, on the eve of the Second Crusade, which was led by King Louis VII of France (1137-1180). It is a confirmation of all the past gifts of his family to the Augustinian house of St. Martin at Ypres, addressed to the prior, Helmarus. Thierry confirms his family's relationship to the abbey "as a remedy for my soul and that of my wife Sybil." The witnesses include two well-known clerics of the 1140s, St. Bernard of Clairvaux, who preached the Second Crusade, and Bishop Milo of Thérouanne (Morinorum).

NOTES ON THE CHARTER

St. Martin's

In the tenth century there was a chapel near the city of Ypres consecrated to the Virgin and to the apostle Andrew. In 1012 Count Baldwin IV of Flanders (988-1035) installed secular canons and founded the priory of St. Martin's there. Count Robert I built the church to replace the old chapel in 1088. The priory was reformed by Jean de Warneton, bishop of Thérouanne (1099-1130) in 1101, after which it was a community of regular canons living by the Augustinian rule. Helmar was prior 1139-1158.[1]

Thierry

Thierry of Alsace was the son of Robert the Frisian's daughter Gertrude, whose claim to the fief was recognized in June of 1128 after a dispute between the king of France and the Flemish nobility. Robert the Frisian (count of Flanders 1071-1093) had made a famous pilgrimage to Jerusalem 1086-1090; his heir, Count Robert II (1093-1111), had joined the First Crusade. Thierry married the daughter of the king of Jerusalem, Sybil, in 1134, and he made the journey to the Holy Land four times: 1138/9, 1147/9, 1157/9, and 1164/6.

For the Second Crusade, Thierry took the cross at Vézelay, on 31 March, 1146, with King Louis VII and a crowd of knights which included Enguerran II de Coucy. Thierry was at the siege of Damascus in 1148, where a dispute arose over who would take possession of the city if it could be captured. Thierry perhaps had the strongest claim among the contenders, but the crusaders were unable to reach consensus, and the siege was abandoned. According to the chronicler William of Tyre the failure should be attributed to Thierry, who had previously visited the shrines at Jerusalem and became eager to abandon the siege and return to Flanders.[2]

---

[1] *Monasticon belge*, vol. 3: 937-45.
[2] For a discussion of Thierry's role in this crusade, see Setton, vol. 1: 469, 487, 506-10;

Thierry's family had ties to the reform papacy through Robert II's wife, Clementia of Burgundy, whose brother was Pope Calixtus II (1119-1124). Clementia was instrumental in installing an Augustinian reformer as bishop of Thérouannne, an involvement which may help to explain Thierry's reputation as a patron of the church, and especially of Augustinian canons like the ones at St. Martin. Thierry's son, Philip of Alsace (1167-1191) went on crusade three times. His great-grandson, Baldwin IX of Flanders (1195-1206), was emperor of Constantinople after the Fourth Crusade of 1204.[3]

Sybil

Count Fulk of Anjou's children by his first wife, Eremburge of Maine, were Sybil of Flanders and Geoffrey Plantagenet. Geoffrey married the only daughter of Henry I of England, thus consolidating an "Angevin empire" which included England, Normandy, and Anjou. Fulk's second marriage to Melisende, the heiress to the Kingdom of Jerusalem, in 1129, was intended to continue the dynasty of Baldwin II, one of the members of the First Crusade. Fulk was the first king of Jerusalem to be married in the church of the Holy Sepulchre, and ruled from 1131-1143. When Fulk died in a hunting accident in 1143, his widow Melisende became effective ruler of the kingdom for their son, Baldwin III, who was only 13. The fall of the city of Edessa to the Muslims in 1144 was the signal for the Second Crusade, which was proclaimed by both Pope Eugenius III (1145-1153) and King Louis VII of France (1137-1180) in 1145.[4] King Louis was Thierry's feudal overlord. There was a tradition of crusading in Thierry's family, and the interests of his wife's family was an additional reason for him to undertake the expedition of 1147/8. Sybil remained in Flanders as regent, and was forced to defend Bruges from the combined attack of the counts of Hainaut and Namur during her husband's absence. She did make

---

and more recently, Jonathan Phillips, *Defenders of the Holy Land: Relations between the Latin East and the West 1119-1187* (Oxford, 1996), appendix.

[3] All of the information on Thierry and his family comes from David Nicholas, *Medieval Flanders* (New York and London, 1992), 56-71, 441. His bibliography is a good starting place on Flanders, and his history includes both maps and genealogical tables. For Flanders and the Augustinian reform, see the introduction; for other charters issued by Thierry see nos. 7, 10, and 19 in this collection. There is also a charter dealing with the advocate of Thérouanne, no. 18.

[4] For Sybil see H. E. Mayer, *The Crusades*, trans. John Gillingham (Oxford, 1972), 86-96. For Melisende, there are a number of articles, notably Bernard Hamilton, "Women in the Crusader States," *Studies in Church History, Subsidia* 1 (1978): 155; and Rudolf Hiestand, "Königin Melisendis von Jerusalem und Prémontré," *Analecta Praemonstratensia* 71 (1995): 77-95.

the journey to Jerusalem with Thierry in 1157, where she entered the convent of Saint-Lazare in order to end her life in the Holy Land.[5]

ob remedium anime mee

Thierry made this confirmation "as a remedy for my soul and that of my wife Sybil." According to Bouchard this phrase signifies "a certain kind of gift, in which the layman expected general spiritual benefits in return for the property he gave the monks ...."[6] Here the phrase connotes the relationship of Thierry and his family as patrons of the canons, being renewed on the occasion of the crusade. Like the transaction in the preceding charter, this one uses a precise formula, indicating the terms of that relationship. Many donations have been investigated as if they were actually sales, the proceeds of which could be used to finance the expedition. Bouchard's point is that monasteries were not "shy" about calling a sale a sale, and the terminology of the charter is a reliable indication of the donor's intention. Here the ongoing relationship is stressed because it is a confirmation, issued not to benefit either party in a concrete way, but rather to offer protection to the priory's possessions in the event of Thierry's death.

I am not sure what the term "scabinatus" or, in French, "echevinage" means in this charter. The term *scabini* or *échevins* dates back to a term for Carolingian officials charged with either administrative or judicial powers. Eventually the term could be used to mean representatives of the central power, whether king, count, or city commune. I assume that the counts of Flanders routinely invested abbots, for instance, with rights or powers as comital representatives in their areas, and that this confirmation is referring generally to whatever rights the priors of St. Martin held.

THE WITNESSES

Milon Morinorum episcopus: Milo, bishop of Thérouanne (1131–1158), had been the abbot of the Premonstratensian house of St. Josse. He is credited with founding the house, and with being the patron of Dommartin, the men's abbey which split off from the original double foundation. He was the patron of four other Norbertine houses: Licques, Marcheroux, Selincourt and St. Augustine in Thérouanne. There is a letter addressed to him describing the crusade to Lisbon of 1147, which implies his help in organizing that expedition.[7]

---

[5] Le Glay, *Flandre*, 232, 239.
[6] Bouchard, *Holy Entrepreneurs*, 76.
[7] On Milo see F. Petit, "Milon de Sélincourt, évêque de Thérouanne," *Analecta Praemonstratensia* 48 (1972): 73–93; Martène et Durand, *Ampliss. Coll.*, vol. 1: 800; and E.

Bernardus Clarevallensis abbas: St. Bernard, abbot of Clairvaux (1116–1153), was one of the principal organizers of the Second Crusade and a pivotal figure in the mid-twelfth century. There is an extensive literature on his life and writings. He was involved in the prosecution of Peter Abelard for heresy, in establishing the rule of the order of the Templars in 1129, and in the disputed election of Pope Innocent II (1130–1143). During his life the Cistercian order expanded rapidly, at least partly because of his influence. In 1115, just after he joined the order, there were five houses, and in 1153 there were three hundred and forty-three. A twelfth-century Premonstratensian writer called Milo, Bernard, and Norbert the most outstanding clerics of their day: Norbert for faith, Bernard for love, and Milo for humility.[8]

Walterus Audomarensis castellanus: Walter, castellan of St. Omer (1145–1173), was in the Holy Land in 1152–53, and returned in 1157–60 to marry Eschiva of Tiberias.[9] He was a frequent attestor at the court of the kings of Jerusalem, using the title "Tiberias" or "St. Omer". He died in 1173.[10]

Gilbert Bergensis: Gilbert I was castellan of Bergues 1128–1155, steward at Thierry's court 1148–1155, and standard-bearer for the count's army in 1153.[11]

Brouette, "La date de décès de Milon Ier, évêque de Thérouanne," *Bulletin trimestriel de la Société académique des Antiquaires de la Morinie* 21 (1970): 335–40.

[8] On St. Bernard, see Michael Gervers, ed., *The Second Crusade and the Cistercians* (New York, 1992), which includes an extensive bibliography; Jonathan Phillips, "St. Bernard of Clairvaux, the Low Countries and the Lisbon Letter of the Second Crusade," *Journal of Ecclesiastical History* 48 (1997): 485–97; Peter Raedts, "St. Bernard of Clairvaux and Jerusalem," *Studies in Church History, Subsidia* 10 (1994): 169–82; and *Vita Norberti Archiepiscopi Magdeburgensis*, ed. V. R. Wilmans, MGH SS 12 (Hanover, 1856), 672.

[9] Walterus/Galterus or Gautier de Faucomberge, castellan of St. Omer, can be found in Bresc-Bautier, *Cartulaire*, under "Galterius de Galilea"; and in C. K. Slack, "Royal Familiares in the Latin Kingdom of Jerusalem, 1100–1187," *Viator* 22 (1991): 40. See A. Giry, *Histoire de la ville de St. Omer et de ses institutions jusqu'au XIVe s.* (Paris, 1877), 341–46.

[10] Warlop, *Flemish Nobility*, vol. 2: no. 192.

[11] Warlop, *Flemish Nobility*, vol. 1: 212–13. Walter Gonella's name appears in Warlop, vol. 2: no. 93, with no information.

4
1147, ROBERT I DE BOVES

Gallia Christiana, edited by the Congregation of St. Maur (Paris, 1751; reprint Farnborough, Hants., 1970), vol. 10, "instrumenta," cols. 310–12, no. 31. Compare with Charles Du Cange, *Histoire de l'état de la ville d'Amiens et de ses comtes* (Amiens, 1840), 292–97, no. 1. The original is a document entitled "Charta Theoderici episcopi de possessionibus sancti Acheoli," from the Cartulary of St. Acheul, held by the British Library, as Add. ms. 15604, cartulary no. 21, fols. 13–15.

Ego Theodericus Deo gratia Ambianensis episcopus tam praesentibus quam futuris in Christo fidelibus in perpetuum. Quoniam omnium debitores sumus, omnium et maxime pauperum Christi necessitatibus ex ecclesiasticis facultatibus summa diligentia providere debemus, quatenus a cura et sollicitudine necessitatum corporalium, sine quibus haec vita transigi non potest, relevati, viam propositi sui gressibus inoffensis incedant, et ad meditationem divinae legis, et expletionem spiritualis servitutis liberiores fiant. Ea propter, fili Galtere abba venerabilis sancti Acheoli in Christo plurimum dilecte, tibi tuisque successoribus, et ecclesiae tuae unum manipulum decimae casae de domno Vedasto, et alterum de Cancy, quia utrumque altare dono praedecessoris nostri G. bonae memoriae ecclesia tua possidebat, in perpetuum possidendos concedimus: collatas etiam ecclesiae tuae a devotis viris eleemosynas, ut pontificalis auctoritatis munimine firmiores habeantur, praesenti pagina significare curavimus quarum eleemosynarum nomina cum donationibus suis subscripsimus; altare videlicet de Baliscourt, quod Elisabeth vobis reddidit praesente viro suo Iberto et concedente: ipsa enim illud ab eo in feodo in conjugio suo acceperat, praesentibus etiam filiis suis, et ipsum donum ore et manu confirmantibus Waltero clerico, Iberto milite, Odone, Willelmo et filia Cothsinde; sextam etiam partem decimae de *Rastel* a quodam milite Alelmo cognomine Grenario receptam, praedictae ecclesiae assignamus.

1. Sciendum etiam quod in Bothua castro de reditibus molendinorum quatuor modios tritici ex eleemosyna comitis Ingeranni ipsa eadem ecclesia antiquitus possedebat; sed maledictorum vocibus filius ipsius Ingeranni, Thomas, & Robertus filius eiusdem Thomae commoti ipsam eleemosynam

I, Thierry, by the grace of God bishop of Amiens, to the faithful in Christ, both present and future, forever. Because we are the debtors of all, and we must provide with great diligence from ecclesiastical holdings for the necessities of all and especially of the poor of Christ, so that freed from care and solicitude for the necessities without which one cannot pass through life, they may with unoffending steps proceed on their chosen way and be freer for meditation on the divine law and the fulfillment of their spiritual service. Therefore to you, my son Walter (Gautier), much beloved in Christ, abbot of the venerable monastery of St. Acheul, and to your successors, and to your church, we grant to be possessed in perpetuity one *manipulus* of the tithes of the house of Lord Vedast, and another of Cancy (Cagny?), because your church possessed both altars by the gift of our predeccessor G. of good memory. And so that they may have more surely, under the protection of episcopal authority, the alms conferred on your church by devout men, we take care to list on the present page the names of those alms with their donations: namely, the altar of Baliscourt, which Elizabeth gave to you in the presence of her husband Ibert who granted his consent. She had received it from him in fief when they were married; their children were also present. This gift was confirmed in word and writing by Walter, a cleric; Ibert, a knight; Odo; William (Guillaume) and his daughter Cothsinde. We assign to the same church a sixth part of the tithes of Rastel, received from a certain knight Alelmus, whose cognomen was Grenarius.

    1. It is to be known that the same church long ago possessed four modii of wheat from the rents of the mills in the fort of Boves by the alms of Count Enguerran. However, moved by the voices of the malcontents, his son Thomas, son of Enguerran, and Robert, son of the same Thomas,

eidem ecclesiae violenter abstulerant. Nuper vero idem Ambianensis comes Robertus Jerosolymam profecturus, consilio religiosorum virorum commonitus, compunctus est, et praesente matre sua domina Milesende, religiosis etiam viris astantibus, in conspectu abbatis supradictae ecclesiae culpam suam recognovit; et absolutione quaesita & impetrata, ipsos quatuor modios tritici de reditibus molendinorum recipiendos, sub testimonio hominum suorum, quorum nomina subscribentur, eidem ecclesiae perpetua possessione per manum nostram confirmavit.

Wido quoque de Mesliressart et uxor eius Emmelina, et Hugo filius eorum cum reliquis filiis, quidquid in territorio villae de Huy ex sua sive ex parte Petri de Saloco possidebant; totam videlicet terram suam cum terragio et omni decima, quibusdam mansis censualibus exceptis, concedente domino Widone de Longo cum Mathilde uxore sua, et filio eorum Alelmo, de cuius feodo terra illa pendebat, praesente etiam multitudine tam clericorum quam laicorum, eidem ecclesiae absque ulla calumnia per manum nostram liberrime contulerunt. Praefatus siquidem Petrus pro matre sua ipsius ecclesiae conversa ex eadem terra campum unum iam contulerat. Quidam vero miles Adam nomine de Glisi, pro matre sua conversa in ipsa villa dedit eidem ecclesiae mansum, pomerium et quidquid infra viam est ab ipso pomerio usque ad mansum Firmini, cum ipso manso, et tantum terrae arabilis quae modio tritici posset seminari, hoc ipsum concedente Ambianensi comite domino suo Roberto de Bova. Praeter haec omnia Radulfus Dalfins, ad cuius dominium altare de Gissocourt laicali iure pertinebat, quidquid per se vel per subiectos sibi homines in ipso altari possidebat, et quidquid in posterum a suis in territorio eiusdem altaris saepe fatae ecclesiae conferetur, uxore sua et filio donum affirmantibus, pro sua suorumque animabus in eleemosyna per manum nostram libentissime concessit.

2. Odo etiam de Wiencourt filius Sorreiae, unum campum terrae sancti Quintini in villa de Baienviller excoluerat, quem omnibus heredibus concedentibus Jerosolymis (*sic*: printed version) proficiscens in eleemosyna praefatae ecclesiae contulit, eo tenore ut terragium et cetera quae debentur, domino ipsius terrae solvantur; Hugo quoque de Geldincourt campum alium, cum medietate terragii similiter Jerusalem tendens, bono animi voto pro salute animae suae, orationum et eleemosynarum eiusdem ecclesiae particeps effectus, domino suo Radulfo de Bacouel, quia in terra illa in territorio de Placi ad suum feodum pertinebat, donum firmante, uxore quoque, et filio, et ceteris heredibus idipsum confirmantibus, per manum nostram contulit ipsi ecclesiae. Ut hoc igitur ratum et inconcussum permaneat, tibi frater Galtere abba, tuisque fratribus sub regula sancti Augustini Domino militantibus, scriptum istud facimus, et sigillo nostro corroboramus, et

violently took away these alms from that same church. Recently however, the same Count of Amiens, Robert, was about to set out for Jerusalem. Moved by the counsel of devout men, he was contrite, and in the presence of his mother, the lady Melisende, and of various religious men, in the sight of the abbot of the above-mentioned church, he acknowledged his fault, and having sought and been granted absolution, in the presence of his men whose names will be subscribed below, he confirmed through our hand to the perpetual possession of the same church those four modii of grain received from the rents of the mills.

Likewise, in the presence of a multitude of clerics and laymen, Gui of Meliressart and his wife Emmelina, and Hugh their son with the rest of their children, confer on the same church through our hands freely and without any contentious claim, whatever they possess in the territory of the village of Huy* either on their own part or by Peter (Pierre) of Saleux:* namely, all their land, with its rents and all tithes, except for certain rental dwellings, with the consent of Lord Gui of Longueaux* and Mathilde his wife, and their son Alelmus, from whose fief that land depends. The aforementioned Peter had already granted a field of that land for his mother, a *conversa* of that church. A certain knight, Adam, named de Glisy,* gave to the same church for his mother, a *conversa*, a house in that same village, with an orchard and whatever is within the road which runs from that orchard to the house of Firmin, together with the house itself and as much arable land as can be sown with a modius of grain; this he did with the consent of the count of Amiens, his lord, Robert of Boves. Besides all these, Radulph Dalfins, to whose domain the altar of Gissencourt pertains by secular law, most freely granted as alms by our hand whatever he possessed in that altar personally or through the men subject to him, and whatever might be conferred later by his people in the territory of the same altar of that oft-mentioned church. This he did with the agreement of his wife and son to the gift, for his soul and the souls of his family.

2. Odo of Guyencourt, son of Sorreia, farmed one field of land of St.-Quentin in the village of Baienviller, which as he set out to Jerusalem, with the agreement of all his heirs, he granted to the aforementioned church, in such wise that the land-tax and other things which were due would be paid to the lord of that land. Also Hugh of Guyencourt, who was also heading for Jerusalem, granted through our hand to that church another field, with a half of a land-tax, out of the goodness of his heart for the salvation of his soul, as one made a sharer of the prayers and alms of the same church. His lord, Radulf of Bacouel,* confirmed the gift, for that land in the territory of Placi pertained to his fief. His wife and son also confirmed the gift. So that this may remain ratified and unchallenged, to you, Brother Walter, abbot, and to your brothers fighting for the Lord under the rule of St. Augustine, we make this written document and confirm

perturbatores huius nostrae confirmationis excommunicamus, et ad majorem huius rei certitudinem, testium nomina subassignamus. Signum mei ipsius Theoderici Ambianensis episcopi, S. Radulphi decani, S. Radulfi et Balduini archidiaconorum, S. Guarini praepositi et thesaurarii, S. Fulconis praecentoris, S. Achardi capellani, Adelelmi *et etc.* sacerdotum, S. Dodomanni, Arnulfi et Richerii diaconorum, S. Wermundi, Rogeri et Willelmi subdiaconorum, S. Widonis, Roberti et Wermundi acolythorum. Signum Theobaldi abbatis sancti Martini de Gemellis, S. Droconis abbatis sancti Johannis, S. Gigomari abbatis sancti Fusciani, S. Mainardi Gardiensis abbatis, S. Adam abbatis sancti Judoci de Nemore, S. Gualteri abbatis de Selincourt, S. Droconis prioris de Lihuns, S. Hugonis prioris sancti Ansberti de Bothua, S. Herberti prioris sancti Fusciani. Signum Droconis militis de Sissolin, S. Adae filii eius, S. Hevelonis de *Rourchel*, S. Roberti fratris eius, S. Petri de Guincourt, Hosmundi de Sanctis, Ragineri filii Roberti miltum, Thomae et Roberti praepositum. Actum Ambianis anno Dominicae Incarnationis M. CXLVII., indictione X, praesulatus autem domini Theoderici episcopi III feliciter. Amen. Simon cancellarius per manum Roberti Gigantis notarii scripsit et subscripsit.

confirm it with our seal. And we excommunicate those who would challenge our confirmation. To give this matter a higher degree of certainty, we affix the names of the witnesses: My sign Bishop Thierry of Amiens (1145–1169). Sign of Raoul de Heilly, doyen (1140–1178). Sign of Raoul archdeacon of Amiens (1125–1149) and Baudouin, archdeacon of Ponthieu (1135–1149). Sign of Guérin de Breteuil, provost (1141–1160) and treasurer (1135–1148). Sign of Foulque, precentor (1135–1164). Sign of Achard, chaplain, of Adelelmus, etc., priests. Sign of Dodomann, Arnulf and Richer, deacons. Sign of Wermundus (Guarmundus), Roger and Willaim, subdeacons. Sign of Gui, Robert, and W/Germund, acolytes. Sign of Theobald, abbot of St.-Martin of Gemlis. Sign of Drogo, abbot of St.-Jean.* Sign of Gigomar, abbot of St. Fuscian.* Sign of Mainard, abbot of le Gard. Sign of Adam, abbot of St. Jude of Nemor. Sign of Walter, abbot of Selincourt. Sign of Droco, prior of Lihons-en-Santerre. Sign of Hugh, prior of St.-Ansbert of Boves. Sign of Herbert, prior of St. Fuscian. Sign of Drieux, knight of Sessoliu.* Sign of Adam, his son. Sign of Hevelon of Rourchel. Sign of Robert, his brother. Sign of Peter de Guyencourt, Hosmund de Sains-en-Amiénois,* Raginer, son of Robert, knights; Thomas and Robert, provosts. Transacted at Amiens, year of the Lord's Incarnation, 1147, indiction 10, in the third year of Lord Thierry the bishop, happily in office. Amen. Simon, the chancellor, wrote this by the hand of Robert Gigans, the notary, and signed it.

SUMMARY OF THE CHARTER

This charter was issued by Thierry, bishop of Amiens (1145–1169), in 1147 for the Augustinian house of St. Acheul at Amiens. All donations previous to 1147 are mentioned, three of which are donations made by crusaders. The donors and their men and heirs were in most cases present, so that their names are included as witnesses. There are two sections I have set into paragraphs and numbered for special attention. In 1, Enguerran II of Coucy's brother and companion on the Second Crusade, Robert of Boves, is mentioned (for Enguerran, see charter 1). The text recalls the gift by their grandfather, Enguerran I of a tax of four *modii* of grain from his mills at Boves.[1] However, because of "evil counsel," both Enguerran I's son, Thomas, and then his grandson, Robert, had refused to pay the tax. Now Robert, who had become count of Amiens, being about to leave for Jerusalem, repented, having been counseled by religious men who were present, along with his mother Melisende. Robert therefore acknowledged his fault before them and the abbot of St. Acheul, seeking absolution and confirming the original gift. His men were to be witnesses. Further along, in the paragraph labeled 2, two other crusaders make gifts to the abbey in the presence of their heirs. Odo de Guyencourt, son of Sorreia, gave a field, and Hugh de Guyencourt another, both as "gifts"—no money is mentioned as being raised for the journey. Presumably these two men took crusade vows with their overlord, Robert of Boves, count of Amiens, in order to join the Second Crusade, led by King Louis VII and Thierry of Alsace, count of Flanders (see the previous charter). This is a fairly common type of charter, in which confirmation is made and the gifts listed, but the section dealing with Robert recalls the first two charters in this collection. Again, a reconciliation between a secular land-holder and the local church is being sealed with a crusade vow.

NOTES ON THE CHARTER

Coucy/Boves

The most important work on the Boves family is still Auguste Janvier, *Boves et ses seigneurs* (Amiens, 1877). See also the Coucy sources, from

---

[1] GC, vol. 10, "instrumenta," cols. 293–94, no. 12: ". . . Ego quidem Ingelrannus comes Ambianis et Bothuensis advocatis, patri et matri mihi que et successoribus meis utiliter providens, de molendinis meis Bothuensibus singulis mensibus sextarios quatuor de tritico mensurae illius ecclesiae sanctae Mariae et sanctorum martyrum Acei et Acheoli in perpetuum trado. Ego vero Eustachius vicedominus Ambianensis, de redditu sextarii nostri in Ambianica civitate sextarios duos de frumento, uxore mea et filiis meis annuentibus, omni mense ecclesiae praedictae in perpetuum trado." This charter is dated 1085.

charter 1, and Alberic de Calonne, *Histoire de la ville d'Amiens*, 2 vols. (Amiens, 1899-1900).[2]

St. Acheul, like Prémontré, was a new house of Augustinian canons, partially founded by the Coucys, attacked by the Coucy heirs, and the recipient of a peace-making gift on the eve of a crusade. In both cases the agreement between the family and the canons may have been negotiated by the local bishop. Like Prémontré, St. Acheul was founded by a bishop near the cathedral town to serve as a retreat for canons wishing to convert to the reformed rule and life. In 1085, Bishop Rorico (1080-1085) of Amiens founded the house, and Enguerran I gave the new abbey a monthly rent of four muids of grain.[3] Robert had refused to honor his grandfather's donation, but he repented of this, and of other attacks on cathedral property in 1146.[4] Robert's "repentance" of 1146, as well as his vow of 1147, represent an effort to conciliate the local church. Robert held Boves from the bishop of Amiens and the abbot of Corbie, which would give him a strong motive for reconciliation. Like the other members of the Coucy family, Robert inherited a lordship based on the violent acquisitions of Enguerran I and Thomas de Marle, and consolidated his holdings by conciliating the church and the crown. In 1146, Robert not only made donations to the church, he also married Beatrice, the daughter of Hugh, count of St.-Pol, whose rival claim to Amiens was recognized by King Louis VII.[5]

Robert incurred excommunication in either 1146 or 1147. It is not clear whether he was censured for his behavior towards the local church, or for failing actually to leave on crusade. His name does not appear in any of the crusade chronicles. The excommunication is known only through a letter from Suger, abbot of St. Denis and regent during Louis VII's absence, to Bishop Thierry of Amiens, in which the abbot scolds the bishop for lifting the punishment on Robert too easily. Suger calls Robert a "diabolical man," in a general condemnation of his actions which leaves the exact rea-

---

[2] Some information can also be found in R. Fossier, *La terre et les hommes en Picardie jusqu'à la fin du XIIIe siècle*, 2 vols. (Paris-Louvain, 1968; new ed. Amiens, 1987); and Charles Du Cange, *Histoire de l'état de la ville d'Amiens et de ses comtes* (Amiens, 1840). See also William Mendel Newman, *Le Personnel de la Cathédral d'Amiens (1066-1306)* (Paris, 1972) and *Les seigneurs de Nesle en Picardie*, vol. 1: 94-99 for further notes on the family and a geneaological chart.

[3] Joseph Roux, *Histoire de l'abbaye de Saint-Acheul-lez-Amiens* (Amiens, 1890) 21, 32; GC, vol. 10, cols. 293-94, above; and cf. Janvier, *Boves*, 25. See also A. Ledieu, "Ache et Acheul," DHGE.

[4] Joseph Roux, ed., *Cartulaire du chapitre de la cathédrale d'Amiens*, 2 vols. (Amiens, 1905-1912), vol. 1: 31-33, no. 23. This cartulary contains a confirmation of Robert's settlement with St. Acheul, issued by his son Enguerran de Boves in 1192: 115, no. 86.

[5] Robert: Auguste Janvier, *La Picardie historique et monumentale*, vol. 1: *Amiens* (Amiens, 1898-1899), 251, 59-61; Enguerran: Janvier, *Boves*, 25, 23.

son for the excommunication unclear.[6] What does seem clear is that his donations to the church in 1146 are similar to his brother's of 1138 and 1146 (see charter 1, above). They represent a negotiated settlement of long-standing disputes rather than an effort to raise money for a crusade expedition. As such, they are technically penitential acts or alms, and clearly motivated by "repentance" as the issuers of the charters claim. Whatever spiritual motivation was being claimed by the word "repentance" is irrelevant to the fact that these charters show a literal "turn-around," a moment when the Coucys changed their method of dealing with the local church, and their holdings became more secure as a result.

Enguerran II was able to continue a program of conciliation of church and crown, with excellent results in terms of the stability and expansion of his lordship. Robert's career looks more like his father's, with similar consequences. He attempted to deseize his nephews in 1154, became notorious for his treatment of his wife, was censured by Pope Alexander III (1159–1181), and finally exiled to Sicily, where his conspiracies against the throne led first to imprisonment and then to a hasty return to Boves. Once home, he helped to foment a quarrel between Count Philip of Flanders, his overlord, and King Philip II Augustus (1180–1223). In 1184, Boves was under siege by a royal army, just as La Fère had been in 1131. Philip II had no more success than Louis VI. In the negotiated truce, Robert did acknowledge the final loss of Amiens, but he kept Boves, holding it from the crown; so that he was able to inform his erstwhile overlord, the count of Flanders, that they were now peers at court. Robert died on the Third Crusade, in 1190 at Acre.[7] One of Robert's nephews also issued a charter for the Second Crusade, charter 5 below.

THE WITNESSES

Besides Robert's mother and brother, the reconciliation the charter records took place in the presence of the abbot of St. Acheul, Walter/Gautier (1146–1175), who is mentioned in the final paragraph, Bishop Thierry, and of many of the members of the cathedral chapter, who are listed as witnesses. There are other abbots present:

Theobald, St.-Martin de Gemellis (Gembloux? if so, O. Ben. 1145–1163)
Drogo, St.-Jean (Amiens? if so, O. Praem., and the name should be Fulco, 1134–1157)*

---

[6] Janvier, *Amiens*, 59–61; *Epistolae Sugerii Abbatis S. Dionysii*, no. 154 (RHGF, vol. 15: 486): "hominem diabolicum."

[7] For the story of Robert's life, see Janvier, *Boves*, 61–75; and *Ex Gisleberti Montensis praepositi Hannoniae chronico* (RHGF, vol. 18: 382a).

Gigomar, St.-Fuscian, O. Ben. (1145–1155). This abbey was founded or reestablished by Robert's grandfather, Enguerran I, lord of Coucy and count of Amiens, who gave the monks part of the village of Sains in 1105. He is buried in the nave of the abbey church.[8]

Mainard, le Gard, O. Cist. (1138–1147)

Adam, St. Judocus in Nemore, otherwise known as Dommartin, O. Praem. (1131–1166)

Walter, Selincourt, O. Praem. (1131–1164)

---

[8] Daire, *Amiens*, vol. 2: 164–66. The prior in 1145 was "Wigomar," 167.

* See stars by place names in the English translation of the charter. Place names marked can be found in the *Dictionnaire historique. . . . Picardie*, vol. 1, *Paris/Amiens*: Bacouel (278–79), a lordship from the 650s, patrons of St. Acheul, and by the 1300s lords of Taisnel; Glisy (214–16), an "old" family to whom Enguerran III (?) de Boves confirmed Glisy and its dependencies in 1219 when Pierre de Glisy accompanied him to the Holy Land; Huy (100), the tithe of Huy was given to St. Acheul by Bishop Rorico in 1085, the lordship in 1215 by Thomas le Monnoyer and Guy de la Croix; Longueau (144 ff); Sains (236), a lordship shared by the lords of Boves and St. Fuscien, by donation of Enguerran of Boves; St. Fuscien (239–42), a Benedictine abbey in the parish of Sains, originally founded in the sixth century and restored by Enguerran I de Boves in 1105; Saloco/Saleux (246–49), a lordship belonging to the vicomtes of Amiens and the Picquigny family (see the following charter); Sessoleium/Saint-Sauflieu (242–46), a lordship in the twelfth century on a level with Picquigny, for which Drieux and Adam are the only ones listed until 1190.

5
1147/1151, ALELMUS DE FLICHECOURT

Bibliothèque nationale, Collection de Picardie 257, fol. 18.[1] This is an eighteenth-century copy. Cf. Charles Du Cange, *Histoire de l'état de la ville d'Amiens et de ses comtes*, 298-99, note 1. Part of the charter is printed in Chesne, *Coucy*, "preuves - additions & corrections," 669.
    The charter is dated 1151, but refers to the expedition of 1147.

Ego Allelmus Flescicurtis dominus, & Ambianis civitatis princeps quartus, recognosco, et ad posterorum memoriam conscribi facio, et ut in perpetuum ratum permaneat, sigilli mei impressione confirmo, quia in anno quo Jerosolimam cum exercitu Francorum profecturus eram, ego et sorores mee Flandrina, Milesendis, & Mathildis, laudavimus et concessimus donationes et eleemosinas quas Wido, pater meus, & Mathildis mater mea, & parentes nostri, & homines eorum pro anima Alelmi avunculi mei & pro animabus suis longo tempore ante donaverant ecclesie Sancti Ioannis Baptiste Ambianensis, scilicet altare de Marchel [Martel?] cum tota decima et terra dotali, et curtem liberam, et nemus circa curtem, quo ipsa clauditur et arationes terrarum quas in territorio de Marcel habet prefata Ecclesia cum pascuis et decimam quam dedit Robertus clericus apud Vadencourt: altare ad campum sancti Germani cum decima, et altare de Ultrbais, et altare de Vadencourt cum tota decima et terra dotali. Campum et curtile sancti Petri de Gaudiaco et campum Ulmorum, et terram quam in eodem territorio Walterus de Vadencourt, Petrus, Emelina, Giroldus de Petraclas, et Crispinus prefate Ecclesie, retento sibi terragio, sub chyrographo cum pascuis donaverunt, altare de Sauieres cum mansione fratrum, et nemus circa mansionem, et curtile juxta nemus et terram quam in territorio de Sauieres Ymarus et Ingelmarus eidem ecclesie assensu heredum suorum, retento sibi terragio sub chyrographo cum pascuis donaverunt. Molendinum de prato, et ipsum pratum in quo illud manet, et campum sancti Petri apud Driencourt, que Hugo Bonaldi prefate ecclesie cum domo sua dedit, decimam quam dedit Robertus clericus apud Hundercurt, et tertiam partem

---

[1] It has been suggested by Professor Hiestand, based on the note at the bottom of the copy "from a codex formerly at the 'Petavianae' library, then of the Queen of Sweden," that the original of this charter exists in the Vatican Library, fonds Reg. Lat. I have not been able to follow this up.

I, Alelmus, lord of Flichecourt and fourth prince of the city of Amiens, certify and cause to be written down as a reminder for my descendants, and so that it may be ratified in perpetuity, confirm with the impress of my seal that in the year in which I was about to set out for Jerusalem with the army of the Franks, I and my sisters Flandrine, Melisende and Mathilde, confirmed and granted the donations and alms which, for the sake of the soul of my uncle Alelmus and for their own souls, Gui, my father, and Mathilde, my mother, and our relations, and their men had long ago donated to the church of St.-Jean Baptiste in Amiens: namely, the altar of Marchel with all the tithes and land endowment, the free court, the forest next to the court by which the court is enclosed, and the lands which the aforementioned church has in the territory of Marcel; together with the pastures and tithe which Robert, clerk of Vadencourt gave: an altar at the field of St. Germain with a tithe, the altar of Ultrbais, and the altar of Vadencourt with all its tithe and land endowment. The field and court of St.-Pierre-a-Gouy* and the field of Aumatre,* and the land in the same territory which with its meadows Walter/Gautier de Wadencourt, Peter/Pierre, Emelina, Girold de Petraclas, and Crispin gave by a charter to the same church, reserving to themselves the power of *terrage*, the altar of Savières* with the house of the brethren, the woods around the house, and the court next to the woods, and the land in the territory of Savieres with its pastures which Ymarus and Ingelmarus gave to the same church in a charter with the consent of their inheritors, keeping for themselves the right of *terrage*. The mill down in the meadow, the meadow in which it stands, and the field of St. Peter near Driencourt, which Hugo Bonaldi gave to the aforementioned church with his house. The tithe which Robert

decime de Hornast, et sextam partem decime de Romeria. Et hoc quod habet domus vallis Widonis in territorio de Mairu, et vadimonium terre, et nemoris quod fecit Waldricus Hugoni Bonemont apud Brouecurt, et quicquid pater meus et mater mea, et homines ad me pertinentes de possessionibus suis prefate Ecclesie concesserunt vel donaverunt.

Consuetudines quoque que ab vulgo dicuntur Travers in Vignacourt, prefate ecclesie indulgeo ...

Actum hoc anno incarnati verbi MCLI regnante in Gallia glorioso rege Francorum Ludovico. Ambianis, in domo Theodorici Episcopi. Testes sunt Theodoricus Ambianensis episcopus. Robertus Ambianensis comes, avunculus meus, & plures alii.

the cleric gave at Handicourt,* the third part of the tithe of Hornast, and the sixth part of a tithe of Romeria. And whatever [the house of the valley of Wido] [*sic*] has in the territory of Mairu, and the promise of lands and woods which Waldricus made to Hugh Bonemont near Brouecurt, and whatever of their possessions my father and my mother, and the men pertaining to me granted or donated to the aforementioned church.

I also grant the aforesaid church the customs which are commonly called "a fief in Vignacourt ..."

Completed in the year of the Incarnate Word 1151, when the glorious king of the Franks, Louis, was reigning in Gaul. Amiens, in the house of Thierry the bishop. The witnesses: Thierry, bishop of Amiens. Robert, count of Amiens, my uncle, and many others.

SUMMARY OF THE CHARTER

Alelmus of Flichecourt (Flixecourt), one of the four lords of Amiens, issued this charter with witnesses and his seal, to confirm a gift made in the year he went on crusade to Jerusalem with the king of France. In that year, he and his sisters, Flandrine, Melisende, and Mathilde, had confirmed gifts given by their parents Guy and Mathilde, for the soul of a relative, Alelmus. Vassals of the family had also made donations at that time. The recipient was the church of Saint-Jean-Baptiste at Amiens, and most of the donations are listed. Unfortunately, the end of that list is illegible. It looks as if that portion records the gift of Alelmus himself.

The charter is dated 1151, and was written in the episcopal palace, during the reign of King Louis VII (1137-1180) and the term of office of Thierry, bishop of Amiens (1144-1165). Robert of Boves is listed as Alelmus's uncle and a witness.

NOTES ON THE CHARTER

Flichecourt and St.-Jean

The Premonstratensian house of St.-Jean was founded in the city of Amiens in 1115 by Mathilde of Flichecourt and the bishop of Amiens, Enguerran. In 1124, the then Augustinian house became affiliated with the order of Prémontré, and in 1136 the abbey was moved to a new location outside the walls of the city, thanks to substantial gifts from the lords of Picquigny.[2] The house was a double monastery until 1148, when the women were moved to another, short-lived, foundation. The four lords of Amiens were the bishop, the count (in this case Robert of Boves), the vidames (the lords of Picquigny), and the chatelains (the lords of Flichecourt), three of whom were involved as founders of the original double monastery.[3]

The family relationship between Alelmus and Robert has been the subject of some debate. Robert is said here to be Alelmus's uncle, but the

---

[2] St.-Jean: Ardura, *Dictionnaire*, 69–74; Maurice Du Pré, *Annales de l'abbaye de Saint-Jean d'Amiens, ordre de Prémontré*, trans. and ed. Auguste Janvier (Amiens, 1899), 13, 21–23; M. Godet, "Amiens, iv: St.-Jean," DHGE; Louis-François Daire, *Histoire de la ville d'Amiens*, 2 vols. (Paris, 1857), vol. 2: 236–44.

[3] Alberic de Calonne, *Histoire de la ville d'Amiens*, 3 vols. (Amiens, 1899–1906), vol. 1: 127–30. For Robert of Boves, see the previous charter. For the Picquigny family, see F. Irénée Darsy, *Picquigny et ses seigneurs, vidames d'Amiens* (Abbeville, 1860; repr. in facsimile, St.-Pierre-de-Salerne, 1981). Warmund of Picquigny was patriarch of Jerusalem from 1118 to 1128. Alelmus is listed by Calonne, in *Dommartin*, 279 n. 7, as one of the patrons of that Premonstratensian house, and as "... l'un des fondateurs de l'abbaye de Saint-Jean-Amiens."

charter evidence for the genealogy is contradictory.[4] A charter of 1146, issued by Bishop Thierry, says that Alelmus held his fief from Robert of Boves, and implies that his reason for joining the crusade of 1147 may have been very similar. Alelmus was also under excommunication that year, and for crimes against the church of Amiens. He had apparently not yet inherited, since he is styled "Alelmus of Amiens," and his parents are mentioned. In the charter of 1146, he makes substantial gifts to Amiens in order to lift the excommunication.[5] It looks as if Enguerran of Coucy, Radulph Canis, Robert of Boves, and Alelmus of Flichecourt were all in the same situation. They had attempted to revoke gifts made to the local church by their parents. Their bishops then attempted to establish that gifts made to the church are irrevocable. All four charters have to do with new orders of canons, and with houses established by the bishops of Laon and Amiens. In each case the church won, at the cost of lending legitimacy to new lordships. All four lords relinquished inherited property,

---

[4] Janvier, *Amiens*, 13, seems to make the most sense. He said that Guy married Mathilde, who was the daughter of Adam, chatelain of Amiens. Her brother was the original Alelmus mentioned in this charter, after whom her son, the issuer, was named. This brother married Thomas de Marle's daughter Melisende, and died without heirs in 1115, the year his sister founded St.-Jean. That marriage made Robert of Boves, Thomas's son, Alelmus of Flichecourt's uncle. But for alternate explanations, and the difficulties of the Flichecourt genealogy, see: Daire, *Amiens*, vol. 1: 35–37; Janvier, *Boves*, 56; Calonne, *Amiens*, vol. 1: 145; n.a., *Maison d'Amiens. Généalogie des Princes châtelains d'Amiens* (St.-Pol-sur-Ternoise, 1934); Jean Massiet Du Biest, "Les châtelains d'Amiens de la maison de Flixecourt-Vignacourt, leur forteresse urbaine, leurs fonctions, leurs domaines urbains et ruraux (XIe–XIVe siècles)," *Revue du Nord* 37 (1956): 143–45; Fossier, *Picardie*, vol. 2: 501–3. In BN, Collection de Picardie 225, fol. 175, there is a confirmation charter for St.-Jean, mentioning Alelmus and Gerard of Picquigny, issued by Raoul, count of Vermandois; and in the same Collection, 257, fols. 6–7, there is a charter of 1150 for St.-Lucien, Beauvais, which is issued by Alelmus and mentions his wife "Ade." The *Maison d'Amiens* lists Ada as a Picquigny (p. 23).

[5] A fragment of the charter of 1146 is printed in Daire, *Amiens*, vol. 2: 370–71: "Ego Theodoricus ... Episcopus ... Notum facimus quod Alelmus de Ambianis cum ab Ecclesia Ambianensi propter rapinas quod adversus eam exercuerat, diu excommunicatus fuisset, tandem ipse et parentes eius Guido et Mathildis ante nostram constituti praesentiam, pro absolutione illius, Ambianensi Ecclesiae annuam piscium capturam quae vulgari nomine appellatur nocturna, ac dimidium banni per quindecim dies circiter festum Beati Joannis, totumque pratum de Francavilla et medietatem prati de Forest cuius altera pars eiusdem erat Ecclesiae, et terram de Casneto perpetuo jure donaverunt, et donationem illam fide et Sacramento firmaverunt, annuente hoc Roberto Comite Ambianensi de cuius feodo pretexata pendebant, concedente etiam ob remedium animarum suarum habitatoribus Sancti Mauricii et Vallis, omnibusque ad Ambianensem Ecclesiam pertinentibus, pascua herbarum in territoriis suis in perpetuum." Another charter, of 1150, marks a reconciliation between Alelmus and St.-Lucien, Beauvais, again negotiated through Bishop Thierry: BN, Collection de Picardie 257, 5–6. It is witnessed by Walter, abbot of Selincourt, Fulk, abbot of St.-Jean-Amiens, and Enguerran, brother of Gerard de Picquigny, among others. It is another piece of evidence to document a rupture with the clergy of Amiens, which was smoothed over by donations and a crusade vow.

added new donations, and took a crusade vow, apparently to seal the new relationship.[6]

Laudatio parentum

Stephen White has discussed a feature which many of the charters have in common, and which is explicit here, the *laudatio parentum*, or formal agreement of members of the donor's family to the gift.[7] According to White, the practice of having members of the family witness and/or consent to donations was widespread in the eleventh and twelfth centuries, dying out in the late twelfth to early thirteenth centuries. It is difficult to devise a rule that would have regulated the circumstances or choice of family members, since the practice as recorded in the charters varies considerably. However, the initial gift or settlement is often formally approved. Confirmations often are not. Family members regularly received countergifts as a symbol of their acquiescence (see charter 2, above). In some cases relatives seized property, challenging the original gifts on the grounds that they "or their wives had not approved them."[8] Clearly, a gift of land to a monastery worked to the material disadvantage of the relatives of the donor, and gaining their consent helped to protect the gift. Legally the consent of relatives who otherwise would have been heirs was indispensable, and well worth procuring in advance. White and other scholars have seen the relationship between the family and the religious house as one of mutual benefit, which was expected to continue indefinitely, and thus have a continuing impact on the family, and especially the heirs of the donor.[9]

THE WITNESSES

For Theodoricus, bishop of Amiens, and Robert, count of Amiens, see charter 4, above.

---

[6] A further similarity is the role played by Melisende, mother of Enguerran and Robert, and Mathilde, mother of Alelmus. Both women founded double monasteries: Melisende at Rozières (originally part of Prémontré), and Mathilde at St.-Jean (Ardura, *Dictionnaire*, 69, 466). The family of Ralph Canis was in a subordinate position, but if the *Obituaire de Prémontré* is correct, Ralph's mother is listed as a major donor to the house as well (ed. Waefelghem, 134–35 and n. 1).

[7] Stephen White, *Custom, Kinship, and Gifts to Saints: The "Laudatio Parentum" in Western France, 1050–1150* (Chapel Hill and London, 1988).

[8] White, *Laudatio Parentum*, 51, and see the discussion in chapter three generally for the definition of this practice.

[9] White, *Laudatio Parentum*, 26–27.

* See stars by place names in the English translation of the charter. Place names are identified in *Dictionnaire historique . . . Picardie*, vol. 3: Aumatre (22–30), a village and lordship held from the abbey of St. Riquier; Saint-Pierre-a-Gouy (300–4), a Benedictine priory founded in 1066 whose prior is lord of the village; Savières (586), a chapel and lordship held by St. Jean of Amiens.

6
1147, BURCHARD DE GUISE

Archives départementales de l'Aisne, Laon, H. 797. There is another copy in BM Soissons 7, fol. 58.

† Quia labili memorie hominum facile excidit rerum gestarum cognitio, dignum est ut scripto tradantur que ad posterorum noticiam transmittenda iudicantur. Iccirco (Idcirco?) ego Burchardus domini patientia dominus de Guisia que in diebus meis premonstrate ecclesie vel a me ipso vel ab hominibus meis me concedente collata sunt dignum duxi in unum compingere ut nemini in posterum pateat super his locus contentionis aut calumpnie. Notum igitur esse volo tam futuris quam presentibus quod anno Dominice Incarnatione M°. C°. XXXV°. ego et frater meus Godefridus contulimus in elemosinam eidem premonstrate ecclesie perpetuo possidendum alodium de Germania ab omni exactione liberum, assensu matris nostre Adeluse ob remedium anime nostre et predecessorum nostrorum. Sub his testibus: Hugone abbate de Huombleriis, Roberto cognomine Muto, Reinero filio eius, Widone de Vspaiz, Widone de Beloris, Reinero de Romon, Werrico Hauart.

Anno quoque Domini M°. C°. XXXVIII°., Albricus miles de Nouiomo et filii eius Petrus et Robertus contulerunt in elemosinam eidem ecclesie territorium Hanapie quod a me in feodo tenebant sicut predecessores eorum a predecessoribus meis tenuerant. Ego autem et frater meus totum ipsium territorium cum appenditiis suis libere concessimus. Sub his testibus: Waltero et Reinoldo sacerdotibus, Nicholao clerico, Waltero dapifero et Rothardo fratre eis, Drogone de Dulcilon, Roberto de Stablis.

Interea quidam homo Richerus nomine uillicationem Hanapie sibi uendicare contendebat qui tamen postea me agente et fratre meo recognouit et quiete ac libere remisit eidem premonstrate ecclesie. Sub his testibus: Gerardo decano, Waltero et Reinoldo sacerdotibus, Nicholao clerico, Clarembaldo et Rohardo et Odone de Wadencurt, Hugone uillico de Dorenc.

Item alii duo Guiffridus et Arnulfus terras et pratum in ipso territorio reclamantes tandem coram me et fratre meo in causa uenerunt et quicquid

Because the knowledge of past deeds easily escapes the fleeting memory of men, it is right that those things which are judged proper to be transmitted for the knowledge of posterity be handed on in writing. Hence, I, Burchard, lord of Guise by the patience of the Lord, have deemed it proper to list together in one place the things which have been given in my days to the church of Prémontré either by myself or by my men with my permission, so that in posterity there will be no occasion for contention or slander for anyone. Therefore, I wish it known to those in the future and those here present that in the year of the Lord's Incarnation 1135 I and my brother Godfrey conferred as alms to the same church of Prémontré as a perpetual possession, the domain (allod?) of Germania, free from any exaction, with the consent of our mother Adeluse, for the remedying of souls, both our own and those of our predecessors. Before these witnesses: Hugh, abbot of Huombleriis (Homblière); Robert, whose cognomen is Mutus; Reiner, his son, Gui Uspaiz; Gui de Beloris, Reiner de Romon, Werric Havart.

Also in the year 1138, Albric, knight of Noyon, and his sons Peter/Pierre and Robert conferred as alms on the same church the territory of Hanapie which they held in fief from me, just as their predecessors had held it from my predecessors. For our part, my brother and I freely grant this entire territory and all that is connected with it. With these witnesses: Walter/Gautier and Reinold, priests; Nicholas, a clerk; Walter, a steward (dapifer) and Rothard his brother; Drogo de Dulcilon; Robert de Stablis.

Meanwhile, a certain man, Richer by name, strove to claim the domain of Hanapie for himself. However, through the effort of my brother and me, he signed off and quietly and freely gave it to the same church of Prémontré. Before these witnesses: Gerard, deacon; Walter and Reynold, priests; Nicholas, a clerk; Clarembald and Rohard; Odo de Vadencourt; Hugo, steward de Dorenc.

Likewise, another two men, Guiffridus and Arnulf, laying a claim to the lands and meadow in this territory finally brought their case before me

calumpniabantur quiete dimittentes, super altare Sancte Johannis Baptiste eiusdem ecclesie in elemosinam posuerunt et pro hoc a fratribus in communione orationum et beneficiorum suscepti sunt astantibus et testantibus: Gerardo decano qui etiam excommunicauit omnes qui hanc querelam deinceps resuscitarent; Waltero et Reinoldo sacerdotibus, Nicholao clerico, Sigero de Casteneriis, Balduino Furnel, Everardo de Orini, Clarembaldo et Rohardo et Odone de Wadencurt.

Sub eodem tempore contuli prefate ecclesie capellam Sancti Nicholai apud Sanctum Quintinum liberam cum pertinentiis suis. Sub his testibus: Herberto sacerdote, Nicholao clerico, Guimundo laico, Hezelone et Meinardo conversis.

Anno autem Domini M°. C°. XLVII°. profecturus Iherosolimam augere uolens elemosinam contuli eidem ecclesie ubicumque extra castrum consistit terras Segardi quas sicut alodium libere possidebam assensu coniugis mee Adelidis et fratris mei Godefridi. Sub his testibus: Clarembaldo, Drogone de Dulcilon, Stephano de Sessi, Waltero Dulcet.

Post haec vero anno Domini M°. C°. LV°. concessi etiam prefate ecclesie ecclesiam de Dorenc cum pertinentiis suis quas a me tenens in feodo Rogerus castellanus cum fratribus suis et matre eidem ecclesie contulerunt. Annuente uxore mea Adhelide et fratre meo God[frido]. Cuius concessionis testes sunt: Reinoldus decanus, Arnulfus et Petrus clerici, Matheus de Sciers, Clarembaldus, Drogo de Dulcilon, Werricus Hauarus.

His omnibus testificandis et confirmandis sigillum meum apponere non incongruum judicaui.

and my brother. Renouncing whatever was in contention, they placed it as alms upon the altar of St. John the Baptist in the same church, and for this reason they were received into a communion of prayers and spiritual blessings by the brethren. There were present as witnesses: Gerard, a deacon, who excommunicated all who would revive this conflict; Walter and Renaud, priests; Nicholas, a cleric; Siger de Caterniis; Baldwin Furnel; Everard de Orini; Clarembald and Rohard and Odo of Vadencourt.

At the same time I conferred on the aforementioned church the chapel of St. Nicholas in St. Quentin, free of restriction, with all that pertains to it. Before these witnesses: Herbert, a priest; Nicholas, a cleric; Guimundus, a layman; Hezelone and Meinard, *conversi*.

In the year of the Lord 1147, about to set out for Jerusalem and wishing to increase my alms, I conferred upon the same church wheresoever outside the castle there were lands of Sequéhart which I held as free domain. I did this with the consent of my wife Aélide and my brother Godfrey. Before these witnesses: Clarembald, Drogo de Dulcilon, Stephen de Sessi, Walter Dulcet.

After these things, in the year of the Lord 1155, I granted to the aforesaid church the church of Dorenc with what pertains to it. Robert the castellan holding them in fief from me with his brothers and mother conferred them on the same church. This I did with the agreement of my wife Aélide and my brother Godfrey. The witnesses of this grant are Renaud, deacon; Arnulf and Peter, clerks; Matt[eu]s de Sciers; Clarembald; Drogo de Dulcilon; Weric of Havarus. I have judged it not inappropriate to affix my seal in witness and confirmation of all these things.

SUMMARY OF THE CHARTER

In a charter dated 1155, Burchard of Guise confirmed his previous donations to Prémontré. Among the various donations, each with its own date and witness list, there is one for 1147, written just before his departure for Jerusalem. Burchard, with the consent of his brother Godfrey and his wife Aélide, gave the abbey the territory of Sequéhart (earlier gifts include the territory of Hanapie, and the church of Dorenc).[1]

NOTES ON THE CHARTER

Guise

Guise belonged to the "bailliage" of Vermandois, and is located on the Oise River, in the arrondissement of Vervins. The history of the family is known from about 1058, and is based on the possession of a castle of unknown date. The lords of Guise were neighbors of the Coucys and had difficulties with local clergy very similar to those of the Coucy family, and at about the same date. In fact, the archbishop of Trèves appealed to Bishop Barthélemy of Laon to mediate in the 1120s.[2] Burchard's mother entered the order of Prémontré in 1141, a year before Melisende of Coucy founded a house of Premonstratensian nuns. Burchard and Godfrey were donors to the Premonstratensian house of St. Martin, Laon, in 1137, and frequent donors to Prémontré itself, from 1138 to 1155. In one case, Burchard appears as advocate for the abbey.[3] Bishop Barthélemy seems to have exerted a powerful influence over the family after 1121, judging from the resolution of the local disputes, the gifts to Prémontré, and the replacement of the secular canons in the castle of Guise with monks from Fesmy, a house with which the bishop had close ties. Burchard took the cross in 1147, returned before 1152, and died in 1156, leaving Guise in the hands of his brother. The family continued to be patrons of the Norbertines.[4] Beyond the similarities to Coucy/Boves in family history, there was contact between the two families, since Guise, on the Oise River, was close to the castle of Le Fère. Enguerran II was at war with Burchard in 1135, but on crusade with him in 1147.[5] This is not surprising, since one

---

[1] Auguste Matton, *Histoire de la ville et des environs de Guise*, 2 vols. (Laon, 1897–1898), vol. 1: 14; cf. *Obituaire*, ed. Waefelghem, 131 and n. 1.

[2] Matton, *Guise*, vol. 1: 5–6; Matton, *Archives*, H793; Guyotjeannin, *Episcopus et comes*, 219–20.

[3] Matton, *Archives*, H793, H797, H872; Matton, *Guise*, vol. 1: 10. On the women of the two families, see charter 5: "Flichecourt," above.

[4] Matton, *Guise*, vol. 1: 10, 15–18; Matton, *Archives*, H929; Hugo, *Annales*, vol. 1: 418, 526; *Obituaire*, ed. Waefelghem, 131.

[5] Janvier, *Dictionnaire*: s.v. "Guise"; Barthélemy, *Coucy*, 524.

of the purposes of the crusade movement, according to the accounts of Pope Urban II's speech at Clermont in 1095, was the reconciliation of feuds in France through a redirection of hostility, now to be aimed at Muslims in Palestine.[6] Moreover, even a small collection of charters shows that most crusaders traveled to the Holy Land with their neighbors.

Again, although not as much is known about the Guise family as is known about the Coucys, the reason for crusading, reconciliation with the local clergy as a step towards legitimizing family holdings, seems to be the same.[7]

THE WITNESSES

Burchard's Court: The witnesses are not known to me, beyond the "principal members of Burchard's court" (those whose names appear most frequently as witnesses to his documents): Renaud, doyen of the chapter of Guise; Gérard, chaplain; Mathieu, castellan, and Agnès, his wife; Arnoul, clerk of Faty; Drogon de Dulcelon; Weric Havartus; and Clarembaud and Richard de Faty.[8]

---

[6] For an English translation of Urban's speech, see Peters, ed., *The First Crusade*, 12.

[7] I do not know of a history of the family before 1500. For their later history, see Jean-Marie Constant, *Les Guise* (Paris, 1984).

[8] See Matton, *Guise*, vol. 1: 14–16, where Burchard's seal is described, with a drawing on page 16.

7
1157, THIERRY, COUNT OF FLANDERS

Thérèse de Hemptinne and Adriaan Verhulst, eds. *De Oorkonden der Graven van Vlaanderen (Juli 1128–September 1191)*, II. Uitgave - Band I: *Regering van Diederik van de Elzas (Juli 1128–12 Januari 1168)* (Brussels, 1988), 273–74, no. 172.

Noverint tam presentes quam futuri, quod ego Theodericus, Dei gratia Flandrensis comes, et comitissa una cum filio meo Philippo, Atrebati, cum peregrinationis iter aggressi essemus, cum aliis plerisque affuimus, ubi Jordanus, castellanus de Dixmudis, Yprensi ecclesie per manum meam ac Philippi septem firtonum redditus absque omni exactione imperpetuum iure hereditario possidendos assignavit.

Et ut rata foret assignatio, eam sigilli mei impressione corroboravit.

Actum est hoc anno Domini M° C° LVII°.

Testes: Milo Morinorum episcopus, Geraldus Tornacensium episcopus, abbas de sancto Bertino, Desiderius Insulanus prepositus, Robertus Ariensis prepositus, abbas de sancto Amando, Rogerus castellanus Curtracensis, Galterus Formozellensis, Galterus Duacensis castellanus, Arnaldus de Rupelmunda, Gilelmus de Paschendala, Joseph de Dixmudis, Volcraven filius eius, Lambertus de Jathbeka.

Let people both present and future know that I, Thierry, by the grace of God count of Flanders, was setting out on a pilgrimage journey with the countess, and my son Philip. We were with many others at Arras when Jordan, castellan of Dixmude, assigned the church of Ypres by my hand and that of Philip, seven *firtones* income, without any tax, to be possessed in perpetuity and by hereditary right.

So that this donation would be legally ratified he confirmed it by the impression of my seal.

This was done in the year of the Lord 1157 [error in the printed text: 1057].

Witnesses: Milo, bishop of Thérouanne; Gerald, bishop of Tournai; the abbot of St.-Bertin; Desiderius provost of Lille; Robert provost of Aire; the abbot of St.-Amand; Roger, castellan of Courtrai; Walter/Gautier of Voormezele; Walter, castellan of Douai; Arnald of Rupelmunda; William de Paschendala; Joseph of Dixmude; Volcraven, his son; Lambert de Jathbeka.

SUMMARY OF THE CHARTER

For Thierry, count of Flanders, see charter 3, above. This donation is made, as the one in 1147 was, to the Augustinian house of St. Martin, Ypres. Here the donation is made with Thierry's wife, Sybil, and his son, Philip, and is essentially a confirmation of a gift made by one of Thierry's vassals, Jordan de Beveren, castellan of Dixmude. Thierry made his third trip to Palestine in 1157, and this seems to be a confirmation of the same type as the one of 1147, protecting the rights of the abbey in case of the count's death.

NOTES ON THE CHARTER

Philip and Thierry

Philip of Alsace (1157–1191) was installed as count by Thierry in 1157, in spite of the fact that he was only fourteen at the time. During Thierry's two-year absence, Philip issued charters and appointed advisors, and even after his father's return he continued to make administrative decisions. Philip has been called "probably the most remarkable ruler of medieval Flanders."[1] Thierry's career could serve as an introduction to the decisive events of the mid-twelfth century. In 1134, after marrying Sybil, he held a council at Ypres to promulgate the Peace of God, which was attended by the bishops of Tournai, Arras, Thérouanne, and Cambrai. He then departed for Jerusalem, where he joined King Fulk in the defense of Damascus. He was again at Damascus in 1147 (see charter 3, above), and returned home in 1150 with a relic he believed to be a drop of the blood of Christ. In 1154, he attended the coronation of Henry II of England, and in 1157 he was again in Palestine. There he joined Reynald of Antioch and King Baldwin III (1143–1163) in a successful attack on the Muslim fortress of Harenc in February 1158.[2] Curiously, the pattern established at Damascus in 1147 was repeated. The siege of Shaizar was discontinued because of a dispute over who would hold the city in the event of its capture. Once again, the king of Jerusalem promised it to Thierry but the opposition of the nobles of the Latin Kingdom led to the abandonment of the siege. Thierry returned to Flanders without Sybil, who entered the convent of Saint-Lazare in Jerusalem. Thierry received Thomas Becket in Flanders in 1163, and also made a final visit to the Holy Land in that year. He died in 1168, leaving his son Philip of Alsace as heir.[3]

---

[1] For Philip, see David Nicholas, *Medieval Flanders* (New York and London, 1992), 71.

[2] Mayer, *Crusades* (first edition, 1972), 116.

[3] For details of Thierry's career in Flanders, see Le Glay, *Flandre*, 223–42. For his crusades, see Setton, *History of the Crusades*, vol. 1: 521, 541; and above, charter 3.

Dixmude and St. Martin's

Dixmude is a Flemish port city, sixteen kilometers from Furnes and about thirty-eight kilometers from Bruges. There were castellans, representatives of the counts of Flanders, at the castle there from 964. From the 1130s, the castellans often were also counts of Alost. Jordan was castellan (1128–1165), as well as chamberlain at Thierry's court.[4] The abbey of St. Martin, Ypres, had been founded as part of a reform of the clergy promoted by Jean, bishop of Thérouanne (1099–1130), and Clémence, the wife of Count Robert II (1087–1111). Under their influence, several secular chapters of canons were converted to communal houses, using the rule of St. Augustine, and two new houses were founded: Warneton and St. Martin.[5] There were six converted houses; one, Furnes, is represented by charter 18, below.

THE WITNESSES

For Milo Morinorum, see charter 3, above.

Geraldus Tornacensium episcopus: Gerald, bishop of Tournai (1149–1166), was a former Cistercian monk.

Abbas de sancto Bertino: St. Bertin, in the diocese of Tournai, was a Benedictine abbey. Leo was abbot from 1138 to 1163, and appears as a correspondent in St. Bernard of Clairvaux's letters (nos. 324, 242, 382).

Desiderius Insulanus prepositus: Insulanus means of Lille, about thirteen kilometers from Turnhout. The church in the village was dependent on the bishop of Cambrai in the twelfth century. There was also an abbey, Notre-Dame de l'Abbiette, but so far I have found no Desiderius listed as abbot or provost.

Robertus Ariensis prepositus: Robert of Aire was appointed by Philip in 1157, against Thierry's wishes. He was the son of a smith from Chartres, but rose rapidly, accumulating offices (provost of Aire, St.-Marie at St.-Omer, St.-Amatus at Douai, and of the church of St.-Donatian at Bruges) with Philip's patronage, until he was elected bishop of Cambrai in 1174. He was beaten to death in that same year at Condé by order of a nobleman of Hainaut, Jacques of Avesnes.[6]

Abbas de sancto Amando: St. Amand, a Benedictine house, was headed by Hugo II (1142–1168/9), who had been elected on the advice of St. Bernard of Clairvaux.

---

[4] Warlop, *Flemish Nobility*, vol. 2: no. 23.

[5] F.-L. Ganshof, *La Flandre sous les premiers comtes* (Brussels, 1944), 83–84.

[6] Warlop, *Flemish Nobility*, vol. 1: 325, 326, 374, vol. 2: no. 172, 274 note 3; *Lambert Ardensis ecclesiae presbyteri chronicon Ghisnense et Ardense*, ed. D. C. de Godefroy Menilglaise (Paris, 1855), 47, 51, 61; *Monasticon belge*, vol. 3: 932–89 on St. Martin's.

Rogerus, castellanus Curtracensis: Courtrai (or Kortrijk) is about fifty-three kilometers from Bruges. In 990 a castle was constructed there by the counts of Flanders, after a rebellion by the castellan. It was rebuilt in 1199 by Philip of Alsace. Roger I was castellan from 1128/33 until 1190, and might have gone on crusade in 1177.[7]

Galterus Formozellensis: Voormezele, five kilometers from Ypres, had a college of canons, St.-Marie, founded in 1068/9, and placed under the rule of St. Augustine by Jean de Warneton, bishop of Thérouanne, in 1100. Walter II was lord of Voormezele from 1138/69 to 1187.[8]

Galterus Duacensis castellanus: Douai is in northern France. Walter II is listed as castellan c. 1120–1157/8.[9]

Rupelmunda: Rupelmonde was a port city which took its name from the river Rupel, and in the twelfth century belonged to the counts of Flanders. There are no records of a lordship there until the 1600s. The castle there was used by the counts to detain their enemies; in 1219, Burchard d'Avesnes was decapitated there.

Paschendala: Passchendale, twelve kilometers from Ypres, was the site of the abbey of Saint-Bertin, mentioned in the witness list. There was a "William, baron" (1157–1187).[10]

Jathbeka: Jabbeke, eleven kilometers from Bruges was a fief of the counts of Flanders, mentioned in various sources from 621. Lambert held the lordship from 1157 until 1161.[11]

---

[7] Warlop, *Flemish Nobility*, vol. 2: no. 121.

[8] Berlière, *Belge*, vol. 3: 698–99; Warlop, *Flemish Nobility*, vol. 2: no. 220.

[9] Warlop, *Flemish Nobility*, vol. 2: no. 61.

[10] Warlop, *Flemish Nobility*, vol. 2: no. 165.

[11] Warlop, *Flemish Nobility*, vol. 2: no. 172, 274, note 6. Information on the place-names in the witness list comes from *Dictionnaire historique et géographique des communes Belges*, ed. Eugène de Seyn, 2 vols., 3rd ed. (Turnhout, n.d.). For St. Amand cf. St. Omer.

8
1164, KING LOUIS VII OF FRANCE

Charles Louis Hugo, *Sacri et Canonici Ordinis Praemonstratensis Annales* (Nancy, 1734–1735), vol. 2: lxxii–lxxiv: "Diploma Ludovici VII. Regis Galliae, pro Abbatia Marchasii-Radulphi. 1164." A. Luchaire, *Études sur les actes de Louis VII* (Paris, 1885), 260, no. 506: 12 April 1164–3 April 1165.

In nomine sanctae et individuae Trinitatis. Amen. Ego Ludovicus Dei gratia Francorum Rex. Ad regiae dignitatis officium dignoscitur pertinere, Ecclesias Dei quae in regno nostro sunt constitutae, vigilanter custodire, ut quantum in nobis est praecaveamus ne interior quies, exterioribus molestiis vacillet, et his quorum manus celeres sunt ad rapiendum, murum deffensionis apponamus. Notum itaque facimus universis, praesentibus pariter et efuturis fidelem nostrum Ansculphum de Senotz, cum Jerosolimam iturus esset, praesentiam nostram adiisse, et pro Ecclesia sancti Nicolai de Tellis quae vulgo Marchasium-Radulphi dicitur, quam in propria terra sua fundaverat, humiles nobis porrexisse preces. Huius rationabili petitioni benignam accomodantes aurem, Ecclesiae illi quam in custodia et protectione regia volumus esse, eleemosynas quas idem Ansculphus, sive de proprio, sive de feodo suo contulerat ei, et quidquid in praesenti die eadem Ecclesia possidebat in pace et rationabiliter tam in agris, quam in pascuis, et landis, et boscis et vineis, seu aliis quibuscunque redditibus, quantum in nobis erat contulimus, salvo omnium jure, tam nostro quam alieno; et scriptura et sigillo nostro praecipimus confirmari, addicto caractere nominis nostri. Actum publice apud Pontisiacum, anno incarnati Verbi MCLXIV, astantibus nobis quorum subscripta sunt nomina et signa, id est Comitis Theobaldi Dapiferi nostri; id est Guidonis Buticularii, id est Camerarii, Constabulerio nullo. Datum per manum Hugonis Cancellarii, et episcopi Suessionensis.

In the name of the holy and undivided Trinity. Amen. I, Louis, by the grace of God, King of France. It is recognized that it belongs to the office of the royal dignity to vigilantly watch over the churches of God which are established in our realm, so that as much as it is in our power, we make sure that their interior quiet is not upset by external disturbances and also erect defenses against those whose hands are ready for plunder. And so we make known to all, present as well as future, that our loyal vassal Ansculph de Senotz, when he was about to depart for Jerusalem, came into our presence and addressed to us his humble prayers for the church of Saint-Nicholas-en-Thelle, which is commonly called Marcheroux, which he had founded on his own land. We granted a favorable hearing to his reasonable petition and on that church, which we wish to be under royal care and protection, we conferred, insofar as it was in our power, the alms which the same Ansculph, whether of his own or by his fief, conferred on it, and whatever at the present time the same church possesses peacefully and reasonably, both fields and pastures, and lands and woods and vineyards, or any other incomes, save the rights of all, our own or another's, and we caused this to be confirmed in writing and with seal, and under our own signature. This was transacted publicly at Pontifiacum in the year of the Incarnate Word, 1164, in the presence of those whose names and signs are below: Count Theobald, our steward; Gui the butler, who was chamberlain, there being no constable. Given by the hand of Hugh, the chancellor, and bishop of Soissons.

SUMMARY OF THE CHARTER

In the introduction to the charter, Louis recognizes the royal responsibility to protect the church in France. He then confirms the gifts of a certain Ansculph de Senotz, identified only as a vassal to the king, to the Premonstratensian abbey of Marcheroux. The property donated is not specified, but confirmed as whatever the abbey had received from Ansculph from his own possessions or from his fief (presumably held from Louis), including land under cultivation, pasture, woods, vineyards, and whatever else the abbey held. Ansculph was about to make the journey to Jerusalem, in 1164, and it was in the interest of the abbey to confirm the status of all his previous donations before he left. According to the charter, Ansculph came to Louis to obtain royal confirmation for the protection of the abbey he had founded.

NOTES ON THE CHARTER

Marcheroux and Ansculph

The document contains the location Pontoise, and the abbey was in the diocese of Rouen (now Beauvais), in the commune or parish of Beaumont-les-Nonnains. Its name was formally Saint-Nicolas-en-Thelle, as it had been founded in 1122 at a chapel of that name by one of St. Norbert's original companions, Ulric. According to Bernard Ardura in his *Dictionnaire*, the original community was a "double" one, containing both men and women. At about the time that the order decided to stop admitting women, 1145–1147, the men from this community moved to a new site, called Marcheroux, "leaving" a community of canonesses at St. Nicholas. The women's house was renamed Beaumont-les-Nonnains, and the new installation at Marcheroux became affiliated with the Norbertine abbey of Saint-Josse-au-Bois. Both the original double foundation, a type which was common in the first twenty years of the order, and the new establishment of the mid-1140s, were made possible by a donor who is identified by Ardura only as Ansculphe de Fay, lord of Senotz.[1] Ponthieu, where Ansculph

---

[1] There is no further identification of Ansculph in accounts of the house: A. Sabatier, "L'abbaye de Marcheroux de l'Ordre de Prémontré et de la filiation de Saint-Josse-au-Bois ou de Dommartin," *Mémoires de la Société académique d'archéologie, sciences et arts du département de l'Oise* 6 (1865–1867): 614–23; Backmund, *Monasticon*, vol. 2: 556–57; A. Versteylen, "Beaumont-les-Nonnains," DHGE. Luchaire, *Actes de Louis VII*, lists two other charters in which Ansculph's name can be found: no. 8, 100–1, which is a confirmation by Louis VII of donations made by various people, including Ansculph, to Notre-Dame-du-Val in 1137/38; and no. 463, 248–49, issued for the bakers of Pontoise, saving the rights of Anscoul de Sénotz, in 1162/3. Pierre Louvet, *Histoire de la ville et cité de Beauvais*, 2nd ed. (Beauvais, 1635), 58, credited Ansculph with founding another Premonstratensian house in Pontoise, Ressons, in 1125. This was also a double monastery, dependant on St.-Jean of

held land, was royal domain from 1064, and was the site of a castle built by Louis VI, as well as of the royal monastery of St. Martin. Presumably, then, Ansculph held land directly from the king.

The history of Marcheroux would allow for Ansculph to be the founder because of his support of the move of the 1140s. He witnessed only three of Louis's charters (see the footnotes), beginning with a donation of 1137, and ending with a pilgrimage to Jerusalem in 1164. These dates would give him an effective career of about thirty years, as a relatively unimportant fief-holder in royal domain, since his name appears so seldom as a witness at Louis' court. A journey at the end of his life, perhaps even with the intention of dying in the Holy Land, would be typical of medieval lords, who became increasingly concerned with the afterlife as they grew older.

Louis VII (1137–1180) led the disastrous Second Crusade of 1147/8. One of the many donations he made on the eve of his departure was to the Norbertine abbey of Dilo, founded by his father in 1132. This royal foundation also was originally a double monastery, and was separated into two establishments in the 1140s. The first church at the men's site was consecrated in 1168 by Thomas Becket.[2] Louis' support for Prémontré would be imitated by his vassals; the patronage of the king could create a sort of "fashion" for particular orders. Both the king and his brother, Henry, archbishop of Reims, in their turn were influenced by St. Bernard of Clairvaux, who did so much to promote both the Second Crusade and the new order of Prémontré. Henry was born in the early 1120s, and was a subdeacon by 1136. He collected livings in the church, in a way that was typical of noblemen whose families had designated them for a career there, until he met St. Bernard in 1146. He then took orders as a Cistercian monk, and retired to the cloister for three years. In 1149, his brother insisted that he accept election to the see of Beauvais, and then in 1162 to

---

Amiens. The men did not move from the original location at Aumont, in the forest of Tillières, until 1221. Cf. Ardura, *Dictionnaire*, s.v. "Ressons." GC, vol. 11, col. 328, lists the founder of Marcheroux as "Ansculfus Montis-Capreoli," and also as "de Senort," in vol. 7, col. 59, no. 72. Senort is in the canton of Chaumont, Beauvais. The abbey of St. Quentin, Beauvais, held land from the domain of the neighboring lordship of Fay from its foundation in 1067 (Durvin, *St. Quentin de Beauvais*, 34–35).

[2] Ardura, *Dictionnaire*, see the notices on Dilo, Beaumont-les-Nonnains, and Marcheroux, with further bibliography on each house. On Dilo, see also Jean-Luc Dauphin, *Notre-Dame de Dilo. Une abbaye au coeur du Pays d'Othe* (Villeneuve, 1992). On the Second Crusade and St. Bernard of Clairvaux, there is a large bibliography. Beyond the description in Setton's *History of the Crusades*, a good place to start is Michael Gervers, ed., *The Second Crusade and the Cistercians* (New York, 1992). On his connection to Prémontré start with B. S. James, *The Letters of Bernard of Clairvaux* (London, 1953), no. 328; and T. J. Gerits, "Les actes de confraternité de 1142 et de 1153 entre Cîteaux et Prémontré," *Analecta Praemonstratensia* 40 (1964): 192–205.

Reims. The influence of St. Bernard remained strong thoughout Henry's career; he was a notable patron both of regular canons and of the new military orders.[3]

Double Monasteries

Prémontré accepted women and the foundation of double monasteries from 1121. At the original community, under the guidance of St. Norbert, women were put in charge of the hospital, near the men's house, and given the care of the poor, the sick, and travelers. They had their own chapel, and may have provided clean linen and food for the whole establishment. Adelvie Machanie, the mother of Burchard de Guise (charter 6), entered the community of women at Prémontré in 1135. There is no text of a rule mandating the separation of the double monasteries, only a policy, which was started at the mother house, and spread through the order in the 1140s. Historians of the order have guessed that there must have been a decision made in a general chapter—the annual meeting of abbots of the order—to stop recruiting women and to separate the double houses. The first text recording this decision comes from 1180, and was ratified by Pope Innocent III in 1198. Early histories emphasize the large numbers of women who entered the order; later, at least one commentator complained of a sinful laxity in the relations between canons and nuns.[4] It was a widespread belief among those who lived in religious communities that the mere presence of members of the opposite sex offered a distraction which was hard to resist. Like any lay patron, Ansculph would have depended on the purity of the community for the efficacy of its prayers on his behalf. It would be in his interest to support the decision of the abbot or general chapter to improve discipline by separating the double houses.

THE WITNESSES

Comitis Theobaldi Dapiferi Nostri: I am assuming that this refers to Count Thibaut V of Blois and Chartres (1152–1191), who was made royal seneschal in 1154. See charter 12.

Gui III de Senlis, the boutieller/butler, who was also serving as chamberlain.

---

[3] For Henry, see P. Demouy, "Henri de France," DHGE. For King Louis, there is a large bibliography, and recently Yves Sassier, *Louis VII* (Paris, 1991).

[4] All the information on double monasteries is from Martine Plouvier, "Les soeurs de l'abbaye de Prémontré," CERP 17 (1991). For more general information on women and the church in the Middle Ages see Caroline Walker Bynum, *Jesus as Mother* (Berkeley and Los Angeles, 1982) and *Holy Feast and Holy Fast: The Religious Significance of Food to Medieval Women* (Berkeley and Los Angeles, 1987).

Hugh II de Campo-florido/Champfleury, royal chancellor and bishop of Soissons (1159–1172).[5]

---

[5] Hugh de Champfleury was archdeacon at Arras, and canon at Paris, Orleans, and Soissons. He was involved in the famous trial of Gilbert of Poitiers in 1147. He attended the council of Paris and was made royal chancellor in 1150. In 1159 he was made bishop of Soissons, but was deprived of office in 1172 because of allegations made by Henry archbishop of Reims. He died 4 Sept. 1175 (Perrichet, *La grande chancellerie de France*, 504). Luchaire, *Actes*, 50, shows that the constable's office was vacant during part of 1164.

9
1168, RAOUL I DE COUCY

Jules Tardif, ed., *Monuments historiques,* **Archives de l'Empire. Inventaires et Documents, 122 (Paris, 1866; reprint, Nendeln, 1977), 308-9, no. 613:** Noyon, 1168. Donation faite par Raoul, sire de Coucy, à l'église de Nazareth, d'une rente de dix livres à prendre sur ses revenus de Laon.

Quoniam decurrente humane fragilitatis conditione, gesta presentium, nisi scripto recolantur, ad noticiam non perveniunt posterorum, eapropter ego Radulfus domnus Cociaci, litteris adnotari feci, quod ex dono patris mei Ingeranni dedi et concessi ecclesie de Nazareth, in qua corpus eius requiescit, pro eius anima et pro mea et pro animabus antecessorum et successorum meorum, decem libras Proveniensium in wionagiis meis Lauduni, in festo beati Remigii per manus fratrum de Templo, singulis annis accipiendas. Et hoc factum est assensu Agnetis uxoris mee. Rogatu etiam Lodovici regis Francie et meo, domnus meus Galterus Laudunensis episcopus hoc donum laudavit. Quod ne ab aliquo infirmari possit, sigilli mei impressione et testium subscriptione munivi. Signum Lodovici regis Francie, S. Henrici Remensis archiepiscopi, S. Henrici Silvanectensis episcopi, S. Eustachii Canis fratris de Templo, S. Johannis de Cociaco, S. Blishardi de Firmitate, S. Aitoris de Lauduno, S. Symonis de Cociaco, S. Petri de Sancto Medardo.

Actum Noviomi, anno incarnati Verbi M°.C°.LX°.VIII°.

Because of the fragility of the declining human condition, the deeds of the present age, if they are not called to mind in writing, will not come to be known by future generations. So I, Raoul, lord of Coucy, caused it to be officially put into writing that from the gift of my father, Enguerran, I gave and granted to the church of Nazareth in which his body rests, for his soul and for mine, and for the souls of my ancestors and successors, ten *libras* of Provins from my wionage at Laon, to be received each year on the feast of Blessed Rémi by the hands of the brothers of the Temple. This is done with the consent of my wife, Agnes. At the request of King Louis of France and at my request, my lord Walter/Gautier, bishop of Laon, has certified this gift. Lest anyone find a way to challenge this gift, I have signed it with my seal and the signatures of the witnesses. The sign of Louis, king of France. The sign of Henry, archbishop of Reims. The sign of Henry, bishop of Silvanectensis. The sign of Eustace Canis, brother of the Temple. The sign of Jean de Coucy. The sign of Blishard de Firmitate. The sign of Aitor de Laon. The sign of Simon de Coucy. The sign of Peter of Saint-Medard.

Issued at Noyon, in the year of the Incarnate Word, 1168.

SUMMARY OF THE CHARTER

This is the only charter in the collection which does not show a donation made in preparation for a crusade. This one was made as the result of a crusade. The charters in this collection show King Louis VII, Count Thierry of Flanders, and Enguerran II of Coucy on crusade in 1147. In 1168, Enguerran's son is arranging for an annual rent to be paid to the canons of the cathedral of Nazareth, where Enguerran was buried. The money was to go through the Templars, who had a chapel in Laon, to the Holy Land. Three of the phrases highlighted in previous charters are explicit here: *pro* eius *anima* et pro *mea* (for his soul and mine), *lauda*vit (both Louis VII and the bishop "approved" the gift, as well as Raoul's wife, Agnes), and *wionagiis*. The Coucys taxed merchants who used "their" road for trade in and near Laon (*Lauduni*). The tax must have yielded at least ten *libras* of Provins annually, which was to go to Nazareth. (A *libra* is the Roman pound, of 12 ounces.) The list of witnesses suggests that Raoul attended a court held by Louis in Noyon, where the charter was issued.[1]

NOTES ON THE CHARTER

Nazareth and the Coucys

Enguerran II issued charter 1, above, in 1138, and joined the Second Crusade of 1147. He died in 1148 in the Holy Land, and was buried at the crusader cathedral in Nazareth. He was the son of Thomas de Marle, who went on the First Crusade and died attacking Louis VI in 1131. Enguerran's mother, Melisende, founded a house of Premonstratensian nuns, where she presumably spent the last years of her life (see the introduction). Enguerran himself was a patron not only of Prémontré, but also of the Norbertine house of Thenailles. Both houses were founded under the auspices of Bishop Barthélemy of Laon, and Enguerran may have favored them less out of piety than as part of a negotiation over his excommunication in the 1130s. He had continued his father's quarrel with his overlord, Louis VII, and with the local church. As part of the resulting negotiations, he married Agnes of Beaugency, a distant cousin of the king's.[2]

Nazareth was a shrine church, one of the major pilgrimage sites in Palestine, which was rebuilt by the crusaders and elevated to a cathedral. After 1114, when the Holy Sepulchre was converted from a house of secu-

---

[1] M. Lecomte, "Baldwin III," DHGE, does not mention a council in his brief account of the bishop of Noyon's unremarkable career 1167–1174/5.

[2] For Enguerran, see the notes to charter 1, and Chesne, *Coucy*, 206–12. For Thenailles, see the listing for that house in Ardura, *Dictionnaire*.

lar canons to regulars under the rule of St. Augustine, the major shrines, including Bethlehem, Nazareth, Hebron, Tripoli, Quarantaine, the Mount of Olives, Mount Zion, the Templum Domini, St. Habacuc, St. Samuel, and St. George's, Antioch, also adopted the reform.[3] Nazareth held property in western Europe, including a small hospital at the foot of the hill on which Laon is situated, called Chambry, which was in existence between 1160 and 1180. The further history of this small hospital is unknown, including its connection, if any, with the Coucys.[4]

Templars

The Templars were a military order founded in imitation of the community of canons serving the Holy Sepulchre in Jerusalem.[5] Their founder, Hugh of Payens, came from Champagne, but there were connections with northern France. One of Hugh's companions was Godfrey of Saint-Omer, and the patriarch to whom the original Templars took their vows was Warmund of Picquigny, whose family were lords of Amiens.[6] Bishop Barthélemy of Laon was present at the council of Troyes (1129) where the Templar rule was written, and donated land to them after he returned to his city.[7] The Templar chapel in Laon survives today on the grounds of the city's museum.[8] It is not surprising that Raoul should have chosen them as carriers of his gift to Nazareth. They offered protection and hospitality to pilgrims to Jerusalem, and acquired property rapidly in Europe and the Holy Land after their foundation in 1120. By 1187, when they could use the resources of their European holdings to support their army in the East, they could field six hundred knights and two thousand mounted sergeants, in some cases hiring mercenaries to maintain these

---

[3] For the conversion of the bishoprics, see Bernard Hamilton, *The Latin Church in the Crusader States: The Secular Church* (London, 1980), 116, for religious communities, see his index. More information on religious communities in crusader Palestine can be found in H. E. Mayer, *Bistümer, Klöster und Stifte im Königreich Jerusalem*, Monumenta Germaniae Historica, Schriften, 26 (Stuttgart, 1977); and Jotischky, *Perfection of Solitude*. For the Nazareth church, see Jaroslav Folda, *The Nazareth Capitals and the Crusader Shrine of the Annunciation* (University Park, Pa. and London, 1986).

[4] Jean Richard, "Hospitals and Hospital Congregations in the Latin Kingdom during the First Period of the Frankish Conquest," in *Outremer*, ed. B. Z. Kedar et al. (Jerusalem, 1982), 89–100.

[5] William of Tyre, *Chronique*, ed. R. B. C. Huygens et al., Corpus Christianorum, Continuatio Mediaevalis, 63, 63A (Turnhout, 1986), book 12, 7; Marion Melville, "Les débuts de l'Ordre du Temple," in *Die Geistlichen Ritterorden Europas*, ed. Josef Fleckenstein and Manfred Hellmann (Sigmaringen, 1980), 23–25. For the Templars, see Malcolm Barber, *The New Knighthood. A History of the Order of the Temple* (New York, 1994).

[6] For Picquigny, see the notes to charter 5, above.

[7] Alain La Meyre, *Guide de la France templière* (Poitiers, 1975), 258.

[8] BN, Collection de Picardie 267, fol. 26 contains a donation from Louis VII to the Temple at Laon from 1140.

numbers.[9] Their army, their expertise, and their wealth as an order enabled them to play a major role in the history of the crusader kingdoms.

THE WITNESSES

Lodovici regis Francie: Louis VII, King of France. See charter 8, above.

Henrici Remensis archiepiscopi: Henry of France, archbishop of Reims. See charter 8.

Henrici Silvanectensis episcopi: Henri, bishop of Senlis.

Eustachii Canis fratris de Templo: See charter 2, above, and especially note 3.

Petri de Sancto Medardo: St.-Médard, Tournai, was converted to a regular house in 1125. There was a house of the same name at Soissons.

---

[9] Rudolf Hiestand, "Kardinalbischof Matthäus von Albano, das Konzil von Troyes und die Entstehung des Templerordens," *Zeitschrift für Kirchengeschichte* 99 (1988): 295–325.

10
1178, RAOUL I DE COUCY

Archives de la Société archéologique, historique et scientifique de Soissons 1, pièce 13. Another copy: Bibliothèque municipale de Soissons, 7, fol. 21. Charles Hugo, *Sacri et Canonici Ordinis Praemonstratensis Annales*, 2 vols. (Nancy, 1734-1735), probationes, xxi-xxiii and the confirmation of 1207, xxiii. The charter has also been partially edited by Chesne, *Coucy*, "preuves," 349-50.

In nomine patris et filii et spiritus sancti. Amen.

Ego Radulfus dominus Cociaci. Notum fieri volo tam presentibus quam futuris quod amore Dei ductus et desiderio salutis mee et predecessorum pariterque heredum meorum recognovi et concessi inperpetuum elemosinas et aisentias quas avus meus Thomas et Ingelrannus pater meus contulerunt fratribus premonstrate ecclesie perpetuo possidendas. Videlicet quicquid iuris vel consuetudinis habebat avus meus predictus in loco qui premonstratus dicitur remisit fratribus ibidem deo servientibus et servituris. Valles etiam omnes premonstrato adiacentes et proclivia montium sicut valles perportant ex quibus fratres parum sartaverant et residuum se posse sartare asserebant sed obtinui apud eos, quod deinceps in eis non sartabitur sed nemus vallium et pendentium ad opus edificiorum suorum et aliarum necessitatum suarum reservabunt. Concessit etiam idem avus meus eis usuarium de mortuo nemore in foresta de Voois et pascua animalibus suis. Dedit quoque ipsis locum qui Rosieres dicitur et de propria terra unam carrucatam que omnia predicte ecclesie fratres in diebus eiusdem avi mei et in diebus patris mei quiete possederunt. Cum autem locus prefatus ampliari cepisset et per uniuersos fines tocius orbis dilatari pater meus qui loco illum plurimum dilexit paterne liberalitatis emulator concessit eiusdem loci fratribus terragium et decimam de Veruin, terragium de Aegnies, terragium de Couci villa exceptis duobus modiis hiemalis annone qui persoluuntur ecclesie Beate Marie Nongenti. Viuarium etiam cum molendino iuxta eandem villam videlicet Couci feodum quoque et partem decime de Vassen. Remisit etiam eis wionagium in omni loco terre sue ubi ab alienis accipiebatur nisi de re que ematur ut iterum venalis exponanda deferatur. Ego itaque qui beneficia et elemosinas avi mei sive patris mei minuere non appeto neque servientes Deo super elemosinis sibi collatis vexari desidero ea que

In the name of the Father and of the Son and of the Holy Spirit, Amen.

I, Raoul, lord of Coucy, wish it known to those present and those to come that, led by the love of God and by a desire for my salvation and that of my ancestors and heirs, I grant and concede in perpetuity the alms and dependencies which my grandfather, Thomas, and my father, Enguerran, granted to the perpetual possession of the brothers of the church of Prémontré. Namely, whatever my above-mentioned grandfather had by law or custom in the place which is called Prémontré he remitted to the brothers who serve or will serve God in that same place. All the valleys lying adjacent to Prémontré and the draws on the mountains, as well as all valleys which run through them which the brothers clear, and the rest which they said they could clear. But I obtain from them that henceforth they will not clear, but instead they will reserve for the buildings and other needs the woods of the valleys and unsettled areas. My grandfather also granted to them the use of the dead wood in the forest of Vois and pasturage for their animals. He also gave them the place which is called Rozières and from his own land one carrucate. All these the brothers of the aforesaid church possessed peacefully in the days of that same grandfather of mine and in the days of my father. When, however, the aforesaid place began to be extended to all parts of the world, my father who loved that place very much, as an imitator of his father's liberality, granted to the brothers of the same place a terrage of land and the tithes of Vervins, a terrage of Aegnies, a terrage of the village of Coucy, except for two *modii* of winter grain which is granted to the church of St.-Marie de Nogent. Also the pond with the mill which is next the same village of Coucy, and the fief and part of the tithes of Vassen. He also granted them remission of the wine tax in every part of his lands where it was received from strangers, unless it was a matter of something to be transported for resale. For myself, I have no desire to lessen the benefices and alms of my grand-

predicta sunt benigne eis recognoui et concessi, et quod eis in pace facerem possidere promisi. Unde volo quod servientes mei et heredum meorum de his omnibus pacem eis ferant. Quod si pro quacumque occasione wageria eorum ceperint vel ad me ea deferant sive adducant apud Couciacum vel in vicinia si presens fuero aut eis recredant usque ad reditum meum et tunc res mihi notificabitur et ut res pacifice et rationabiliter valeat terminari mittam si voluero ad veritatem cognoscendam. Volo enim ut pax eis conservetur et ut a servientibus meis non inquietentur. Quia uero moleste ferebam quod tot nove vie vel ab ipsis vel ab aliis fiebant in foresta mea, vias eis assignari feci per quas bona eorum libere et quiete adduci poterunt et reduci videlicet viam per Anlers, viam per longum Buellum, viam iuxta Rosieres, viam per septem valles, viam que ducit Crispiacum et que ducit ad Sanctum Nicholaum et que ducit per Broiencourt, et que ducit versus Anisiacum has vias concedo liberas et quitas karris eorum et karretis. Quia igitur ea que praedicta sunt et omnia que de feodatis et hominibus meis in omni posse meo tempore huius scripti tenebant benigne eis concessi, ipsi versa vice dederunt mihi advocatiam suam de Sorni. Salvis redditibus et possessionibus eorum et omnibus que ibidem habent preter iusticiam eiusdem ville. Ita sane quod cum grangiam sibi maiorem in eadem villa constituent per singulos annos ad querendos et recipiendos redditus suos liberum habebunt ab omni tallia ab omni exactione et requisitione et si forifecerit per abbatem premonstratensem emendabit aut si nollet per me michi emendaret. Convenit autem inter me et ipsos quod advocatia illa numquam alienabitur a domino de Cuci, sed qui erit dominus de Cuci erit advocatus de Sorni. Ut igitur hec concessio predecessorum meorum et mea rata et inconcussa perpetuo prefate premonstrate ecclesie permaneat presenti scripto et sigilli mei appositione et hominum meorum qui interfuerunt annotatione feci roborari. Actum Lauduini anno Incarnationis Dominice M°. C°. LXX°. VIII°. presentibus hominibus meis:

Radulfo de Hussel
Radulfo Cane[1]
Hectore

Symone de Amigni
Petro camerario
Guidone de Sancto Paulo

[Postmodum autem cum presens scriptum facerem confirmari: recognovi iterum apud Cociacum coram istis Petro capellano meo. Renardo de Foro. Roberto maiore de Coci et Mauberto servientibus meis. Ex parte autem Domni Hugonis premonstrati abbatis affuerunt cum eo Willelmus abbas de Cartauoro, Ellebaudus abbas Loci Restaurati, Symon, Hermannus, Willelmus, fratres premonstrati et sacerdotes.]

---

[1] Note the appearance of Radulf Canis as a witness, and compare with the Radulf Canis of charter 2, above.

father and my father, nor do I desire to disturb the servants of God regarding the alms conferred upon them. Those mentioned above I have confirmed and granted for them, and I have promised to so act that they may possess them in peace. Whence, I wish that those who are my servants or the servants of my heirs will leave them in all these things in peace. But if for some excuse they seize their right to weigh produce let them either bring the matter to me or to Coucy if I am present in the neighborhood, or let them give security until my return when the matter will be brought to my attention and if I wish I will set out to learn the truth so that it will be possible to end the matter peacefully and rationally. I wish that peace be preserved for them and that they not be disturbed by my servants. Because I bore with ill temper the fact that so many new roads were made in my forest by them or by others, I caused there to be assigned to them roads on which they could freely and peacefully take out or bring back goods; namely, the road through Anlers, the road through Longum Buellum, the road near Rozières, the way through the seven valleys, the way which runs to Crispiacum and to St. Nicholas and which leads through Broiencourt, and leads toward Anisiacum. These roads I grant to them free and clear for their wagons and carts. Therefore, because the things just said and everything which concerns my fiefs and men which they held I graciously granted to them as far as it was in my power at the time of this writing, they in return gave to me the position of advocate of Sorny without prejudice to their rents and possessions and all those things which they have except jurisdiction over that town. Likewise, when they set up a bigger grange for themselves in the same village to seek and receive their rents each year, they will have it without any toll, exaction or requisition. And if it forfeits it will make compensation through the abbot of Prémontré, or, if he is unwilling, through me. It is arranged between me and them that the advocacy will never be alienated from the lord of Coucy, but whoever is abbot of Coucy will be advocate of Sorny. That this concession of mine and of my predecessors may be perpetually ratified and unchallenged and that it might remain in the aforementioned church of Prémontré, I caused the present writing to be fortified by the imposition of my seal and the signatures of my men who were present. Given at Laon, the year of our Lord's Incarnation 1178, in the presence of my men: Radulf de Bosell, Radulf Canis, Hector, Simon of Amegia, Peter chamberlain, Guy of St. Paul. Afterwards, when I caused the present document to be confirmed, I reaffirmed it again at Coucy along with these people: Peter my chaplain, Renard de Foro, Robert mayor of Coucy, and Maubert, my servants. On the part of the Lord Hugh, abbot of Prémontré, there were present with him William abbot of Carauvoro, Ullebaudus abbot of Locus Restauratus, Simon, Hermann, Willelogus, brothers of Prémontré and priests.

SUMMARY OF THE CHARTER

Raoul of Coucy (1147–1190) issued this charter for the house of Prémontré to confirm all of the previous gifts of his family, and to establish himself as its lay protector or "advocate." This office is specifically mentioned with regard to the village of Sorni, but implied when Raoul describes how all challenges to the rights of the abbey were to be brought to him so that he "will set out to learn the truth ... to end the matter peacefully and rationally." He recalls the gift of Thomas of Marle of the place of Prémontré itself, and its surrounding valleys, as well as the exemptions from tolls granted by Enguerran II in charter 1, above. He mentions the gift of Rozières among the properties given originally by Thomas, rather than mentioning Melisende as founder. Among the gifts of Enguerran II are the uncultivated lands (terrage) of Vervins and Aegnies. In its first writing the charter does not mention any cleric by name, and the witnesses are all Raoul's "men." Later, when Raoul was at Coucy, he confirmed it with the abbot and witnesses from Prémontré.

This charter establishes the relationship between the family and the abbey which is discussed in the Introduction. That connection went back to Thomas of Marle as founder and First Crusader. This is not a crusade charter in the sense of preparation for an expedition, unless Raoul went to the Holy Land, as his neighbor Yves de Soissons did, in 1178 (see the following charter). It does clarify points made about the family's relationship to the reform movement, and so is included as a companion piece to the introduction and other Coucy charters.

NOTES ON THE CHARTER

Raoul

Thomas de Marle had three children by his third wife, Milesende: Enguerran II, Robert de Boves, and Melisende. The eldest, Enguerran II, married Agnes de Beaugency in 1132, and had three children before his death in 1148: Enguerran, who died before 1160, Raoul I, and Melisende. Raoul married twice. His first wife, Agnes of Hainaut, died in 1173, after which he married Alix de Dreux, the niece of King Louis VII. Their five children were Enguerran III, who inherited Coucy, Thomas, who inherited the lordship of Vervins (mentioned in this charter), Robert of Pinon, Raoul the clerk, and Agnes.[2] In theory, Coucy was held by the archbishop of Reims from the king of France. The family of Coucy essentially took their holdings by force, negotiating with Louis VII for a settlement that involved marriage with a cousin of the king. Raoul solidified this connection

---

[2] Barthélemy, *Coucy*, 56–57.

by his second marriage. He also sanitized the relationship between Prémontré and his family. Originally, the bishop of Laon founded the house, with St. Norbert, and Thomas contributed his approval to this use of uncultivated land between his holdings and those of the bishop. Enguerran almost certainly attacked the property of the canons, and repented of it in 1138, but only after the appearance of the king with an army. Here, Thomas and Enguerran appear as founders and donors, giving Raoul the right to claim the office of advocate for the house. In the view of the historian of the house, the whole process of reconciliation to king and church was managed by the Coucys to mask their origins as usurpers.[3]

---

[3] Barthélemy, "Fondateurs," 192. See the introduction, above, where these relationships were laid out in more detail.

11
c.1178, IVES DE NESLES, COUNT OF SOISSONS

William Mendel Newman, *Les seigneurs de Nesle en Picardie (XIIe–XIIIe siècles): leurs chartes et leur histoire*, 2 vols. (Philadelphia-Paris, 1971), vol. 2: 127–28, no. 55 (1171–1178). BN, nouv. acq. lat. 3064: Cartulaire de St. Léger de Soissons, fols. 34–35. Edited by Louis-Victor Pécheur as *Cartulaire de l'abbaye de Saint-Léger de Soissons* (Soissons, 1870), 89–90, no. 35, undated, but "before 1178." See also BN, Collection de Picardie 257, fol. 208.

Ego Ivo, Suessionis comes, notum fieri volo tam futuris quam presentibus quod Durandus, in peregrinatione transmarina defunctus, domum suam in vico Berengeri ecclesie Sancti Leodegarii pro anima sua in elemosinam dimisit. Pentechosta vero de Amblinio, que domum illam de domino Gervasio de Busenci in feodo ante tenuerat, et liberi et heredes ipsius elemosinam factam laudaverunt; et in augmentum beneficii prefate domus censum qui iuris eorum erat eidem ecclesie concesserunt et, videntibus plurimus, super altare Sancti Leodegarii dimiserunt. Et ut hoc in posterum negari non posset et inviolabile ratumque constaret, ante meam presentiam venerunt et coram multis quod de elemosina factum erat se fecisse cognoverunt. Dominus vero Gervasius, de cuius patrimonio res erat et cuius benivolentiam prenominate ecclesie conventus expetebat, prece et voluntate mea quantum ad ipsum pertinebat, istud beneficium cumulavit et assensu suo et filii sui, sicut michi placuit, hilariter confirmavit. Ut ergo hec venturis temporibus malignorum consiliis, aut subdola adinventione nequeant perturbari, presentem paginam sigilli mei auctoritate et subscriptorum testimonio volui roborari. Huius enim rei testes existunt: Radulfus Nigelle castellanus, Robertus Cigot, Ebalus de Berzi, Wido frater eius, Johannes dapifer, Willermus de super Axonam, Ingelbertus Matifart et Girardus frater eius, Radulfus Al Dent, Philippus de Porta, Martinus filius Acardi, Ivo de Foro, Ernoldus Broiart, Lisiardus Peierans villam. Hii etiam testes et plegii sunt pro ecclesia responsuri, si super hoc deinceps adversus eam querela surrexerit, Adam de Fonteneto, Ansellus de Septemmontibus, Gillebertus, Mathildis, Pentechosta et filie eius. Super hos omnes ego ipse Ivo, comes, advocatus ecclesie, causam illius in mea protectione suscipio et ubi necesse fuerit pro illa respondebo.

I, Ives, count of Soissons, wish it known both to people in the future and to those present, that Durand, who died while on pilgrimage beyond the sea, bestowed his house in the neighborhood of Berenger as alms to the church of Saint-Léger for his soul. Pentechosta of Amblinio, who earlier had held that house in fief from Lord Gervase de Buzancy, and her children and heirs, confirmed the gift. To augment the benefice of the aforesaid house, they granted the rent, which was theirs in law, to the same church. In the sight of many, they granted this on the altar of Saint-Léger. So that this cannot be denied in the future, and may remain inviolable and confirmed, they came before me and in the presence of many witnesses acknowledged the alms they had given. The Lord Gervase, of whose patrimony these things were and whose goodwill in regard to this matter the community of the aforementioned church requested, at my prayer and will gathered these benefactions into one gift, and to my pleasure, gladly confirmed it with his assent and that of his son. In order that these things cannot be disturbed in times to come by the counsels of evil people or by fraudulent invention, I wish to confirm the present page with the authority of my seal and the witness of the signatories. The witnesses of this matter are: Radulf castellan of Nigella; Robert Cigot; Ebal de Berzi; Wido his brother; Jean steward; William de super Axonam; Ingelbert Matifart and Girard his brother; Radulf Al Dent; Philippus de Porta; Martin son of Acard; Ivo de Foro; Ernold Broiart; Lisiard Peierans *villa*. Also these witnesses and respondents will answer for the church, if afterwards any quarrel arises against it regarding this document: Adam de Fonteneto, Ansell de Septemmontibus, Gillebert Mathildis, Pentechosta and her daughter. Besides all these, I, Ives, count and advocate of the church, take the cause of the church into my protection, and where necessary, I will answer for it.

SUMMARY OF THE CHARTER

Ives, lord of Nesles and count of Soissons (1171–1178), confirms the gift of Durand, who died on pilgrimage overseas, to the house of St.-Léger, Soissons.[1] The gift was a house in Berenger Street, which Durand had held in fief from Gervais de Buzancy. Apparently there was a legal claim for all or part of the revenue from it by Pentechosta and her family, who gave up that claim as alms as well. Ives, as advocate for the church, and Gervase, from whom Durand and Pentechosta held fiefs, were able to arrange for both gifts, so that the church could hold the house and revenues free of any conditions. Ives issued the charter as the advocate, or secular protector of the church's interests. Durand is otherwise unknown, with no record of his crusade.

NOTES ON THE CHARTER

Saint-Léger

St.-Léger was a house of regular canons of the order of Arrouaise.[2] Part of the church still exists as the museum of the city of Soissons. The order of Arrouaise, founded in 1097, had connections to the crusade movement. Lambert, bishop of Arras, had been appointed in 1093 by Pope Urban II, and had attended the council of Clermont, where the crusade was first preached in 1095. Arrouaise was founded under Lambert's patronage three years later. It was one of a group of new orders which used a form of the Augustinian rule and which included Prémontré. At least two of the cathedral canons who accompanied their bishop to Clermont reached Jerusalem with or just after the First Crusade: Evremar, who became patriarch of Jerusalem in 1102; and Aicard, one of the original members of the order of Arrouaise, who was prior of the canons of the *Templum Domini* by 1112. Conon, another of the founders of the order, was created bishop of Palestrina and papal legate by 1108, and held a council in Jerusalem in 1111.[3] The new orders maintained strong links with the

---

[1] For Ives, St. Léger, and Prémontré, see Newman, *Picardie*, vol. 2: 94–101, 108–11, 126, 132–33, nos. 35, 36, 41, 42, 54, 58.

[2] GC, vol 9, 467.

[3] Lambert: *Miscellaneorum libri vii*, ed. S. Baluze, 7 vols. (Paris, 1678–1715), vol. 5: 248–51, 255–56; Migne, *PL* 162, 713–20; B. M. Tock, "Les élections épiscopales à Arras de Lambert à Pierre 1er (1093–1203)," *Revue belge de philologie et d' histoire* 65 (1987): 709–21. Arrouaise: L. Milis, *L'Ordre des chanoines réguliers d'Arrouaise*, 2 vols. (Bruges, 1969), vol. 1: 97–98. Evermar: Bernard Hamilton, *Latin Church*, 56–57, 115; Migne, *PL* 162, 677–78, nos. 77, 78. Aicard: Reinhold Röhricht, *Regesta regni Hierosolymitani, MXCVII–MCCXCI*, 2 vols. (Oeniponti, 1893–1904), no. 68; Galterus, archdiaconus, *Vita Johannis episcopi Teruanensis*, MGH SS 15, 1143–44; S. Schein, "Between Mount Moriah and the Holy Sepulchre: The Changing Traditions of the Temple Mount in the Central Middle Ages," *Traditio* 40 (1984):

papacy, and therefore with the crusade movement, throughout the twelfth century (see the introduction). Ives de Nesles was himself in Jerusalem in 1138, and again in 1150.[4] His relationship with St.-Léger in Soissons recalls Raoul of Coucy and Prémontré, in that both were advocates and patrons of houses of new orders in the 1170s (see the introduction). These two orders, Prémontré and Arrouaise, were also the projects of individual bishops, Barthélemy of Laon and Lambert of Arras.

Ives de Nesle

The house of St.-Léger in the city of Soissons had been founded by Renaud the Leper, count of Soissons, as a house of secular canons sometime before 1133.[5] In 1139 Renaud restored the house to the bishop of Soissons, and it was affiliated to the order of Arrouaise. In 1161, Ives was attempting to consolidate his claim to Soissons, and he issued a charter taking the house under his protection.[6]

Ives' claim to Soissons was problematic. Renaud the Leper had no heirs, and in 1141 he asked his overlord, Joscelin de Vierzi, bishop of Soissons (1126–1152), to choose an heir from among a number of Renaud's relatives. Each claimant presented his case before the bishop in the episcopal court: Geoffroy de Donzy, Gautier count of Brienne, Guy of Dampierre, and Ives de Nesle. Another claimant, Mathieu de Montmorency, failed to put in an appearance. The relative claims of these lords and their relationship to Renaud are unknown, but the bishop chose Ives, who had to pay a sum of money to satisfy the other claimants. Ives, whose lineage has been traced back to Richard I, duke of Normandy in 996, was duly confirmed as count of Soissons by the king. He issued a steady stream of charters at least partially to consolidate his position.[7] In 1146, when he took the cross with King Louis VII, Ives was threatened with excommunication by Pope Eugenius III and Abbot Suger of St. Denis for reasons which are not clear. He seems to have been extorting money from the abbey of St. Médard, which was under papal protection. He played a creditable role in the Second Crusade, creating a favorable impression on Louis VII, and returned to France to make an excellent marriage and what

---

181–86. Conon: see Milis, *Arrouaise*; Charles Dereine, "Conon de Préneste," DHGE; and Galterus, abbas, *Fundatio Arroasiensis*, MGH SS 15, 1120.

[4] Ives de Nesle: Newman, *Picardie*, vol. 2: 55 and n. 1.
[5] Gosse, *Arrouaise*, 343.
[6] Newman, *Picardie*, vol. 2: 94–95 and n. 1.
[7] Newman, *Picardie*, vol. 2: 94–95 and n. 1, and especially the following charters to find overlapping with names from Coucy charters: Chauny, Guny, La Fère, Bethencourt, Bonneuil, Prémontré in nos. 35, 36, 41, 42, 43, 58. In Jacquemin, *Soissons*, 78–81, several entries show connections between Joscelin and Bernard of Clairvaux, Milo of Thérouanne, and Alvise of Arras.

his biographer calls a brilliant career, dying in 1178. Presumably the Durand mentioned in the charter had accompanied him on the Second Crusade.[8]

The motivation for the Coucys and the counts of Soissons to cement their ties with these houses seems to be the same: patronage of the church, and especially of the local bishop, as a method of legitimizing the lordship; followed by the claim of advocacy to illustrate the relationship and maintain some control over the church property. In both cases a crusade vow seems to have resolved problems which led to the threat of excommunication.

THE WITNESSES

The witnesses for this charter have been identified by Pécheur, *Saint-Léger*, as:

Radulfus, Nigelle castellanus: Radulf, castellan of Nesles (1134–1153), married Gertrude of Montaigu, niece of Thierry of Alsace in 1143.[9]

Robert Cigot, Eble de Berzy and Gui his brother, Guillaume de Vic-sur-Aisne, Ingelbert Matifart and Guibert his brother, Raoul Audent, Philippe de Porta.

See also Newman's notes to the charter.

---

[8] Newman, *Picardie*, vol. 1: 25–32, and see chart on 288–89. Ives married Yolande, daughter of Count Baldwin IV of Hainaut.

[9] Warlop, *Flemish Nobility*, vol. 2: no. 40. Röhricht *Regesta*, (see note 3, above) lists a Radulfus de Nigella as a witness to two charters of the Latin Kingdom, in 1179 and 1180, nos. 587, 591. He also lists: Drogo de Nigella in 1114, no. 76a; and two other names which are reminiscent of ones on this witness list: Gualterius de Beryto (1178, 1179, nos. 562, 587), and Guy, his brother (1179, no. 585). Cf. "Ebalus de Berzi, Wido frater ejus" above. However, Professor Hiestand has identified Beryto with Beyrouth in Lebanon and Berzy as a French place-name.

12
1178, HENRY, COUNT OF TROYES

Bibliothèque nationale, Collection de Picardie 290, folio 13. The 1178 portion of the charter is edited in Henri d'Arbois de Jubainville, *Histoire des ducs et des comtes de Champagne (VIe–XIe fin)*, 8 vols. (Paris, 1859–1869), vol. 3: 471, no. 151 (cf. 375, no. 281).

Commiseratione divina Laudunensis episcopus. Universis fidelibus Christi presentes litteras inspecturis. Salutem in domino. Noveritis quod nos cartam nobilis recordationis Henrici quondam Trecensium comitis palatini ecclesie premonstrate concessam inspeximus sub hac forma.

Ego Henricus, Trecensium comes palatinus, notum facio presentibus et futuris, quod, cum domui et fratribus de Premonstrato terram Petri de Curcellis laudassem, postea, signo dominice crucis assumpto, cum eosdem fratres et domum eorum visitaturus illuc venissem, eis laudavi quicquid apud Cis et in potestate de Cis et apud Domnum Medardum et apud Ru et apud Praellam dono sive elemosina sive etiam emptione possent acquirere. Eorum etiam que acquisierint, consuetudines, si quas ibi habuero, tam in terragiis, quam in censibus, et vinagiis, eis concessi; et quicquid ibidem de feodo meo acquisierint unde h/dominium non amittam, laudavi.

Quod ut notum permaneat et stabile teneatur in perpetuum, litteris annotatum sigilli mei impressione firmavi. Affuerunt autem huius rei testes: Henricus comes Grandis Prati; Gaufridus frater eius; Willelmus marescallus; Theobaldus Révelarz; Ertaudus camerarius; et Milo de Pruvino. Actum anno Incarnati Verbi M°. C°. LXX°. VIII°. Data apud castrum Theoderici per manum Stephani cancellarii, nota Guillermi.

Datum anno domini millesimo ducentesimo quadraginta quinto. Epacta Quarta ante Epiphaniam Domini.

By divine mercy, Bishop of Laon. To all the faithful of Christ present, that may inspect these documents. Greetings in the Lord. May you know that we have inspected in this form the charter of Henry of noble memory, formerly the count palatine of Troyes, granted on behalf of the church of Prémontré:

I, Henry, count palatine of Troyes, make known to those present and future that when I had approved the land of Peter de *Curcellis* for the house and brothers of Prémontré, afterwards when he had taken up the sign of the Lord's cross, I came there to make a visitation of those brothers and their house, I confirmed for them whatever they could acquire at Cis, and in the power of Cis, and in the lordship of Medard, and at Ru, and at Praellam, whether by gift or alms or even by purchase. If I should have any customary rights on what they acquire, whether in land, rents or vineyards, I grant these to them. I confirm whatever they acquire of my fief provided I don't lose my seigneurial right.

Let this remain as noted and let it be held firmly in perpetuity. I confirm what is written down by the impression of my seal. There were present as witnesses of this matter: Henry, count of Grandpré; Godfrey, his brother; William the marshal; Theobald Révelarz; Ertaud, chamberlain; and Milo de Pevinno. Issued in the year of the Incarnate Word 1178, at Château-Thierry, by the hand of Stephen the chancellor.

Copied by William, issued in the year of the Lord 1245, epact four, before the Epiphany of the Lord.

SUMMARY OF THE CHARTER

This is a copy of a charter issued in 1245 as a confirmation by the bishop of Laon of whatever Prémontré held from the counts of Champagne by 1178. The charter had originally been issued by Count Henry of Champagne and Troyes in that year, primarily to record the gift to the abbey of one of his men, Peter/Pierre, who had gone on crusade. In the course of confirming Peter's gift, Henry reaffirmed his consent to the gifts of his own father Thibaut. By 1140 Thibaut, under the influence of his friend St. Bernard of Clairvaux, had made several gifts to the canons and had installed Premonstratensian canons to serve at the chapel of Château-Thierry, where this charter was issued.[1]

NOTES ON THE CHARTER

The Counts of Champagne

The counts of Champagne are a famous crusading family, about whom much has been written. Any of the sources already mentioned, most notably Setton and the bibliography included in that multi-volume history of the movement, would be a good place to start in English. The counts are also tremendously important to the history of France, and again there is a large bibliography on them which can be accessed through an encyclopedia such as Strayer's *Dictionary of the Middle Ages*, or Tierney's history of the medieval period, or a basic work on medieval France, such as Jean Dunbabin's *France in the Making*. Most recent scholarship on them is in French; see the bibliography under Michel Bur.

Champagne bordered both royal domain and Picardy, making its rulers neighbors of the Coucys and of the king of France. From 1152 to 1234 it included the countships of Blois and Chartres. Troyes, one of the earliest episcopal cities in France, became part of the lordship in the eleventh century. Both Champagne in general and Troyes in particular were known for their fairs, at which goods from all over the continent, and especially from Flanders, could be purchased. These fairs were an important source of income for the lordship, one of the reasons why it became so important to the history of France. There were six fairs in all, including two at Troyes and two at Provins (see charter 8 for the "money of Provins"), and they were timed to provide a continuous market, a year-long event, which had its own laws and magistrates to enforce them.

The counts' role in the crusades was important and colorful. Hugh, who became count c.1093, gave up the lordship to become a Templar in

---

[1] Bur, *Formation*, 354.

1125.[2] The Templars were a crusading order of canons regular; see charter 9. From Hugh the county passed to Thibaut II the Great, count of Blois and Meaux, and guardian to young King Louis VII (see charter 8). In 1152 Thibaut's eldest son Henry inherited the lordship, and married Louis' daughter Marie. He went on crusade in 1178 and was captured by the Muslims, dying in Constantinople soon after he was ransomed by the emperor. His wife became regent for their young son Henry II. This Henry went on the Third Crusade in 1190, married the heiress to the throne of Jerusalem, and died in Acre in 1197. His story is well worth reading, if only for his bizarre death. One of the "dwarves" attached to his court fell out of a window. The man clutched at Henry's clothing in a vain effort to save himself. As a result the count was pulled out of the window as well and died from the fall.

The family was equally involved in the church reform movement.[3] Thibaut was a notable patron of the Cistercians and friend of St. Bernard of Clairvaux. In 1135, during the last illness of Louis VI, Suger of St.-Denis suggested Thibaut and the royal seneschal, Raoul of Vermandois, as guardians for the king's son and heir. Thibaut was a companion to the young Louis VII in 1137, when he was married to Eleanor of Aquitaine and crowned. As Louis became more powerful, he made demands on Thibaut which the count felt were unfair according to feudal law. The two quarreled, and Suger retreated from his involvement in the royal court. In 1141 Raoul of Vermandois divorced his wife, who was Thibaut's niece, in order to marry Queen Eleanor's sister. The king backed his seneschal, and Thibaut appealed to Rome on behalf of his niece. Pope Innocent II appointed a commission to settle the affair, and its members excommunicated the newly married couple, suspended the priests who had approved the divorce, and placed the king's lands under interdict. Legally Thibaut was in the right, but not all medieval cases played out according to the rules. In this instance the king was forced to back down under the combined influence of his most powerful vassal and the church. Thibaut's alliance with the church made it possible for him to continue to humiliate the king and affect royal policy. The quarrel reached its height when Louis attacked Thibaut's castle town of Vitry in 1143, burning the town and fifteen hundred innocent residents who were trapped there. Negotiations were under-

---

[2] Arbois de Jubainville, *Histoire des ducs* . . . , vol. 3: 417, no. 84, contains a charter in favor of Épernay, dated 1114 and notable for a mention of crusading: ". . . quoniam Hugo, comes Campaniae, suo tempore venerabilis atque sibi subditis pius et affabilis, cum ob suorum veniam peccaminum in Jerusalem iturus esset, pluribus ecclesiis pro sua suique patris atque genitricis animabus multa bona contulit, atque subi suppositis multas consuetudines condonavit. . . ." I am assuming this is the house of regular canons at St. Martin's, Épernay.

[3] Arbois de Jubainville, *Histoire des ducs* . . . , vol. 3: 274–75, 277, 292, 354–55.

taken by Bernard of Clairvaux, Pope Celestine II, and Suger. St. Bernard promised that an heir would be born to the childless king if he agreed to a peace with Thibaut. Eleanor's daughter Marie was born in April 1145, and at Christmas Louis announced that he would go on crusade to the Holy Land. (This is the Second Crusade, discussed in charters 3 and 8.) He held a council at Vézelay on 31 March 1146, at which Bernard was able to induce many barons to take the cross, including Henry de Troyes for Champagne. One of Bernard's colleagues in planning and promoting the crusade was Bishop Godfrey of Langres, from whom the counts held considerable lands. Theodore Evergates, whose article on the counts of Champagne is the source for this summary of their history, sees Henry's crusade vow as a result of the influence of Bernard, of Godfrey, and of the Cistercian bishop of Troyes from 1145 to 1169, Henry. Thibaut's young heir left France with a large contingent of his vassals and a letter from Bernard to the emperor in Constantinople, asking that Henry be dubbed a knight by the emperor himself.

Henry fought in Palestine alongside Thierry of Flanders (charter 3), and earned the lasting respect and friendship of the king, in spite of the disastrous results of the crusade. They returned home in 1148/9. In 1153 Louis betrothed his eight-year-old daughter Marie to Henry, and the three-year-old Alice to Henry's younger brother Thibaut V, count of Blois (1152-1191), who became royal seneschal. In 1160 the king, newly widowed, married Henry's sister Adela. The marriages of the two counts with the king's daughters were performed in 1164. The following year Adela produced the long-awaited heir to the Capetian throne, the future Philip II Augustus.

Count Henry again left for Palestine in May 1179, as an escort for Adela's daughter Agnes, who was to be married in Constantinople to the heir to the Byzantine empire, Alexius II. One of his men must have been the Peter mentioned in this charter. Henry was captured in Asia Minor in 1180, and ransomed by the emperor who had knighted him in 1149. He died in Constantinople in March 1181, after seeing his niece crowned as empress.[4]

Bernard of Clairvaux is part of the reform movement that affected the monastic world and papal politics in Europe. He was also an active patron of new orders of Augustinian canons like the Premonstratensians and the Templars (see the introduction). Under his influence, both the kings of France and the counts also patronized reformed canons. Both were involved, for instance, in the Premonstratensian foundation at Dilo, and the

---

[4] Theodore Evergates, "Louis VII and the Counts of Champagne," 109-17 in Gervers, *The Second Crusade and the Cistercians*. See Charles M. Braud, *Byzantium Confronts the West, 1180-1204* (Cambridge, Mass., 1968), 31-49.

counts were also founders of Norbertine houses at Valsecret and Humilimont. The counts of Troyes were patrons of the Premonstratensians at Valchrétien.[5] Henry was generous (he was known as "the Liberal") to the Augustinian house of St. Loup at Troyes, and of course to the Templars.[6] There are recorded donations by him to the Premonstratensian houses of Valsecret, Beaulieu, Septfontaines, Chapelle-aux-Planches, Dilo, and Moncet, as well as to the "regular canons at Saint-Quiriace."[7]

Contemporaries, and especially clerics, celebrated the counts as patrons and protectors of the church, emphasizing their generosity. The modern historian of the family, Michel Bur, sees the relationship with the church as part of a policy of independence. According to Bur, Thibaut, whose reputation is so closely linked with Bernard of Clairvaux, particularly seems concerned with protecting his rights from both church and king. Bur points out that no abbey could be founded in his domains without Thibaut's permission, and that his career was fuelled by his hostility to the increasing demands of the Capetians. In his view, Thibaut adopted the ideals behind the image of the round table of Arthurian legend. The king was only the first among equals, and should devote himself to tasks suitable to that position, such as the defense of the realm. Bur sees Thibaut as one of the organizers of the Second Crusade, as opposed to an obedient servant under the leadership of Louis and Bernard.[8] It is difficult to read the spiritual idealism of Thibaut and Henry at this distance, but Bur at least does not see it as over-riding their political strategy or family loyalty.

THE WITNESSES

Henri de Grandpré married Raoul I of Coucy's daughter Isabelle. Grandpré is in the departement of the Ardennes, in the valley of the Aire River, north of Reims and close to Namur.[9]

---

[5] See Ardura, *Dictionnaire*, and Backmund, *Monasticon*, under the names of individual houses.

[6] Arbois de Jubainville, *Histoire des ducs* . . . , vol. 3: 449–78, lists donations by Henry to these and other houses.

[7] Arbois de Jubainville, *Histoire des ducs* . . . , vol. 3: 329–72 contains a catalogue of Henry's donations. Compare with J.-B. Béraud de l'Allier, *Histoire des comtes de Champagne et de Brie*. 2 vols. (Paris, 1839–1842), 262. For Valsecret and Château-Thierry, see also Jacquemin, *Soissons*, 34–35, 75, nos. 53, 54, 123.

[8] Bur, *Formation*, 282, 283.

[9] Barthélemy, *Coucy*, 56.

13
1180, RADULPH DE DURI

Mémoires de la Société des Antiquaires de Picardie. Documents inédits concernant la province, vols. 14, 18: J. Roux and E. Soyez, eds., *Cartulaire du Chapitre Cathédrale d'Amiens*, 2 vols. (Amiens, 1905, 1912), vol. 1: 85, no. 61.

Ego Ingelrannus, Dei gratia Ambianensis ecclesie decanus, totumque capitulum, tam futuris quam presentibus notum esse volumus quod Radulphus de Duri ad nostram veniens presentiam, assistente et concedente uxore sua Agnete, terras quas habebat in territorio de Duri, sive proprias sive pignori obligatas, que ad nostram pertinent jurisditionem, antequam proficisceretur Jherusalem, sic ordinavit: Siquidem ipse et frater eius Petrus terras illas pro indiviso possidebant. Radulphus autem partem fratris sui pro XXX libris attrebatensium sive parisiensium habebat pignori obligatam. Dimidiam itaque partem que ipsius propria erat concessit Radulphus ecclesie Ambianensi in perpetuum habendam, post suam et uxoris sue vitam; hac inter ipsos et ecclesiam servata conditione, quod si Radulphum premori contigerit, uxor eius terram tenebit, et ad ipsius Radulphi anniversarium celebrandum singulis annis, persolvet vini modium. Post vitam Agnetis, ecclesia terram illam habebit et pro utroque anniversarium celebrabit. Partem vero Petri quam Radulphus et uxor sua tenebant pignori obligatam, ipsa Agnes in manu sua tenebit ad faciendum quod voluerit, donec a Petro vel ejus herede XXX libris redimatur, vel ab ecclesia Ambianensi, si illis deficientibus ecclesia redimere voluerit. Siquidem media pars prefate pecunie ipsius Agnetis erat; reliquam partem concessit ei maritus suus Radulphus in elemosinam. Hec uterque sic ordinata a nobis observari postulavit, et ad conservationem memorie sub cyrographo scribi et sigillo nostro communiri impetravit. Testes sunt: Magister Robertus Paululus, Simon de Mondisderio, Drogo de Sancto Martino, Symon de Sancto Michaele, Ricardus de Gerborreo, Symon de Wadencort, Balduinus de Pas, Ebrardus de Foilloi, Ogerus de Kierru, Rogerus de Remis, Theobaldus de Remis, Willelmus de Borri, Johannes et Theobaldus fratres, Robertus de Abbatisvilla, Petrus de Fonte.

Actum est hoc anno incarnati Verbi M° C° LXXX°.

I, Enguerran, by the grace of God dean of the church of Amiens, and the entire chapter, wish it to be known to people in the future as well as in the present that Radulph de Duri, about to set out for Jerusalem, coming into our presence, in the presence and with the consent of his wife Agnes, made these arrangements for the lands which he has in the territory of Duri, either his own or those encumbered by mortgage, which pertain to our jurisdiction. He and his brother Peter/Pierre possessed these lands indivisibly. However, Radulph held the part of his brother as collateral for a debt of thirty *libras*, either of Arras or of Paris. Radulf granted the half part which was his own to the church of Amiens to be held in perpetuity after the death of himself and his wife. There was this condition to be kept between them and the church: that if Radulph predeceased his wife, she would keep the land and would provide a modius of wine for the celebration of the anniversary of Radulph's [death] each year. After Agnes' death, the church will have that land and will celebrate the anniversaries of both spouses. Peter's part, which Radulph and his wife held as collateral, Agnes herself will keep in hand to do with what she wants, until the thirty *libras* are redeemed by Peter or by his heir, or indeed by the church of Amiens, if Peter and his heirs default and the church wishes to redeem it. One half of their money belonged to Agnes; her husband Radulph granted the remaining part to her as alms. They both ask that these arrangements be observed by us, and to keep memory clear they asked that these arrangements be written down by a scribe and fortified with our seal. The witnesses are: Master Robert Paululus, Simon de Montdidier, Drogo de Saint-Martin, Simon de Saint-Michel [there was a church in Amiens and a chapel in Beauvais with this name], Ricard de Gerborroi [a canon of Amiens], Simon de Wadencourt, Balduin de Pas [subdeacon and then deacon of Amiens], Ebrard de Foilliaco, Oger de Kierru, Roger de Remis [or Rains], Theobald de Remis, William de Borri, Jean et Theobald, brothers, Robert de Abbatisvilla, Peter de Fonte. Issued in the year of the Incarnate Word, 1180.

SUMMARY OF THE CHARTER

This charter was issued by Enguerran, dean of the cathedral chapter of Amiens, for the members of the chapter.[1] It records the disposal of the property of Radulph at Duri in the event of his death. He held land in common with his brother Peter, some of which he wanted to give to the church of Amiens as a gift. He wanted the use of it for his lifetime, and for his wife's, if he predeceased her. In return for the gift, he wanted the anniversaries of their deaths celebrated annually. The financial arrangements of the crusader were recorded by the church partly for the sake of the canons of the chapter, and partly for the sake of the family. There was an outstanding loan due from Radulph's brother Peter, and the arrangements for payment were that the church could redeem it if Peter or his heirs defaulted.

NOTES ON THE CHARTER

Amiens

Amiens has been discussed under the Flichecourt charter, no. 5, above. It is in northern France, on the Somme River, eighty-one miles from Paris. It was an important center as early as the Roman era, and Christianity was preached there in the early fourth century.

In the tenth century the city was held by the counts of Vermandois. Their holdings were bordered by Flanders to the north, Champagne to the east, and royal domain to the south. After the archbishops of Reims, they were the principal losers by Coucy establishment and expansion. By 1117 when he won a battle there, Amiens belonged to Enguerran I de Coucy. However, his claim was denied by Louis VI, who ordered him to return Amiens to the counts. Enguerran's grandson Robert of Boves was disputing the king's decision in 1147 (charter 4). The fief was claimed as well by the counts of Flanders after the marriage of Philip of Alsace and Elizabeth of Vermandois in 1164, and finally reverted to the crown after 1185, to become part of royal domain.[2]

Amiens was also the seat of a bishopric dependent on Reims. Theobald/Thibaut de Heilly was bishop 1169–1204, and attended the third Lateran council in 1179.[3] The council may be relevant to crusade recruitment in Amiens in 1180, since clerics from the Latin Kingdom attended the council and their concern for the defense of the Holy Land would have

---

[1] GC, vol. 10, col. 1146, and "instrumenta," 293–94, no. 12 says this was a regular chapter, one where the canons had been convinced to "reform" and adopt a version of the Augustinian rule. Any information about the witnesses' names was taken from Roux, *Cartulaire*, the index in vol. 2.

[2] Nicholas, *Flanders*, 72; Barthélemy, *L'ordre seigneurial*, 245.

[3] M. Godet, "Amiens," DHGE.

been an important item on the agenda. Over a thousand clerics met in Rome in March of 1179, including fifty-nine French bishops, which may also explain why it is the dean and not the bishop who is issuing the charter.

Radulph and Agnes

I am unable to identify the family or the witnesses in this charter, presumably because they are not notable enough to appear in other charters or in chronicle evidence.[4] It is interesting to note the joint ownership of land by the two brothers, and the consent of Agnes, Radulph's wife, to the transaction which provides for her support in the event of her husband's death. As Constance Brittain Bouchard has pointed out, "one cannot extrapolate from women's appearance in charters to information about the position of women in society in general in the twelfth century."[5] While women, according to her, did not initiate economic transactions while their husbands were alive, neither did young men who had fathers to act for them. Bouchard found women mentioned in charters giving assent to transactions more often than the male heirs, which would seem to indicate that their approval was as, if not more, important. On the other hand, at the moment when a young man inherited, he seems to have been asked for a confirmation of the gifts made by the previous male holders of the property.[6]

---

[4] Roux, *Cartulaire*, vol. 1: 113–14, no. 85 and 118, no. 89 are two later charters which seem to concern this gift. In the former, issued in 1192 by Theobald, bishop of Amiens, Rainer de Duri and his son Peter have contested the donation. In the latter, issued by Theobald in 1195, the sale of Duri by Petrus Cecus is mentioned.

[5] Bouchard, *Holy Entrepreneurs*, 163.

[6] Bouchard, *Holy Entrepreneurs*, 163–64.

14
1184, OSTO DE TRAZEGNIES,
with the confirmation document of 1188

J. Barbier, "Documents concernant Trazegnies, extraits du cartulaire de l'abbaye de Floreffe," *Analectes pour servir à l'histoire ecclésiastique de la Belgique* 7 (1870): 371-72, no. 1; and 372-74, no. 2; 375-76. The cartulary, which survives in a fourteenth-century copy, is held by the Archives de l'Etat at Namur.

[4 Avril 1184] Osto de Traizegnies ratificat donationem ecclesiae de Traizegnies cum attinentiis factam ab avo et patre suo, uti et donationem de Herlaimont.

In nomine sancte et individue Trinitatis. Notum sit omnibus et presentibus et futuris, quod ego Osto, miles de Trasingeis, patrum meorum devotionem imitatus, eleemosynam, quam avus meus Hosto et pater meus Egidius ecclesie beate Marie de Floreffia pro salute animarum suarum et successorum suorum in perpetuum possidendam contulerant, ecclesiam videlicet de Trasingeis cum omnibus, que ad ipsam pertinent, et quidquid terre ac decime inter Pintonem et Calciatam possidebant, pro salute anime mee et predecessorum et successorum meorum, eidem Floreffiensi ecclesie recognovi, confirmavi et perpetuo possidendam concessi, eamque in manus Henrici, comitis Namurcensis, et Balduini, comitis Hainacensis, presentibus quampluribus nobilibus viris, tuendam deposui. Et ne de posteris meis aliquis in futurum hanc confirmationem audeat infirmare, presenti eam scripto mandare, et sigilli mei authoritate communire, et testium subscriptione curavi roborare. Fuerant igitur huius rei testes et fautores; mater mea Damisia, et nobiles ac liberi homines, Sigerus frater meus, Richaldus et Gerardus de Rohenia cognati mei, Willelmus de Hutange, Heinricus de Birbais, Johannes de Goe, Guido de Fontibus, et filius eius Walterus, Robertus etiam de Caniris et Amandus de Papigin, et plures alii. Super haec autem omnia prelibate eleemosyne recognitionem et confirmationem, etiam in presentia Radulphi, Leodiensis episcopi, astante Hermanno, abbate Floreffiensi, et presentibus plurimis, tam clericis quam militibus, in dedicatione ecclesie de Herlamont, que facta est anno ab Incarnatione Domini M° C° LXXXIIII, feria quarta hebdomade pascalis innovavi, et ipsam eleemosynam manibus episcopi imposui, quam ipse protinus super altare, quod in presentiarum sacraverat, posuit et omnes, qui de cetero aliquam Floreffiensi ecclesie de eadem eleemosyna iniuriam facerent, excommunicavit.

[4 April 1184] Osto de Trazegnies ratifies a donation to the church of Trazegnies and what pertains to it made by his grandfather and father, as well as the donation of Herlaimont.

In the name of the holy and undivided Trinity. Let it be known to all both present and future that I, Osto, knight of Trazegnies, imitating the devotion of my parents, donate, confirm, and grant to the same church of Floreffe, for the salvation of my soul and the souls of my predecessors and successors the alms which my grandfather, Osto, and my father, Egidius, granted to the church of St.-Marie de Floreffe. Their gifts were to be held in perpetuity for the salvation of their souls and the souls of their successors; notably the church of Trazegnies with all that pertains to it, and whatever land and tithes they possessed between Pinto and Calciata. I deposit this for safekeeping in the hands of Henry, count of Namur, and Balduin, count of Hainaut, in the presence of many noble men. And lest in the future one of my descendants dares to challenge this confirmation, I am taking care to have it written down and fortified by the authority of my seal and the signatures of witnesses. These are the names of those who witnessed and approved this: my mother Damisia; and the noble and free men Siger, my brother; Richard and Gerard de Rohenia my cousins; William de Hutange; Henri de Birbais; Jean de Goe; Gui de Fontibus and his son Walter; also Robert de Caniris; and Amand de Papigin; and many others. I renewed the acknowledgement and confirmation of all that concerns the alms mentioned above in the presence of Radulph, bishop of Liège, in the presence of Hermann, abbot of Floreffe, and many others, both clerics and knights, at the dedication of the church of Herlaimont, which occurred in the year of our Lord 1184, on Wednesday of Easter week. I placed this same alms in the hands of the bishop, who then put it on the altar which he had consecrated in their presence. He excommunicated all who would do any injury in the matter of these alms to the church of Floreffe.

The Duke of Brabant and the Counts of Namur and Hainaut Confirm Osto's Gift in 1188

Dux Lovaniensis, comes Namurcensis et comes Hainacensis eamdem donationem declarant.

In nomine sancte et individue Trinitatis. Quoniam piis Deo devote famulantium votis pie favere magna pars est devotionis, ac iustis eorum petitionibus acquiescere ipsorumque commodis et paci benigne prospicere ingens fiducia retributionis, ego Godefridus, Dei gratia dux Lovaniensis, et ego Heinricus, comes Namurcensis, et ego Balduinus, comes Hainacensis, pium pariter et salubre, iustum similiter et necessarium duximus per presentia scripta tam presentium quam futurorum memorie commendare, quod dominus Hosto de Trazingeis, vir nobilis et miles egregius, dominicum visitaturus sepulchrum et ad ulciscendam Omnipotentis contumelian sancto profecturus desiderio, ut celesti munitus armatura tutior iret, ac pias Deo famulantium preces fideles patronas et comites haberet individuas, magnam decimam suam de Trazingeis promptissima devotione pro se suisque antecessoribus et successoribus ecclesie beate Dei Genitricis Marie de Floreffia, assensu et favore uxoris sue Mathildis, et primogeniti sui Egidii, et reliquorum filiorum ac filiarum suarum, integre et libere contradidit, et super maius altare ipsam in perpetue beneficium eleemosyne per manum Hermanni, eiusdem ecclesie abbatis, fideliter obtulit et legitime affectavit. Statim autem et ipsa hora idem Osto de manu prelibati abbatis et ecclesie partem eiusdem decime, decimam scilicet de indominicatis suis, culturis videlicet propriis, quas ipsius propria carruca colet, suscepit, censum trium modiorum sigetis ad mensuram modii de Trazingeis eidem ecclesie pro decima recepta annuatim daturus. Segetis autem dimidium siligo, reliquum avena erit. Verum iam dicta ecclesia, ne tantis ingrata beneficiis appareret, et ut tam liberalis eleemosyna perpetui sibi munimentum monumenti pararet, communibus votis et prompta devotione preter generales orationes, tres specialiter missas sepe dicto Hostoni pro ipso et eius antecessoribus et successoribus perhenniter celebrandas concessit, quarum primam in honorem sancti Spiritus, alteram in veneratione gloriose Dei Genitricis Marie in abbatia, tertiam apud Herlaimont, ubi domini Egidii, patris ipsius, corpus humatum requiescit, pro anima eiusdem patris sui et omnium fidelium defunctorum salute celebrari constituit. Huius actionis et legitime affectionis prescripte eleemosyne, petitione et electione sepedicti Hostonis et ecclesie Floreffiensis, testes, tutores et obsides sumus in tantum, quod, si quis de hac eleemosyna, quam spe celestis premii tuendam suscepimus, prelibate ecclesie vel vi vel dolo iniuriam vel calumpniam inferre presumpserit, nos

In the name of the holy and undivided Trinity. Because it is a big part of devotion to piously foster the pious prayers of those who devoutly serve the Lord and to accede to their just petitions, and a great hope of merit to prosper kindly what suits them and gives them peace, I, Godfrey, by the grace of God, duke of Louvain, and I, Henry, count of Namur, and I, Baldwin, count of Hainaut, undertake devoutly and beneficially, justly and necessarily, to commend by the present writing to the memory of those present and those to come the fact that Lord Osto de Trazegnies, a noble man and outstanding soldier, about to visit the Lord's tomb and to set out with a holy desire to avenge the insult given to the Almighty, so that he might have the devout prayers of those serving God as his faithful patrons and comrades, wholly and freely hands over and faithfully offers and legally confers with ready devotion upon the great altar as a benefice of perpetual alms to the church of the Blessed Mother of God, Mary of Floreffe, through the hand of Hermann, abbot of the same church, his great tithe of Trazegnies, for himself, his ancestors and his successors, with the assent and favor of his wife, Mathilde, and of his first-born son Egidius, and of the rest of his sons and daughters. Immediately, at the same hour, the same Osto received from the hand of the same abbot and church a part of the same tithe, namely, the tithe of his demesne, his personal farmlands, which he cultivates as his own carrucate, a tax of three modii of grain (according to the modius measure of Trazegnies), to be given to the same church for the tithes received annually. Half of the grain will be wheat, the rest oats. In order not to seem ungrateful for such great benefices, and so that such generous alms might obtain for themselves the protection of a lasting monument, the same church granted by shared vows and with prompt devotion that besides the general orations, three masses would be specially celebrated each year for this Osto and for his ancestors and descendants. It was agreed that of these the first will be celebrated in honor of the Holy Spirit; the second in veneration of the glorious Mother of God, Mary, in the abbey; the third at Herlaimont, where the body of Lord Egidius, his father, lies buried, for the soul of that same father and for the salvation of all the faithful departed. Of this act and the legal conferral of the aforesaid alms, by the request and choice of the same Osto, and of the church of Floreffe, we are the witnesses, guardians and defenders, in so far as if anyone either by violence or cunning will presume to inflict injury and falsehood regarding this alms which we have received into our care in the hope of a heavenly reward, the church will find us the avengers of her

ecclesia et sue ultores iniurie et sui defensores iuris inveniet. Unde et presentem paginam ad eterni roboris firmamentum nominum nostrorum inscriptione et sigillorum nostrorum auctoritate fecimus communiri et testium probabilium, in quorum presentia hec omnia gesta sunt, subscriptione roborari. Quorum ista sunt nomina: Eustachius de Ruez, Richaldus de Roenia, Johannes de Milench, Servatius de Goe, Simon de Timion, et Henricus frater eius, Gebergis mater eiusdem Hostonis, cuius favore et concessu omnia hec acta sunt, Philippus sacerdos de Trasingeis, Nicholas de Gibeceh, Richaldus, Reinerus Ruschebus, Godifridus de Calmont, Godefridus de Sombreffia, et Jacobus filius eius; liberi homines de familia ducis, Arnoldus de Walhehanc, et Willelmus frater eius, Gerardus de Hedeberges, et Arnoldus frater eius. De liberis hominibus comitis Namurcensis, Clarebaldus de Alta Ripa, et Willelmus frater eius, et cum eis Willelmus de Ugeseers et Johannes Agnus. De hominibus etiam comitis Hainacensis, Nicholaus de Barbencon, Johannes Cornutus de Haineceol, Reinardus de Stripi, Gosvinus de Tulinc, Amandus senescalcus, et plures alii.

Acta sunt hec anno Verbi Incarnati millesimo C° LXXXVIII°, indictione secunda, concurrente vero epacta vigesima.

injury and the defenders of his rights. Hence, we cause the present page to be strengthened for the firmament of eternal strength with the inscription of our names and the authority of our seals, to be fortified with the signatures of reliable witnesses in whose presence all these things have been done. Their names are Eustace de Ruez, Richard de Roenia, Jean de Milench, Servatius de Goe, Simon de Timion, and Henri his brother, Gebergis, the mother of that same Osto by whose favor and consent all these things have been done, Philip, priest of Trazegnies, Nicholas de Gibeceh, Richard, Reinerus Ruschebus, Godifrid de Calmont, Godefrid de Sombreffia, and Jacob his son. The free men of the household of the duke are Arnold de Walhehanc, and William his brother, Gerard de Hedeberges, and Arnold his brother. The free men of the count of Namur, Clarebald de Alta Ripa, William his brother, and with them Willelmus de Ugeseers et Jean Agnus. Also, of the men of the count of Hainaut: Nicholas de Barbencon, Jean Cornutus de Haineceol, Reinard de Stripi, Gosvin de Tulinc, Amand the seneschal, and many others.

Issued this year of the Incarnate Word, 1188, the second indiction, concurrent epact 20.

SUMMARY OF THE CHARTERS

In the first charter, Osto, knight of Trazegnies, in imitation of the devotion of his father, confirms the gifts made by his grandfather Osto, and his father Egidius, to the Premonstratensian house of Floreffe, for the salvation of their souls, and of their successors. The gifts include the church at Trazegnies, with all that pertains to it, as well as whatever lands and tithes had been given at *Pinto(nem)* and *Calciata(m)*. The confirmation was made with the approval, and in the presence of Osto's overlords, Count Henry II of Namur (1139–1194) and Count Baldwin V of Hainaut (1150–1195), as well as Osto's mother, Damisia, and a group of nobles and free men. Radulph, bishop of Liège, and Hermann, abbot of Floreffe, were also present, with many clerics. The occasion of the assembly was the dedication of the church of Herlaimont. The charter was made to ensure that the family would not trouble the canons; anyone who did was liable to excommunication.

In the second charter, these gifts, called the tithe of Trazegnies, are confirmed by Duke Godfrey III of Louvain/Brabant (1143–1190), as well as by the counts of Namur and Hainaut. The document records an assembly of crusaders, who are making or confirming gifts on the point of departure. Osto, desiring to visit the tomb of Christ, and in order to obtain the favor of the Almighty, confirmed his gifts at the altar of the church at Floreffe, in the presence of the abbot, Hermann (1173–1193/4), and the assembly of other crusaders. He had the approval of his wife, Mathilda, of his heir, Egidius, and all of his other sons and daughters. His mother is again mentioned, this time in the witness list, where she is called *Gebergis*. In return for the gifts of the family, the abbey agreed to include them in their prayers, and to say special masses for them. Osto's father had been buried at Herlaimont, the church belonging to Floreffe that was mentioned in the first charter, and the anniversary of his death was to be celebrated there. The three overlords set the seal of their authority on the charter for the protection of the abbey's rights, and witnesses are recorded, including the priest of the church at Trazegnies, members of the duke's court, and vassals of the two counts.

NOTES ON THE CHARTERS

Floreffe and the Lords of Trazegnies

There is evidence that Floreffe, which was second in importance in the early history of the order only to the mother house of Prémontré, was a center of crusade recruitment and fund-raising in the twelfth century. Its history is bound up with the history of the Premonstratensian order in the Holy Land.[1] According to Sigebert of Gembloux, Bishop Barthélemy of

---

[1] Compare C. K. Slack, "The Premonstratensians and the Crusader Kingdoms in the

Laon and St. Norbert founded Floreffe in 1121, in a church donated by Ermesende, countess of Namur.[2] C. L. Hugo, who edited the foundation document, credited Count Godfrey (1105-1139) and his wife Ermensende with the foundation of the house, and the family continued to be patrons.[3] The village of Floreffe is only 10 kilometers from Namur, and became the favorite residence of Count Henry l'Aveugle, who fortified the place in the 1150s. Meanwhile, King Baldwin II of Jerusalem (1118-1131) was negotiating with St. Bernard of Clairvaux to found a house of Cistercians in the Holy Land. Bernard refused, but offered to send Premonstratensian canons instead. A group of canons left for Jerusalem in the 1130s, with a letter of introduction from Bernard to Baldwin's daughter and heir, Melisende. Eventually, Norbertine canons were established at two major shrines in Palestine, St. Habacuc and St. Samuel. After the fall of Jerusalem to the Muslims in 1187, the canons were forced to move to Acre, one of the few cities which remained in European hands. The abbots of Prémontré maintained a vigorous claim to their possessions in Palestine. Abbot Hellinus of Floreffe (1209-1219) accompanied the famous preacher, Jacques de Vitry, to Acre in 1216, and died on Cyprus, at the abbey's new house, Bellapaix, in 1219. He was sent, not only to look after the order's interests, but because he had been preaching the Fifth Crusade in Europe, and had gone with Jacques for what they described as a preaching mission to prepare the disheartened refugees in Acre for the new crusade.[4]

It is not surprising to find that the abbey hosted an assembly of crusaders in 1188. Its patrons had long-standing connections to the crusades movement. The register of the cartulary of Floreffe shows a series of donations from the lords of Trazegnies, fief-holders of the dukes of Brabant. Osto I donated land for a house of canonesses at Herlaimont, and was buried there in 1137 (as the confirmation charter above recalls).[5] His son, Egidius, or Gilles, seems to have joined the Second Crusade, returning in 1148. By 1163, Gilles had died, and his son, Osto, is mentioned in a confirmation grant for Herlaimont. This seems to be the same Osto who issued the 1184 grant, above, and who is described as a crusader about to

---

Twelfth and Thirteenth Centuries" *Analecta Praemonstratensia* 67/68 (1991/1992): 76-110, 207-31; with Rudolf Hiestand, "Königin Melisendis von Jerusalem und Prémontré. Einige Nachträge zum Thema: Die Prämonstratenser und das Hl. Land," *Analecta Praemonstratensia* 71 (1995): 77-95.

[2] Sigebertus Gemblacensis, *Chronica*, ed. D. L. C. Bethmann, MGH SS 6: 459.

[3] Hugo, *Annales*, vol. 1, index.

[4] For Hellinus, see Slack, note 1, above; and Joseph Barbier, *Histoire de l'abbaye de Floreffe*, 2 vols. (Namur, 1888), vol. 1: 99-101. See Jotischky, *Perfection of Solitude*, on the cross relics in Crusader Palestine.

[5] On Herlaimont, see L. C. Van Dijck, DHGE.

depart in the confirmation of 1188. Several of the witnesses issued their own charters of donation to Floreffe at the same time. In 1192, Osto was in the Holy Land, and he is mentioned in Ambroise's chronicle of the Third Crusade. Joseph Barbier, who edited the register and wrote the history of Floreffe, thought that Osto made two separate trips to Palestine between 1188 and his death in 1193. In 1195, Osto's son Gilles confirmed his father's gifts to Floreffe, mentioning that he was repenting his attempt to revoke those gifts. This charter is interesting first because it records the kind of struggle between religious houses and the families of the donors that has been the theme of so many of the charters in this collection, but also because Gilles mentions an impressive relic Osto brought back from Jerusalem. Gilles says that he took an oath as a sign of reconciliation with the canons, and that he swore on the relics his father brought back, including "the wood of the Lord's cross."[6] In another charter, again confirming Floreffe's property, Gilles styles himself "lord of Trazegnies, son of Osto, who died overseas as a knight of the cross of Christ."[7] Gilles

---

[6] Barbier, "Trazegnies," no. 3: (1195) Osto's son Gilles (Egidius) confirms the same donation, mentioning that he had witnessed the original gift. Gilles also says that he himself contested that donation, but has now repented, and is promising on the wood of the cross, brought back by his father to the altar of Floreffe, that he will cease to trouble the abbey: "In nomine sancte et individue Trinitatis. Notum sit omnibus tam presentibus quam futuris quod ego Egidius, dominus de Trasineis, magnam decimam ipsius ville de Trasineis, quam ecclesie Floreffiensi digne recordationis dominus Hosto, pater meus, in perpetue beneficium eleemosyne pia devotione et legitima donatione, me presente et favente, contradidit, in meos usus non sano ductus consilio per aliquod tempus iniuste et violenter converti; sed demum mei penitens erroris, ipsam decimam eadem libertate et integritate, qua eam pater meus Floreffiensi ecclesie donaverat, eidem ecclesie recognovi, concessi et contuli, et, tactis sacrosanctis reliquiis maximeque salutifero dominice Crucis ligno, quod de transmarinis partibus pater meus advexerat, iurisiurandi sacramento super altare beate Dei Genitricis Marie insolubiliter pollicitus sum et statui, quod neque pro ipsa decima vel alia aliqua iniusta querela vel opressione Floreffiensem ecclesiam, vel quevis ad ipsam pertinentia, de cetero inquietarem, sed etiam predicte decime vel eleemosyne donationem ante ducem Lovaniensem et comitem Hainacensem, et per ipsos firmissime confirmarem, fratresque meos huic traditioni favere facerem. Insuper etiam, ne ab huius iuramenti et pacti firmitate, levitate aliqua ductus, resilire possem, testes idoneos huic facto meo advocavi, qui Floreffiensi ecclesie de veritate actionis huius et coram prescriptis principibus, et ubicumque oportuerit, etiam contra me, si necesse fuerit, constanter testimonium se laturos, fide interposita, promiserunt. Quorum hec sunt nomina: Theodericus de Gocileis, Godefridus de Tuin, Egidius de Roenis, Johannes de Goe, Walterus et Ywannus de Roenia, Bernardus de Melench, Philippus quoque sacerdos de Trazineis, et Nicholaus clericus, et plures alii. Acta sunt hec anno Verbi Incarnati Mº Cº LXXXVº."

[7] Barbier, "Trazegnies," 376–77, no. 5: (1200) "Ego Egidius, dominus de Trasingeis [sic], filius Hostonis, qui in partibus transmarinis legitimus miles crucis Christi defunctus est, notum facio omnibus tam presentibus quam futuris, quod ecclesia de Trasengies [sic] cum minuta decima et dote sua, omnia scilicet ad ius presbyterii pertinentia, ecclesie beate Marie de Floreffia pro salute anime domini Egidii, que ipsi olim collata et tempore patris mei quieta possessa, eidem ecclesie absolute recognovi, et, quidquid iuris habebam vel habere poteram in ecclesia de Trasengeis ad ius presbyterii pertinens, totum supradicte ecclesie Flo-

took the cross in 1200, left with Baldwin IX of Flanders for the Fourth Crusade, and died at the siege of Constantinople in 1204.

Popular belief held that the cross had been hidden from the Muslims and then divided into many pieces for safekeeping long before the arrival of the First Crusade. There were pieces of what the crusaders believed to be the original in the Holy Land. A piece of the cross had been sent by King Baldwin II to Bernard of Clairvaux as part of the negotiations of the 1130s, for instance. Ambroise, who wrote the chronicle of the Third Crusade, says that Osto was with King Richard the Lionheart when the Cistercians of St. Elias gave the king a piece of the cross.[8] Gilles's charter records the presence of a piece at Floreffe by 1195. Alternately, C. L. Hugo recorded that Count Baldwin IX's brother, Count Philip of Namur, procured a piece of the cross after Constantinople fell to the crusaders of 1204.[9] What is known is that Floreffe had a relic, supposed to be a piece of the cross, by 1254, when the abbey became a pilgrimage site and the center of a festival of the Holy Cross. The annals of the house record a miracle in that year: drops of blood were seen issuing from the relic. Sometime in the thirteenth century, possibly after this miracle, the wood was housed in a new reliquary, of gold and enamel, in the form of a triptych showing Christ crucified. The director of the department of Objets d'Art at the Louvre (Paris) gave a talk in September 1994 on the history of the acquisition of the reliquary, which is on display there. In 1824, the abbey had sold the reliquary; eventually it was purchased by Adolphe de Rothschild, who then donated it to the museum.[10]

The Trazegnies family hosted a famous tournament in 1251, and arranged a marriage with the family of the dukes of Brabant in 1255. Their

---

reffiensi legitima donatione in eleemosynam perpetuam contuli. Verum, ne in posterum successoribus meis malignandi relinquatur occasio, huic cartule cum munimine mei sigilli, testium probabilium, in quorum presentia hec omnia facta et confirmata sunt, annotari nomina necessarium duxi. Hec igitur sunt nomina testium: Walterus frater meus, canonicus in maiori ecclesia Cameracensi, Balduinus et Arnoldus sacerdotes, Mattheus clericus de Angiens, Godefridus de Tudinio, Johannes de Goe, et filius eius Johannes, Johannes de Heripont, Bernardus de Melench, Egidius de Hoja et Nicolaus clericus, frater eius. De familia comitis Namurcensis, Everardus de Veteri Villa, Valterus, Godinus, et alii plures. Actum anno ab Incarnatione Domini M° CC°."

[8] Ambroise, *The Crusade of Richard the Lion Heart* (New York, 1941), 287, 330, 372n. The editor, John LaMonte, says on 372n. that this is not Osto de Trazegnies. Cf. Hans van Werveke, "La Contribution de la Flandre et du Hainaut à la troisième Croisade," *Le Moyen Age* 78 (1972): 55–90, esp. 61, 71, 88 n. 60. Cf. Jonathan Riley-Smith, "King Fulk of Jerusalem and 'the Sultan of Babylon'," in *Montjoie: Studies in Crusade History in Honour of Hans Eberhard Mayer*, ed. B. Z. Kedar et al. (Aldershot, 1997), 55–66.

[9] Hugo, *Annales*, vol. 1: 80. On the relic, see F. Courtoy, "Les reliques de la passion dans le comté de Namur, au XIIIe siècle," in *Mélanges Félix Rousseau* (Brussels, 1958).

[10] There is a photograph of the reliquary in Ph. Jacquet et al., *Floreffe, 850 ans d'histoire. Vie et destin d'une abbaye de prémontrés* (Floreffe, 1973), 191.

relations with Floreffe continued to be troubled by disputes. In 1270 the women at Herlaimont were replaced by canons, and by 1289 the heir to Trazegnies, another Osto, demanded the return of the property on the grounds that the intention of the original gift had been violated by the removal of the nuns. He went so far as to briefly imprison the abbot, but eventually relented and confirmed the original donation.[11]

---

[11] The history of the Trazegnies family is contained in the history of the abbey of Floreffe, based on charters which are analyzed by the author. See Barbier, *Histoire* (note 4, above), vol. 1: 38, note 3, which gives an annotated genealogical table, 39–93, analysis of the charters of 1135–1203, 141–58, details of the thirteenth-century quarrel, and vol. 2, a register of the charters: nos. 4, 40, 60, 65, 78, 89, 159, 384, 385. See also Léopold Devillers, "Trazegnies, son château, ses seigneurs et son église," *Annales de l'Académie [royale] d'archéologie de Belgique* 39 (1883): 161–91; and "Trazegnies, Oston II de," Edouard Poncelet, in the *Biographie Nationale de Belgique*. There are two newer works I have not been able to see, both by Jules Plumet: *Les seigneurs de Trazegnies au moyen âge. Histoire d'une célèbre famille noble du Hainaut, 1100–1550* (Mont-Sainte-Geneviève, 1959); and "Essai sur les seigneurs de Silly-Trazegnies," *Annales du Cercle royal d'histoire et d'archéologie d'Ath et de la région et musées Athois* 36 (1952): 1–50.

15
1188, SIMON DE THIMÉON,
and confirmation document

Joseph Barbier, "Documents concernant la Paroisse de Thiméon, extraits de la cartularie de Floreffe," *Analectes pour servir à l'histoire ecclésiastique de Belgique* 9 (1872): 262–65, nos. 2 and 3. Barbier, *Histoire*, vol. 1: 78; vol. 2: 14, no. 67. See charter 14.

Donatio dominii de Thymeon

In nomine sancte et individue Trinitatis. Quoniam frequenter etiam in bene gestis et justissime consummatis oblivio ceca et litem generat et scandalum parit, ego Hermannus, Dei patientia Floreffiensis abbas, et totus conventus eiusdem ecclesie tam presentium quam futurorum commendamus memorie, quod presenti pagina omnium ingerimus notioni, quod charissimus Simon de Thymion, vir nobilis et miles industrius, in expeditione militum Christi, pio voto Jerosolymam profecturus, bonorumque suorum terrenorum Dominum relinquere deliberans heredem, ut celestium potiretur consortio, quartam partem ecclesie et decime minute et grosse de Thymeon (sic), et quidquid in eodem allodio in terris, silvis, pratis et pascuis, cultis et incultis, servis et ancillis, reditibus et censu possidebat, sine exceptione aliqua, totum integraliter et perpetualiter ecclesie beate Genitricis Marie de Floreffia, et Domino inibi famulantibus, si ei in eadem expeditione occumbere contingeret, in eleemosynam sancta devotione contradidit, et, astante ipsius ecclesie toto conventu, et presentibus quam plurimis nobilibus viris, et de familia et conditione servili, super maius altare ipsius ecclesie per ramum et cespitem legitime affectavit. Huius autem libere donationis et legitime affectationis testes idonei affuerunt de nobilibus Eustachius de Ruz, Hosto de Trasingeis, Godescalcus de Moralmeis, Rigaldus de Roevia, Johannes de Goe et filii eius Walterus et Arnoldus, Liebertus et Wilelmus de Florifuch, Philippus sacerdos de Trasingeis, predictus Simon de Thymeon huius rei author et testis, et frater eius Henricus de Senzelle, et plures alii. Verum, ut huius pagine auctoritas inconvulsa et munitissima perpetuo perseveret, cum testium probabilium astipulatione et sigilli nostri appensione ad maioris augmentem roboris domini

In the name of the holy and undivided Trinity. Because it frequently happens, even in deeds well done and rightly concluded, that blind forgetfulness generates contention and gives birth to scandal, I, Hermann, by the patience of God the abbot of Floreffe, and the whole community, present and future, of the same church, commend to memory what by the present page we present to the knowledge of all, namely that the most dear Simon de Thiméon, a noble man and energetic soldier, about to set out for Jerusalem in accord with his devout vow in the expedition of the soldiers of Christ, deciding to leave to the Lord the inheritance of his goods and lands, in order to have a stronger claim to fellowship with the inhabitants of heaven, donates a fourth part of the church and of the small and large tithes of Thiméon, and what he possesses in the same holding of lands, woods, meadows and pastures, cultivated and unclutivated, male and female servants, rents and taxes, without any exception, whole, entirely and perpetually to the church of the Blessed Mother Mary of Floreffe, and those serving the Lord there, if on that expedition it should happen that he die, and in the presence of the whole community of that church he lawfully ratifies this in the presence of many noble men, and of men of his household and of servile state, upon the main altar of this church through branch and turf (through **ramum et cespitem**). Suitable witnesses of this free donation and lawful conveying include the nobles Eustace de Ruz, Osto de Trazegnies, Godescalc de Moralmeis, Rigald de Roevia, Jean de Goe and his sons Walter et Arnold, Liebert and William de Florifuch, Philip priest of Trazegnies, the aforesaid Simon de Thiméon author and witness of this matter, and his brother Henri de Senzelle, and many others. Indeed, so that the undisturbed and fortified authority of this page may be preserved perpetually, with the accord of the credible witnesses and the addition of our seal, for an augmenting of greater force we append as nec-

advocati et tutoris nostri comitis Namurcensis sigillum huic scripto necessarium duximus appendere.

Acta sunt hec anno ab Incarnatione Domini millesimo centesimo octogesimo octavo, indictione vi, concurrente vero epacta xx^a.

Henry, Count of Namur and Luxembourg, Confirms Simon's Donation

Ratificatio donationis per comitem Namurcensem

In nomine sancte et individue Trinitatis. Quoniam omnis potestas ab omnipotente Deo est, qui, cum ipse potens sit, potentes tamen non abiicit, necessarium est, ut qui potestate ab ipso concessa uti salubriter desiderat, et ipsi Domino dominorum in timore servire, et ei servientes timorate servare studeat. Huius summi et solius Domini timoris et amoris intuitu servientium et adherentium ipsi tam paci quam commodis ego Henricus, Dei gratia comes Namurci et Luzeleburch, providere et prospicere in perpetuum cupiens, tam presentium quam futurorum presenti scripto transmitto et committo memorie, quod Simon de Timiun, miles et actu et genere liber, expeditione christiani exercitus sancta devotione Jerosolymam iturus, bonorumque suorum Dominum relinquere deliberans heredem, ut pro terrenis eterna reciperet, quartam partem ecclesie et decime minute et grosse de Thymeon, et quidquid in eodem allodio in terris, silvis, pratis et pascuis, cultis et incultis, servis et ancillis, reditibus, et censu possidebat, sine exceptione aliqua et diminutione, totum integraliter et perpetualiter ecclesie beate Dei Genetricis Marie de Floreffia et Domino inibi famulantibus, si ei in prefata expeditione occumbere contingeret, pia devotione libere et absolute contradidit, et, adstantibus ipsius ecclesie tam abbate quam toto conventu, presentibus etiam quam plurimus nobilibus viris, et de familia et, de conditione servili, super maius altare eiusdem ecclesie, manu propria offerens per ramum et cespitem legitime affectavit. Huius autem libere donationis et legitime affectationis testes idonei affuerunt: Eustachius de Ruz, Hosto de Trasingeis, Godescalcus de Morelmeis, Rigaldus de Roevia, Johannes de Goe, et filii eius Walterus et Arnoldus, Libertus et Wilelmus de Florifurch et Henricus de Senzelle, predicti Simonis huius eleemosyne autoris, frater Philippus sacerdos de Trasingeis, et plures alii. Nos quoque, qui predictam Floreffiensem ecclesiam, utpote a progenitoribus meis fundatam, et omnia ad ipsam pertinentia iure advocati ut propria conservare, manutenere et tueri et volumus et debemus, cum testium probabilium astipulatione presentem paginam sigilli nostri auctoritate communivimus, ne cuiquam de cetero liceat de prescripta eleemosyna vel vi vel fraude sepedictam ecclesiam perturbare.

Acta sunt hec anno ab Incarnatione Domini millesimo centesimo octogesimo octavo, indictione sexta, concurrente vero epacta xx^a.

essary for this document the seal of our lord, advocate, and tutor, the Count of Namur.

Issued in this year of the Incarnation of the Lord 1188, indiction 6, concurrent epact 20.

Ratification of the donation by the count of Namur.

In the name of the holy and undivided Trinity. Because all power is from the all-powerful God, who, although he is powerful, does not throw down the powerful, it is necessary that whoever desires to use in a healthy way the power granted by God should strive both to serve the Lord of lords in fear and conserve faithfully those serving him. In consideration of the fear and love of this highest and sole Lord and seeking to provide for and look out for the peace and needs of those serving and clinging to him, I, Henry, by the grace of God count of Namur and Luxembourg, transmit by the present writing and commit to the memory of people both present and future, that Simon of Thiméon, knight both by declaration and by birth, about to go to Jerusalem with holy devotion on an expedition of a Christian army, and deciding to leave the Lord as heir of his goods, so that he may receive eternal ones for earthly ones, gives over out of pious devotion freely and absolutely a fourth part of the church and small and large tithe of Thiméon, and whatever he possesses in the same property (*allodio*) in lands, woods, meadows, and pastures, cultivated and uncultivated, male and female servants, rents and taxes, without any exception or diminution, totally, integrally, and perpetually to the Church of the blessed Mother of God, Mary of Floreffe and to those serving the Lord there, if it happens that he die on the said expedition; and, in the presence of the abbot and the whole community of that church, in the presence as well of many noble men, both those associated with his family and those of servile condition, he affirmed this legally upon the high altar of the same church offering by his own hand branch and turf. There were present suitable witnesses of this free donation and lawful intent. Eustache de Ruz, Osto of Trazegnies, Godescalc of Morialmais, Riegald de Roevia, John de Goe, and his son Walter and Arnold, Libertus, and William de Florifurch and Henry of Senzelle, the author of this alms of the said Simon, Brother Philip, priest of Trazegnies, and many others. We also, we ought and wish to preserve, maintain, and guard as our own by right of advocate the said church of Floreffe, and all the things which pertain to it since it was founded by my ancestors. With the testimony of credible witnesses we reinforce this document with the seal of our authority, so that no one may distrub the said church regarding the prescribed alms either by force or by fraud.

Given in this year of the Lord's incarnation 1188, the sixth indiction, concurrent epact 20.

SUMMARY OF THE CHARTERS

The first charter was issued by Hermann, abbot of Floreffe, and records the assembly documented by charter 14. Among the witnesses are Osto of Trazegnies, charter 14, and Godescalc of Morialmeis, charter 28. In it Simon, a nobleman and energetic knight, has joined the expedition to Jerusalem of the army of Christ, and, in hope of God's favor, has given the abbey a fourth part of the tithes of the church at Thiméon, as well as property including land, timber, and pasturage, cultivated and uncultivated. The donation was ratified at a solemn assembly in the church at Floreffe, in the presence of the canons and a large group of witnesses who had gathered in preparation for an expedition to the Holy Land. The ceremony ratifying the donation included the feudal custom by which the donor placed a green branch and a tuft of grass (**ramum et cespitem**) on the main altar as a symbol of the transfer of property.

The second charter is issued by Henry II l'Aveugle, count of Namur and of Luxembourg (1139–1194), and repeats the original donation; in places, word for word. Both charters refer to Henry as the advocate and protector of the abbey; Henry's recalls that his ancestor founded it.

NOTES ON THE CHARTERS

Thiméon

Thiméon is in the province of Hainaut, ten kilometers from Charleroi, in the diocese of Tournai. The village was part of an area that belonged to the county of Namur, but Simon owned it as an allod, without feudal obligations, and so was able to give it to Floreffe. He seems not to have owned the whole village, since Lambert de Maizeret gave part of it to the abbey in 1130. Simon's father and mother had given Floreffe the tithe and church of St.-Martin at Viller-deux-Églises in c.1177.[1]

If Osto of Trazegnies was a notable person, the third crusader in his family, Simon and Godescalc, witnesses at the assembly of 1188, must have been lesser knights, since the donation charters for Floreffe seem to be the only source of information about them. Simon's overlord and ancestors had been patrons of Floreffe, and the former was about to leave on crusade.

In 1187, the Latin Kingdom of Jerusalem was essentially lost to the Muslims, leaving a small band of coastal territory near Tyre in the hands of the crusaders. At the end of October, a papal appeal was issued for a new crusade. In January of 1188 Philip of Flanders took the cross at a

---

[1] Barbier, *Histoire*, vol. 2: 4, vol. 1: 78 and note 3; and cf. Genicot, "L'evolution," 140, 141n. 2, who says that the word allod is used to mean exemption from certain charges, but the degree to which the property was exempt could vary. See also the catalog of Floreffe's possessions in Jacquet et al., *Floreffe, 850 ans d'histoire*.

meeting between the kings of France and England in Gisors, Normandy. The expedition, led by Richard of England, did not leave until August, 1190. Meanwhile, the Germans, led by Emperor Frederick I, left promptly in May 1189.[2] Simon would seem to have been a member of one or the other of these parties, as part of the entourage of Henry of Namur and Luxemburg.

Namur

Namur is a southern province of what is now Belgium; in the 1190s it was an imperial fief. Henri of Namur married the daughter of the count of Flanders in the early 1150s. There were no children from the marriage, which was dissolved in 1163. Since he was without heirs, Henry transferred the inheritance to his sister Alice, the wife of Baldwin IV of Hainaut. Her son Baldwin V inherited Hainaut, Flanders, and Namur by 1191. Henry had renewed the transfer on several occasions, notably in the winter of 1182/3, during the illness which cost him his vision. However, he also remarried, and although he and his second wife seldom lived together, they did eventually produce an heir, Ermesinde, who was born in 1186. Henry changed his mind about the inheritance, but knew he would need a strong ally to effect Ermesinde's claim. He betrothed her, at the age of one year, to Henry II, count of Champagne and nephew to the king of France (see charter 12). The case was referred to the Holy Roman Emperor, who confirmed Baldwin's rights in May, 1188. This was not surprising, for otherwise the fief would have passed to the control of France. Henry gave in, and in fact abdicated from the administration of his county, passing it on immediately to the control of Baldwin. Meanwhile, however, he was secretly encouraging Henry of Champagne, who was raising an army with the help of the kings of France and England. Several feints were made at a war involving France, Flanders, and the Empire. Numerous short-lived truces were concluded until finally the kings of France and England were distracted by their increasing enmity and their crusade vows, combined with their hesitance to try the resources of Emperor Frederick I Barbarossa (1152-1190). Isolated battles were fought in preparation for what just missed becoming a major expedition, and Floreffe was badly damaged by one of them in 1188. By September of 1190 both the emperor's party and that of Flanders were on the Third Crusade, and a peace had been arranged by which Baldwin V's claim to Namur was upheld. Henry l'Aveugle's last attempt to regain Namur was in 1194, after his return from the Holy Land, but he was defeated by Baldwin, who was able to pass the county on to his son.[3]

---

[2] Jonathan Riley-Smith, *The Crusades* (New Haven and London, 1987), 109-11.
[3] F. Baix, "Baudouin V, comte de Hainaut," DHGE. One of Baldwin V's sisters, Yolande of Hainaut, married Ives de Nesle in 1178 (see the notes for charter 11).

16
1189, THREE CRUSADE CHARTERS FOR BASSE-FONTAINE

Charles Lalore, *Collection des principaux cartulaires du diocèse de Troyes*, 6 vols. (Paris, 1875-1890), vol. 3: *Cartulaire de l'abbaye de Basse-Fontaine*, no. 59, 79-80.

1: Galther de Larcicurte (1145-1161)

Ego Henricus, Dei gratia Trecorum episcopus, notum facio presentibus et futuris, quod, cum Galtherus de Larcicurte promisisset Jhero[so]limis adorare Dominum, largitus est ecclesie de Basso Fonte, quicquid habebat in decima Noveville in presentia Galtheri, comitis Brene, de cuius feodo decima pretendebat, laude et assensu filiorum eiusdem comitis, laudantibus etiam liberis prefati Galtheri et uxore sua. Residuum vero decime dedit eidem ecclesie Ruticus, vicecomes Roniaci, laude et assensu liberorum suorum et uxoris sue, laudante predicto comite cum filiis suis. Hec elemosina utriusque legitime facta, recognita et recapitulata est in presentia mea. Eapropter, nequis hoc donum honeste factum aliquo modo obliquare vel obliterare in gravamen ecclesie presumeret, sigilli mei impressione roborari precepi. Huius elemosine testes sunt: Garnerus, canonicus Belli Loci; Herbertus, canonicus Cartobrii; Rogerus, conversus Cartobrii; Robertus de Mastellio; Escotus de Brena; Paganus de Altissiodoro; et alii plures. Testes autem cognitionis curie nostre: Falcho, Guerricus, archidiaconi; Engelmerius, Bernardus, Trecenses canonici; Guerricus, monachus; servientes: Otramnus, Matheus, prepositus.

Lalore, *Cartulaire de l'abbaye de Basse-Fontaine*, no. 88, 114-15.
2: Aicard, lord of Cacenniacus (1183)

Bonum est litteris exarare, que aliquando oportet retractare. Visis enim litteris, cito revocantur ad memoriam, que oblivioni tradita fuerant per temporum prolixitatem. Proinde ego Airardus, dominus Cacenniaci, uxore mea Felicitate laudante, tam ad notitiam modernorum quam futurorum presentibus litteris inscribi volui, quod ecclesie Beate Marie Bassi Fontis in

I, Henry, by God's grace bishop of Troyes, notify all, present and future, that when Gautier de Lassicourt promised to worship the Lord in Jerusalem, he made a gift to the church of Basse-Fontaine of whatever he held in the tithe of Neuville-les-Brienne, in the presence of Gautier count of Brienne, to whose fief the tithe belonged. This gift was made with the permission and assent of the children of the count, as well as with the permission of the children of the donor, Gautier and his wife. Ruticus, viscount of Rosnay, freely gave what remained of the tithe to the same church, with the consent of his wife, as well as of the aforesaid count and his sons. Both of these donations were legitimately made, recognized and recapitulated in my presence. And so, lest anyone in any way presume to distort or abolish this honest gift to the damage of the church, I command it to be confirmed with the wax impression of my seal. To this donation the witnesses are Garner, canon of Beaulieu; Herbert, canon of *Cartobrius;* Roger, conversus of *Cartobrius*; Robert de Mastellius; Escotus de Brienne; Pagan de Altissiodorus [Auxerre]; and many others. Moreover there were witnesses from our [the bishop's] court: Falchus and Guerricus, archdeacons; Engelmerius, and Bernard, canons of Troyes; Guerricus, monk; [*servientes:*] Otramnus; Matthew the provost.

It is a good thing to write down in letters things that one must at some time re-examine. For when the letters are looked at, there quickly are recalled to memory things that had by passage of time been given over to oblivion. Wherefore I, Airard, lord of Chacenay, with the permission of my wife Felicitas, wish it to be inscribed in the present letters for the notice both of contemporaries and of those to come that I have granted to

elemosinam dedi apud Vitriacum terram, in qua concessi, ut una grangia fieret de nemoribus meis, pro qua michi duodecim nummi censuales in festo Sancti Remigii debentur. Concessi insuper, ut omnia necessaria ad reparationem grangie in nemoribus meis acciperentur. Omnes vero donationes et elemosinas, quas predecessores mei pretaxate ecclesie fecerunt, laudavi. Ovibus quoque et omnibus animalibus ecclesie Sancte Marie Bassi Fontis in omnibus pascuis meis, in nemoribus et in planis plena usuaria concessi. Quando vero Jerosolimam perrexi, devectus precibus matris mee, prefate ecclesie concessi, quod vineam Rufe de Couvegnon cum omnibus appendiciis suis haberet, si mater mea vineam illam in aliquo tempore ei dare vellet.

Actum est hoc anno Incarnati Verbi millesimo C° octogesimo tertio.

Lalore, *Cartularie de l'abbaye de Basse-Fontaine*, no. 89, pp. 115-16.
Confirmation, issued after 1183

Notum sit omnibus, tam presentibus quam posteris, quod ego Agnes, Dei pacientia domina de Cachennaio, liberorum meorum assensu, concessi ecclesie Beate Marie Bassi Fontis grangiam meam de Vitriaco cum area ob remedium anime mee et domini mei Jacobi perpetuo possidendam. Concessi etiam fratribus ecclesie Bassi Fontis, ut ipsi omnia necessaria ad reparationem dicte grangie, quotiens necesse fuerit, accipient in nemoribus meis, sicut filius meus Erardus eis concessit, quando perrexit Jerosolimam. Dedi etiam in elemosinam prefate ecclesie Bassi Fontis vineam Ruffe de Covegnon cum omnibus appenditiis suis perpetuo jure possidendam. Ne igitur aliquis sequentium hoc meum scriptum violare presumat, sigillo fratris mei Brenensium comitis roborari volui. Huius rei testes sunt: Johannes, dominus Cachennaii; Lambertus, Johannes de Aguileio, Gillebertus, presbiteri; Gonterus, et filius eius Iheronimus; Bancelinus, et filius Bancelini Everardus de Cherrevi; Petrus et Haymo, filii Gaufridi; Hugo de Funtus, et frater eius, Petrus; Hugo de Posticio, et frater eius, Milo; Guerricus de Aguilleio; Milo de Presbiterorum Villa, et filius eius Hugo; Henricus de Cachennaio, et filius eius, Johannes; Hugo d'Alibun; Guiardus de Vitriaco.

Lalore, *Cartulaire de l'abbaye de Basse-Fontaine*, no. 23, 27-28.
3: Simon de Villa Episcopi for Basse-Fontaine (1189)

Quoniam vetustate temporum, subreptione malorum aut oblivione rerum, etiam in rebus bene statutis controversie solent exoriri; ad hoc evitandum ego, E., comes Brene, brevibus apicibus adnotari volui, quod Simon, miles de Villa Episcopi, iturus Jherusalem, terram de Busum, que de casamento

the church of Blessed Mary of Basse-Fontaine for an alms in the land of Vitry in which I have conceded that a *grangia* be made of my woods, for which twelve *nummi censuales* are to be given to me on the feast of St. Rémy [1 October]. Additionally I have agreed that everything necessary for repairing the *grangia* be obtained in my woods. But I have permitted all donations and alms that my predecessors have made to the aforementioned church. And I grant free range to the sheep and all animals of the church of St. Mary of Basse-Fontaine in all my pastures, in woods and meadows. But when I went off to Jerusalem, moved by my mother's entreaties, I granted to the aforementioned church that Rufe de Couvegnon should possess the vineyard with all its appurtenances, if my mother wished at any time to give that vineyard to him.

This was done in the year of the Incarnate Word 1183.

Let it be known to all, both present and to come, that I, Agnes, by the mercy of God lady of Chacenay, with the assent of my children, have granted to the church of Blessed Mary of Basse-Fontaine my *grangia* of Vitry with its land to be a possession in perpetuity for the salvation of my soul and that of my lord Jacques. I have also granted to the brothers of the church of Basse-Fontaine, that they are to obtain in my woods everything necessary for the repair of the aforesaid *grangia*, as many times as it shall be necessary, as my son Erardus granted to them when he went off to Jerusalem. For I have given as an alms to the aforementioned church of Basse-Fontaine the vineyard of Rufe de Covegnon with all its appurtenances to be possessed in perpetual right. Therefore, lest anyone presume to violate this my writing of the following, I have wished it to be strengthened with the seal of my brother the count of Brienne. Witnesses of this matter are: John, lord of Chacenay; Lambert, John of Aguileio, Gillebert, priests; Gonterus and his son Jeronimus; Bancelinus, and his son Everard de Cherrevi; Peter and Haymo, sons of Gaufridus; Hugh of Funtus and his brother Peter; Hugh of Posticio and his brother Milo; Guerricus de Aguilleio; Milo of Priests' Villa, and his son Hugh; Henry de Chacenay, and his son John; Hugh d'Alibun; Guiardus de Vitry.

Whereas by the antiquity of time, the insidiousness of evil, or the oblivion of affairs controversies are wont to arise even in well-established matters, in order to avoid this I, E(rard), count of Brienne, wish it to be noted down in brief characters that Simon, a soldier of Bishop's Villa, about to

meo est, in omnibus usibus, terris cultis et incultis, prato, censu, et quidquid ad ipsum casamentum pertinet, fratribus Bassi Fontis in elemosinam dedit; et hoc idem uxorem suam, fratres suos, B., N., sororesque suas, ac nepotes suos laudare fecit. Et ut hoc ratum illibatumque permaneat, sigilli mei impressione confirmavi, et hanc ipsam donationem, cum filiis meis G. et G. laudantibus, in manu mea accepi. Huius rei testes sunt: ego, E., comes Brene cum filiis meis; G., magister de Caleta; Odo, sacerdos Pigneii; Harduinus, prior Bassi Fontis; Evrardus, canonicus; Gobertus, miles; Petrus, miles de Hauberci; Radulphus, prepositus Pigneii.

Actum est hoc in presentia J., fratris mei, abbatis Belli loci, anno ab Incarnatione Domini M° C° octogesimo IX°.

go to Jerusalem, has given the land of Busus, which is of my *casamentum*, for any use whatsoever, with lands cultivated and uncultivated, meadow, tolls, and whatever belongs to that *casamentum*, to the brothers of Basse-Fontaine as an alms; and he caused his wife, his brothers B. and N., his sisters, and his nephews to permit this. And so that this may endure ratified and unhindered, I have confirmed it by the impression of my seal, and have taken this same donation in my hand, with permission of my sons G(autier) and G(uillaume). Witnesses of this matter are: myself, E(rard), count of Brienne, with my sons; G., master of Caleta; Odo, priest of Pigneium; Hardouin, prior of Basse-Fontaine; Evrard, canon; Gobertus, soldier; Peter, soldier of Hauberc; Radulph, provost of Pigneium.

This was done in the presence of J., my brother, abbot of Beaulieu, in the year of the incarnation of the Lord 1189.

SUMMARY OF THE CHARTERS

These charters record donations by members of the minor nobility, the lords of Lassicourt and Chacenay, to the Premonstratensian abbey of Basse-Fontaine before the beginning of the Third Crusade in 1189. The first two represent earlier crusades, but which ones are not recorded. These men were vassals of the Brienne family which had founded the abbey. John of Brienne became king of Jerusalem in 1210, and he was one of the Latin emperors of Constantinople (r. 1228–1237) after it was conquered by the Fourth Crusade. John of Brienne corresponded with Abbot Gervase of Prémontré when the latter was serving as papal procurator for the Fifth Crusade (1213–1221). Gervase was also connected with the Coucys; see the charter for him on crusade preaching in 1212, no. 26, below.

NOTES ON THE CHARTERS

Troyes and Prémontré

The hierarchy of the order of Prémontré developed three tiers as the houses multiplied: first the abbot of Prémontré itself, who was also general abbot of the whole order, then the abbots of the main or "mother" houses of the order, then the abbots of individual subsidiary houses. The abbots met annually in a general chapter, which would have been concerned with a number of issues, among them discipline or other problems normally brought before an episcopal court. The order was, however, responsible not to local bishops but directly to the pope in Rome. The Norbertines therefore were technically independent of the secular church, although they had been founded through the patronage of Bishop Barthélemy of Laon. Just as the local bishop became Norbert's patron, the bishops of Troyes founded Premonstratensian houses in their diocese. In 1112 the bishop allowed three of his priests to establish a house which would follow the Augustinian rule (see the introduction), and in 1140, at the urging of Bernard of Clairvaux, this house was affiliated with Prémontré under the name of Beaulieu. The most important patrons of it after the bishops were the counts of Brienne. In 1143 Agnes, countess of Brienne, and her daughter founded Basse-Fontaine very close to the family castle, which was also in the medieval diocese of Troyes. It was a double monastery, for men and women, and was affiliated with the Norbertines at Beaulieu.[1]

The first charter above was issued by Henry, bishop of Troyes 1145–1169. Henry was a member of the nobility who had been brought up at

---

[1] See Ardura, *Dictionnaire*, under the names of these houses for a brief history and bibliography. Also compare the entries under Basse-Fontaine and Moncetz for some discrepancies.

the court of the king of France. He became a Cistercian monk at the abbey of Morimond and then abbot of the new house of Villiers-Betnach in the diocese of Metz. He became bishop at the request of a member of his family, Mathilde de Carinthie, who was married to the count of Champagne.[2] There was a close connection between the Cistercians and the Premonstratensians, as well as between Bernard of Clairvaux and the counts of Champagne.[3] Both the Cistercians and the Premonstratensians were reformed orders, the former for monks, the latter for canons, and both were used by the papacy to preach and raise money for the crusades. The Brienne and Champagne families were famous crusaders, and each contributed a king of Jerusalem.[4] Bernard of Clairvaux led the preaching effort for the Second Crusade, and at the same time actively promoted the new orders of the Templars and the Premonstratensians. The people who made the donations recorded above were vassals of the Briennes who followed them on crusade and in the patronage of new orders. It was apparently under Agnes of Brienne's influence that in 1146 Jacques of Chacenay gave part of the tithe of Bligny to the new house Agnes had founded at Basse-Fontaine, thus opening the relationship between the family and the canons which was perpetuated by gifts like the one in charter 2 above. In 1179 and again in 1182 Erard I de Chacenay was on crusade; he died in Acre in 1191. Gautier II, mentioned as the count of Brienne in the first of the three charters, was Agnes's son. He and his men continued to be patrons of the house, under the approving eye of the bishops who counted with Agnes as founders. In 1185 and 1186 Gautier's son and heir Erard, along with his wife Agnes and his sons Gautier and Guillaume, continued to make gifts of lands and rents to the abbey, in return for which the canons were to supply the hosts for the mass for all the churches in Brienne lands. The final charter records the pilgrimage to Jerusalem of a Brienne vassal, and his gift to the foundation which had become an important part of his overlord's identity.

The holdings, revenues, rights, and other privileges of a lordship in some sense defined the owner, contributed to his importance as a landholder in terms of his ability to put a certain number of men in the field,

---

[2] For "Henri de Troyes," see R. Aubert, DHGE.

[3] See *The Letters of Bernard of Clairvaux*, trans. B. S. James (London, 1953), especially nos. 32, 310, 328; Hugues Lamy, "Vie du Bienheureux Hugues de Fosses," an extract from *La Terre Wallonne*, vol. 13 (Charleroi, 1925); Petit, *Norbert*, 177–78; n.a., "Chronicon," *Analecta Praemonstratensia* 53 (1977): 225, which records a passage from a life of Bernard edited in Migne, *PL* 185, col. 299.

[4] I am not aware of a history of the family with bibliography more recent than the one in DHGE by Louis Bréhier, "Brienne." Chacenay is covered in the appendix to Evergates, *Troyes*, 166–67, with a genealogical chart. Neither Lassicourt nor Vitry are listed.

enhanced his political influence, and so forth. The type and importance of his religious foundations and patronage certainly contributed to that identity, the buildings themselves defining him in the same way that the extent of his castle defense-works did. By the 1140s Norbert was one of the most influential prelates in Europe, backed by the influence of the most important, Bernard of Clairvaux. For instance the latter encouraged his cousin, Bishop Geoffrey of Langres, to make several donations to Basse-Fontaine in the 1140s.[5] The response to Bernard, to the crusades, and to the reform is once again clouded by the issues of prestige, such as influence with the kings and great nobles of France, who participated in both the Second and the Third Crusades, and who set what has been called a "fashion" for particular orders of canons or monks.

---

[5] For all of the donations mentioned, see first the introduction by Lalore to his edition of the charters, and then A. de Barthélemy's article on the "Champenois" on crusade, "Les pèlerins champenois en Palestine, 1097–1249," *Revue de l'Orient latin* 1 (1893): 359 and note 9, 360, note 14, and 362, note 20. Recent editors have cast some doubt on the accuracy of Lalore's transcriptions. I have not seen the originals in this case.

17
1190, RAOUL I DE COUCY

M. E. Mennesson, "Partage Testamentaire de Raoul Ier Seigneur de Coucy et de Vervins," *La Thiérache. Bulletin de la Société archéologique de Vervins (Aisne)* 14 (1890): 39-42. Bibliothèque nationale, Collection de Picardie 7, fols. 11-12.

Ego Radulphus, dominus Couciaci, notum fieri volo tam praesentibus quam futuris, quod cum ad iter accinctus fuissem, ne aliqua inter liberos meos super haereditatis suae portione oriri posset discordia, terram meam, prout mihi monstravit mentio, ad proborum etiam hominum meorum consilium, diligenter assignavi. Concessi itaque Ingelrenno filio meo, quoniam prior natu existebat, omnem terram meam absque aliorum reclamatione pacifice possidendam, exceptis portionibus quae aliis liberis meis fuerunt deinceps assignatae, quae tales sunt. Volui quod filius meus Thomas Vervinum, Fontanas et Landousies absque omni contradictione quiete possideat; et sexaginta libras in wionagiis Vervini et Landousies, talis monetae qualis ad wionagi persolvetur, habeat annuatim; et de iis omnibus erit homo ligius Ingelrenni fratris sui. Radulpho, qui clericali promissus est officio, quadraginta libras parisiensis monetae apud Roiam annuatim capiendas, quandiu ipse vixerit, assignavi. Roberto siquidem omnia illa quae mihi in matrimonio matris suae collata fuerunt diligenter assignavi, et villam meam ad sui aedificationem Pinon videlicet, cum toto censu cuiusdam nemoris, quod transitus ad Pinon vocare solemus; quae omnia de fratre suo Ingelrenno in planum homagium obtinebat. Si autem contigerit quod praefatus Ingelrennus absque haerede moriatur, tota ei facta assignatio ad Thomam fratrem suum deinceps revertetur. Sciendum e contrario quod quicumque ex praefatis liberis absque haerede decesserit, totam eius possessionem prior natu ex integro possidebit. Agneti vero filiae meae 1600 libras atrabatensis monetae ad redditus communes de Marla et de Creci assignavi capiendas. Quae, completis tribus annis post motionem meam insequentibus, octo annis recipientur, uno quoque anno in festo beati Remigii centum videlicet Marlae, et reliquae centum apud Creci: et ad proventus praedictae Agnetis faciendos Praemonstratensi commendabuntur ecclesiae. Si autem in hac peregrinatione me a praesenti vita migrare contigerit, si etiam praefata Agnes filia mea antequam maritetur decesserit quicquid de assignata sibi pecunia comparens extiterit aequaliter partietur: ejus medietatem

I, Raoul, lord of Coucy, wish it to be known to those present and future, that when I was prepared (girded) for the journey, lest some discord could arise among my children over the division of their inheritance, I carefully assigned my land, as memory showed it to me, with the counsel of my proven men. Because he was the firstborn, I granted to Enguerran, my son, all my land, to be possessed peacefully without any claims from others, except those portions which were then assigned to my other children, which are as follows. I want my son Thomas to quietly possess Vervins, Fontanas, and Landousies without any contention; and desire that he have sixty *libras* annually in the districts of Vervins and Landousies, such money as is produced in these territories. And because of all this he will be the liege man of his brother Enguerran. I assign to Raoul, who is promised to clerical office, forty *libras* of Parisian money to be received annually at Roia, as long as he lives. To Robert I carefully assign all that which was conveyed to me at my marriage with his mother, and my farm at his building at Pinon, with all the tolls of the woods which we are wont to call the crossing to Pinon. This he obtains from his brother Enguerran with full homage. If, however, it should happen that the aforesaid Enguerran should die without an heir, all that which is assigned to him reverts to his brother Thomas. Let it be known, on the contrary, that if any of the aforementioned children dies without an heir, the firstborn will have in full his whole possession intact. To my daughter Agnes I assign 1600 *libras* of the money of Arras to be received out of the common rents of Marles and of Crecy. When three years have passed after my departure, for eight years on the feast of Saint Remi what is due on the one part from Marle and on the other from Crecy will be received. As for the ecclesiastical revenues to be made to the aforesaid Agnes, they will be given to the church at Prémontré. However, if on this pilgrimage it happens that I pass from the present life, [or] if the aforesaid Agnes, my daughter, dies before she is married, whatever of the money assigned her that still exists will be divided

mater eius Aelidis, uxor mea, videlicet obtineat: reliqua vero medietas, pro mea et Agnetis anima, Hospitalariis, Templariis atque ecclesiae Praemonstratensi, in eleemosynam conferatur, inter se aequaliter percipienda. Si autem et Aelidim uxorem meam sicut et nos mori contigerit, medietas ista dictae pecuniae filio meo primogenito conferetur: reliqua vero medietas primam ex integro retinebit assignationem. Notandum est quod totius huius divisionis tenor, salva pariter omni possessione mea, et omni jure Aelidim uxoris meae observato, dividitur. Haec enim omnia subscripta quandiu vixero, meae reservo subdita voluntati. Ut autem tota divisio haec, aliter ordinare eam et commutare voluero, rata et indiscussa perseveret praesenti paginae commendari et sigilli mei impressione volui praemuniri. Actum anno incarnationis Dominicae millesimo centesimo nonagesimo.

equally. My wife, Alix, her mother, should receive her half; the other half is to be conferred as alms for my soul and the soul of Agnes, on the Hospitallers, Templars, and the church of Prémontré. However, if it happens that Alix my wife dies and I do too, her half of the aforesaid money will be given to my firstborn son; the other half will retain the same assignment without change. It is to be noted that this entire division is made of all my possessions respecting every right of my wife Alix. As long as I live, I keep everything written above subject to my will. So that this division—until I choose to arrange and to change it—may remain ratified and unchallenged, I wish the present page to be commended and fortified with the impress of my seal. Issued in the year of the Lord's Incarnation, 1190.

SUMMARY OF THE CHARTER

The charter is issued by Raoul I de Coucy (1147–1190), who, on the point of leaving on crusade, wanted to divide his property according to his own wishes and the advice of his "proven men," so that there would be no quarrel on the part of his heirs. To his son Enguerran (d. 1242), the firstborn, he gave his whole property, to be enjoyed peacefully, without interference by the other heirs, save those portions given to them in this document. His son Thomas (d. 1253) was to possess land and rents at Vervins, Fontaine, and Landouzy as vassal to Enguerran. Raoul was destined for the church and had an annual money rent at Roye for his lifetime only. Robert (d. 1235) was to have all that his mother had brought as dowry, plus land and rights over a wood at Pinon, again as vassal of his eldest brother. If Enguerran died before his brothers, his eldest son Thomas was to be his heir. On the other hand, if any of the younger brothers died without heirs, their portions were to revert to Enguerran. His daughter Agnes was to have certain revenues at Marle and Crécy, which were to be administered for her by the church of Prémontré. If Raoul died on crusade, or if Agnes died before marrying, her income was to be divided into two parts, one part to be given to her mother, Alix, and the other as a gift, for the salvation of Raoul's soul and that of Agnes, to the Hospitallers, the Templars, and the church of Prémontré, in equal portions. When Alix died, her portion was to revert to her eldest son. All of these arrangements were made at Raoul's pleasure, none of them were to hamper his or his wife's rights during their lives, and he held himself free to change them at any time. However, barring his own wish to change the dispositions, they were not to be tampered with by anyone else, and so he had the document made up, and sealed it with his seal.

NOTES ON THE CHARTER

Raoul I

Raoul was the son of Enguerran II, and was issuing his will, or *ordinatio*, on the point of departure for the Third Crusade.[1] He had five children by his wife Alix de Dreux, granddaughter of Louis VI. He died in Ascalon in 1191. By the terms of this document, the lordship of Coucy was divided into three parts: Coucy, Vervins, and Pinon. However, the

---

[1] Albricus monachus Trium Fontium, *Chronique*, ed. Paul Scheffer-Boichorst, in MGH SS 23, 868; Barthélemy, *Coucy*, 116; Du Plessis, 146–47, no. 28; Tardif, "Enguerran," 43. Raoul took at least three of his vassals with him: Jean I de Housset (Barthélemy, *Coucy*, 521); Etienne de Vassens (Vernier, *Coucy*, 379, 381); Melleville, *Dictionnaire*: "Vassens"; and Guy d'A(E)rblincourt (de Sars, *Laonnois*, vol. 1: 240 note 3, 241; Gilbert de Mons, *Chronique*, 274; and charter 24, below). On the Third Crusade see charter 15.

eldest son, Enguerran, kept not only the heart of the lordship, but also the wionage of Vervins, a tax which was levied on traffic through his territory to Flanders, Laon, and Champagne. This left him master both of the roads and of the commercial traffic, since the tax carried the obligation of protecting and regulating merchants who passed through.[2]

The charter is not properly called a will, but an *ordinatio*, because it is such an early example of this kind of document that the form for it has not yet solidified. King Philip Augustus of France, for instance, issued a similar charter for the Third Crusade, but with a different purpose. It provided for an interim government in the event of his death, but also registered gifts to churches. Raoul's was issued specifically to avoid quarreling among his heirs. He ensured that the eldest, Enguerran, would inherit the bulk of the lordship, including the three largest castles, and that his daughter would have a dowry, while also providing for the younger sons.[3]

Alix de Dreux and Enguerran III

Raoul's wife exercised his prerogatives as lord of Coucy at least until 1198, when she arbitrated a quarrel between the canons of Prémontré and Gérard de Gras at Leuilly. She died in 1217, and it is possible that she continued to rule the lordship until as late as 1214, when she was again arbitrator for the abbey. The three brothers, Enguerran, Thomas, and Robert, were with King Philip Augustus at the famous battle of Bouvines in 1214. Their close relationship to the royal house was due to their mother. There is a thirteenth-century legend based on Enguerran's role in this battle. Just before the fighting began, the king invited his knights to take communion with him, but only if, as loyal friends, they were prepared to go to their deaths with him. Enguerran was the first to step forward. His loyalty was to embroil him in the disastrous royal expedition to England in 1216 (see charter 22, below).[4]

---

[2] Barthélemy, "Raoul de Coucy et Vervins," *Mémoires de la Fédération des Sociétés d'histoire et d'archéologie de l'Aisne* 27 (1982): 151.

[3] See Barthélemy, *Coucy*, 405, 217–18, who also points out that this was one of the few charters issued by the nobility of France for this crusade which was not registered in the royal archives.

[4] Barthélemy, *Coucy*, 412, 421–22. Cf. *Récits d'un ménestrel de Reims au XIIe siècle*, ed. N. de Wailly (Paris, 1876), 142; *Gesta Senonensis Ecclesiae*, MGH SS 25, 295; G. Duby, *Le dimanche de Bouvines* (Paris, 1985).

18
1190, GERARD, CHANCELLOR OF FLANDERS

Ferdinand van de Putte and Charles Louis Carton, *Chronicon et cartularium abbatiae Sancti Nicolai Furnensis* (Bruges, 1849), 173-74, not numbered, dated 1190.

Privilegium Dompni Gerardi Brugensis Prepositi de Piscatoribus nostris a Renghersdike in Loograght et Venepa Usque ad Ysaram

Ego Gerardus Dei gracia Brugensis prepositus et Flandrie cancellarius, notum fieri volo tam futuris quam presentibus, quod Eustachius filius Walteri, filii Eustachii, capturam anguillarum, quam a Renghesdicke usque ad Ysarum in Lograt, et Venepa, hereditario iure, a progenitoribus possidebat, Iherosolimam profecturus ecclesie beati Nicolai de Furnes, uxore ipsius Elisabet presente, et assensum prebente, cum omni iure et dominio quod in prefata captura anguillarum habebat, in puram et perpetuam elemosinam tradidit. Duo eciam fratres eiusdem Eustachii, Walterus et Xpristianus, quitquid in eadem captura anguillarum habebant, predicte ecclesie, per manum fratris sui Eustachii in elemosinam dederunt. Huius itaque Eustachii, precibus abbatis et fratrum ecclesie sepius dicte, amore ductus, illam elemosinam, quam ad officium de Redeninga pertinebat comprobavimus, et sigilli nostri impressione confirmavimus. Hiis testibus, Jordano cantore, Leonio notario, Sigero castellano Gandense, Flocramno amman, Bernoldo, landmetra, aliisque quam pluribus. Anno Domini M° C° XC°.

I, Gerard, by the grace of God provost of Bruges and chancellor of Flanders, wish it to be known to people in the future and in the present, that Eustace, son of Walter, son of Eustace, about to set out for Jerusalem, handed over to the church of Blessed Nicholas of Furnes in pure and perpetual alms the catch of eels from Renghesdicke to Ysara in Lograt and Venepa, which he possessed by hereditary right from his ancestors, with every right and dominion which he had in the aforesaid catch of eels, in the presence of his wife Elizabeth who granted her assent. Also, two brothers of the same Eustace, Walter and Christian, gave as alms to the aforesaid church through the hand of their brother Eustace whatever belonged to them of that catch of the eels. At the prayers of the abbot and brethren of this oft-referred-to church, led by love, we approve that part of the alms which pertains to the office of *Redeninga* (rekeninge?), and we confirm it with the impress of our seal. There were these witnesses: Jordan the cantor; Leonius the notary; Siger castellan of Ghent; Foilcramn *almoner*; Bernold, surveyor; and many others. In the year of the Lord, 1190.

SUMMARY OF THE CHARTER

Gerard, provost of Bruges and chancellor at the court of Flanders, proclaims that Eustace, on the point of departure for the Holy Land, makes a present of rights held by his grandfather, Eustace, and father, Walter, to Saint Nicholas at Veurne, in the presence of his wife Elizabeth. The rights would appear to be, as the caption says, "fishing rights," and more specifically the capture of eels, which belonged to his family. Gerard appears to approve as the official responsible for the office of, in Flemish, *rekeninge*, or accounts.[1]

NOTES ON THE CHARTER

Furnes

Veurne/Furnes, in Belgium, was a fortification built to stave off Norman invasions. The important church in the town was St. Walburge, built in the 900s and given a piece of the True Cross by Count Robert II of Flanders (1093-1111). St. Nicholas was on the river Colme near the city, and originally was founded as a retreat by canons from St. Walburge who wished to live "the apostolic life". Before 1120 Jean de Warneton, bishop of Thérouanne (1099-1130), recognized it as a house of regular canons, and appointed an abbot for the twelve men who lived there. Between 1135 and 1164, the canons became affiliated with Prémontré due to the urging of Milo, bishop of Thérouanne (1131-1158), who has been mentioned above in charter 3. In 1170 the canons had once again to relocate further from the growing town, and chose the chapel of Our Lady of Oostuut (see charter 28). The abbot in 1190 was a certain William.[2]

Gerard

The office of chancellor had been given in perpetuity to the provosts of the chapter of secular canons at St. Donatian, the cathedral church at Bruges, in the diocese of Tournai, in 1089 under Count Robert I of Flanders (1071-1093). The chancellor presided over a group of notaries who kept accounts and had custody of the comital seal. As provost of the chapter, which had been founded in 961 under Count Arnulf I (918-965), Gerard would have acted as archdeacon of the district, responsible to the bishop. The provosts of St. Donatian's often held the office of provost of Lille as well.[3]

---

[1] I have not seen the original of this charter, and am unable to resolve the problems posed by the place-names.

[2] Backmund, *Monasticon*, vol. 2: 429-33; *Monasticon belge*, vol. 3: 587-629, 653-54; and see note 5, below.

[3] Warnkönig, *Histoire de Flandre*, vol. 2: 86.

Gerard was provost of St. Donatian and chancellor under Philip of Flanders (1168–1191), who died in the midst of his fourth journey to the Holy Land, in Acre on the Third Crusade, and was buried in the church of St. Nicholas there. Gerard may have been Philip's half-brother, an illegitimate son of Count Thierry of Alsace (1128–1168).[4] According to one historian of the house, Furnes received many gifts from the counts of Flanders, and especially from Philip of Alsace, who relied on new orders like the Cistercians and Premonstratensians to open new land for cultivation.[5]

THE WITNESSES

Siger II (1163–1202) was castellan of Ghent in 1189, and then of Cambrai by 1200, when he resigned from office and joined the Templars.[6]
Foilcramn, *almoner*: his office would have been the distribution of alms.

---

[4] Warnkönig, *Histoire de Flandre*, vol. 2: 86, 87 and n. 4, 347.
[5] N. Huyghebaert, "Furnes," DHGE; and see Philips, *Defenders*, 273.
[6] Warlop, *Flemish Nobility*, vol. 2: no. 89. For household officers, see charter 8, for the Templars, charter 9 above.

19
1193, LAMBERT, BISHOP OF THÉROUANNE

Th. Duchet and A. Giry, *Cartulaires de l'église de Thérouanne* (St. Omer, 1881), 70–71, nos. 89–91.

No. 89

Lambertus dei gratia Morinorum episcopus, omnibus ad quos littere iste pervenerint in domino salutem. Arnulfus Morinensis advocatus, homo noster ligius, propter sumptus quos in peregrinatione sancta fecerat, magnis debitis obligatus, et res suas in reditu suo profligatas et male tractatas inveniens, necessitate compulsus, a karissimis nostris canonicis Morinensibus centum marchas mutuo accepit benigna expectatione eorum, post decessum suum de primis fructibus feodi sui ad nos pertinentis plene et integre percipiendas; ita quoque ut si contingeret cum altera vice peregre proficisci in Iherusalem et sumptus facere, pro quibus debito obligaretur, ipsum debitum primo solveretur, proxime vero predictas centum marchas ecclesia nostra Morinensis perciperet. Huic assignationi Elyzabeth uxor sua advocatissa, sorores sue et nepotes sui benigne assenserunt. Nos quoque benignum gratanter adhibentes assensum, in majorem totius negotii firmitatem, presentem paginam sigilli nostri appensione confirmamus. Actum anno domini millesimo centesimo nonagesimo tercio.

No. 90

Ego Arnulfus Tervannensis advocatus, magnis debitis obligatus propter sumptus quos in tanta peregrinatione feceram et res meas in reditu meo profligatas et male tractatas inveniens, hac necessitate compulsus a dilectis dominis meis canonicis Tervannensibus centum marchas mutuo accepi benigna expectatione eorum, post decessum meum de primis fructibus feodi episcopalis ab ecclesia recipiendas, ita ut si contingeret me alia vice in peregrinatione in Iherusalem sumptus facere, pro quibus debito obligarer, ipsum debitum primo solveretur, proxime vero centum marche ecclesie Morinensi solverentur. In hanc assignationem Elyzabeth uxor mea advo-

Lambert, by the grace of God bishop of Thérouanne, to all whom this document reaches, greetings in the Lord. Arnulf, advocate of Thérouanne, our liege man, because of the expenditures he made on his holy pilgrimage, obligated by great debt, and on his return finding his goods squandered and badly handled, moved by necessity, received from our canons of Thérouanne one hundred marks in a mutual agreement in accord with which they have the kind expectation that after his death they will receive from the first fruits of his fief that which pertains to us, fully and integrally, in such a way that if he sets out abroad for Jerusalem again and transacts business for which he will be obligated by debts, that [original] debt would be paid up first, and then our church of Thérouanne would receive the aforesaid one hundred marks. To this arrangement his wife Elizabeth is advocate, and his sisters and nephews generously agree to it. We too, concurring graciously with our assent confirm the present page with the impress of our seal to give greater firmness to the whole transaction. Issued in the year of our Lord 1193.

I, Arnulf, advocate of Thérouanne, incurred great debts on account of transactions which were made for a great pilgimage; and upon my return, found that those who had managed my affairs had been profligate and incompetent. Compelled by necessity, I received from my dear lords the canons of Thérouanne one hundred marks in the mutually understood and kindly expectation that after my decease they were to be repaid to the church from the first fruits of my episcopal fief. Further, if it happened that I again made purchases for a pilgrimage to Jerusalem for which I was obligated by debt, this particular debt would be paid up first, so that the one hundred marks would be paid to the church of Thérouanne. To this arrangement my wife Elizabeth, as advocate, and my sisters and nephews

catissa et sorores mee et nepotes mei benignum prebuerunt assensum. Ad majorem autem confirmationem, presentem cartam sigilli nostri appositione et subscriptorum attestatione communivimus. Signum Martini abbatis Sancti Johannis; signum magistri Ingelrammi Noviomensis; S. Willelmi militis de Novavilla. Actum anno domini M° C° XC° tercio.

No. 91 (1193/4)

Ego Arnulfus Tervannensis advocatus, assignationem a patre meo Arnulfo et matre mea Aelide et sorore mea Elyzabeth in quadraginta quinque marchis argenti et XI libris canonicis Morinensibus factam, pro salute animarum eorundem, hoc modo, dictorum canonicorum benigna concessione, ordinavi: ut duobus primis annis, unoquoque videlicet eorum, duodecim marche infra purificationem sancte Marie predictis canonicis persolvantur; deinceps, singulis annis, sex marche infra purificationem eisdem refundantur, donec summa quinquaginta duarum marcharum prescriptis canonicis integre fuerit persoluta. Quod si me ante solutionem istius summe plenarie factam de hoc seculo migrare contigerit, huius summe residuum cum centum marchis quibus eis teneor de feodo episcopali integre persolvetur. Actum Tervanne, anno domini M° C° XC° III°, mense februario. Signum Martini abbatis Sancti Johannis; S. magistri Ingelrammi Noviomensis; S. Willelmi militis de Novavilla.

grant me their kind consent. To better confirm the present page, I append my seal and add the signs of witnesses: Martin, abbot of Saint-Jean; Master Enguerran de *Noviomensis;* William, knight de Novavilla. Issued in the year of our Lord 1193.

I, Arnulf, advocate of Thérouanne, have made provision for the assignment made by my father Arnulf and my mother Aelide and my sister Elizabeth for forty-five marks of silver and 11 pounds to the canons of Thérouanne, for the salvation of their souls, thus, by kind permission of the aforementioned canons: that in the first two years, viz. in each of them, twelve marks shall be paid to the aforementioned canons at the (feast of the) Purification of St. Mary (2 February); subsequently, in each year, six marks shall be given to them at the Purification, until the sum of fifty-two marks be completely paid up to the aforementioned canons. But if it happens that I leave this world before the payment of this total sum is completely made up, the residue of this sum together with a hundred marks for which I am obligated to them by the episcopal *feudum* shall be completely paid up. Done at Thérouanne, in the year of our Lord 1193, in the month of February. Signature of Martin, abbot of St. John's; of magister Enguerran of Noviomensis; of William, soldier of Novavilla.

SUMMARY OF THE CHARTERS

Lambert II, bishop of Thérouanne (Morinorum) 1191–1207, issues a charter to record the agreement reached with the cathedral chapter's advocate, Arnulf III (1170–1207). Due to his own extravagance on the Third Crusade (1191), Arnulf had contracted several loans with the chapter to a total of a hundred marks, which he was unable to repay. Therefore, they were to be repaid upon his death from "the first fruits of his fief." His wife and heirs agreed to the arrangement.

The second charter is issued by Arnulf himself, and simply repeats the agreement recorded in the first, using the same wording, but adding witnesses.

The third charter confuses the issue. This is a dispute known only from the charters of the chapter of Thérouanne. Here Arnulf, the son of Arnulf and "Aelide," and the brother (not husband) of Elizabeth, makes a gift of money to the canons in return for prayers for his family. The witnesses are the same as for the previous charter, and the charter is issued within a few months of the other two.[1]

NOTES ON THE CHARTER

Thérouanne

Arnulf's history and therefore his crusade motivation are unknown to me. Apart from his concerns, it is worth looking at the possible motives for involvement by the bishop and chapter. Lambert is known as a witness to charters issued by Countess Ida of Boulogne, and to gifts made to the Premonstratensian house of Braine in 1194.[2] Thérouanne was a chapter which had been converted to the Augustinian rule under the influence of Bishop Lambert of Arras in the early twelfth century (see charter 11). Lambert of Arras was partially responsible for the establishment of the new Augustinian order of Arrouaise, as well as for the reform of his own cathedral chapter. One of his canons, Jean de Warnton, participated in the consecration of the church at Arrouaise as bishop of Thérouanne in 1106. Aicard, one of the original canons at Arrouaise, was archdeacon at Thérouanne by 1099 under Bishop Jean, was sent to Jerusalem in 1104, was deacon of the chapter of the Holy Sepulchre by 1110, and prior of the Temple of the Lord 1112–1136.[3] Instead of illustrating the web of family

---

[1] Duchet and Giry, *Cartulaires*, nos. 89, 90, 91, 98, 99. See Warlop, *Flemish Nobility*, vol. 1: 280; and Fossier, *Picardie*, 611. Also cf. De Hemptinne and Verhulst, *Oorkonden*, no. 64; and van Werveke, "Contribution de la Flandre," 72, 84 and no. 27.

[2] See Ardura, *Dictionnaire*, s.v. "Braine."

[3] For Jean, see Migne, *PL* 162, no. 91, col. 682; GC, vol. 10, "instrumenta," 373; Dereine, "Conon." For Aicard, cf. Milis, *Arronaise*, 103 and n. 2; Moeller, "Flamands du Ternois," 196; Röhricht, *Regesta*, nos. 56a, 59, 68a, 80, 89, 90, 91, 105; Hamilton, *The Latin*

relationships or the connection of certain family members to a particular overlord, this charter opens the question of the relationship between religious houses and the local contingents they supported. If crusading families were motivated first by political advantage to be gained from an expedition, and then by the need to retain property won by family members in the Holy Land, reformed chapters can be seen to have similar motivations. The chapters of both Thérouanne and Arras would have had the same almost proprietary interest in Jerusalem as some "crusade families": traditions begun by the earlier expeditions of members of their chapters, offices held or property acquired by chapter members in Palestine. Additionally, the same kinds of political motives family members served by joining particular crusade leaders work for chapter members, who also could hope for patronage as a result of loyal service. Without knowing Arnulf's story it is impossible to reach a conclusion, but the question of why the chapter would finance an expedition is worth pursuing.

Church in the Crusader States, 134. For Arras, see Tock, *Chartes des Évêques d'Arras* and "Elections épisopales à Arras." in the bibliography. I have not been able to consult Bernard Delmaire, *Le diocèse d'Arras de 1093 au milieu du XIVe siècle. Recherches sur la vie religieuse dans le nord de la France au Moyen Âge*, 2 vols. (Arras, 1994).

20
1201, VIARD DE PRÉS

Charles Louis Hugo, *Sacri et Canonici Ordinis Praemonstratensis Annales*, 2 vols. (Nancy, 1734-1736), vol. 2, "probationes," clxxvi-vii: "Donationes facta a Viardo Milite in Terram sanctam proficiscenti. Anno 1201."

In nomine sancte et individue Trinitatis. Ego Viardus miles de Prés notum facio tam futuris quam praesentibus quod contuli Ecclesiae sanctae Mariae de Mirvault et de Fratribus ibidem Deo famulantibus, pro remedio animae meae et praedecessorum meorum quatuor terrae quarterias cum pratis quarteriis adjacentibus laude et assensu sororis meae Alis et mariti eius Hugonis, et filiorum et filiarum eorundem; et sciendum quod si a transmarinis partibus Deus mihi concesserit regressum, jam dictos quarterios in dicta villa de Pargny excolere licebit si potuero et voluero quandiu vixero. Praeterea notum esse volo, quod iam praenominatae Ecclesiae concessi absque omni retentione partem illam quae me contingebat de la Monteigny, et vageriam meam de molendino et partem prati adjacentis ad la Leschire, et partem meam de Valle-viri. Dedi etiam non semel dictae Ecclesiae partem prati mei de Priens quod situm est juxta Lisodium parvum, laude et assensu Domini Viardi de Rignel et haeredum eius a quo in feodo habebam; volo etiam omnibus esse manifestum, quod si eis, vel extra mare, quod Deus avertat, expiravero, boves cum omni cultura pro remedio animae iam concessi dictae Ecclesiae, et ut hoc ratum habeatur sigillo Domini Viardi de Rignel communivi. Ego Theobaldus comes Barri, et Luceburgis omnibus ad quos praesentes litterae pervenerint, notum facio quod Viardus miles de Praello tres quarterios terrae quos apud Pargneium possidebat laude et assensu nostro Ecclesiae Miraevallis contulit in eleemosynam perpetuam; et nos in testimonium huius donationis praesentem paginam sigillo nostro confirmavimus anno 1201. mense Januarii.

In the name of the holy and undivided Trinity. I, Viard, knight of Prés, make known to those to come and those present that I granted to the church of St.-Marie de Mureau and the brothers serving God there, for the salvation of my soul and the souls of my ancestors, four quarters of land, with four quarters of adjacent meadows, with the confirmation and assent of my sister Alix and of her husband Hugh, and of their sons and daughters. Moreover, it is to be known that if God grants me return from the lands across the sea, it will be allowed to cultivate those quarters in the same village of Pargny (Pargny-sous-Mureau, Vosges, Neuf-châteaux), if I can and wish, as long as I live. Moreover, I want it known that I have already granted to the aforesaid church, without any reservation, that part of Monteigny which fell to me and my right to a scales at the mill and part of the adjacent meadow at Leschire, and my part of Valle-viri. To the said church I also gave, at another time, part of the meadow of Priens which is situated next to *Lifordium parvum*, with the approval and assent of Lord Viard of Rignel, and of his heirs, from whom I had it in fief. I wish also to make known to all that, God forbid, should I die on this side of the sea or the other, I have already granted the oxen and all the seignurial land (*cultura*) to the said church as a remedy for my soul, and that this may be considered ratified I have fortified it with the seal of the Lord Viard of Rignel. I, Theobald, count of Bar and Luxembourg, wish to make known to all to whom the present document reaches that Viard, knight of Prés, granted to the church of Mureau in perpetual alms three quarters of land which were possessed at Pargny with our confirmation and consent. In witness to this donation we have confirmed the present page with our seal in the year 1201, in the month of January.

SUMMARY OF THE CHARTER

Viard, knight of Prés, issued this charter in favor of the Premonstratensian house of Mureau for the salvation of his soul and those of his ancestors. His sister Alix, her husband Hugh, and their children, consented to the donation of agricultural land and pasture, on the understanding that Viard would have the use of the property if he returned from the Holy Land. Viard then confirmed other donations he had made to the canons, including land held in fief from his overlord Viard de Rignel, which Mureau was to receive if he died overseas. At the end of the charter, his overlord Count Theobald of Bar and Luxembourg (1189-1214) approved the donation as well.

NOTES ON THE CHARTER

Mureau and Bar

Mureau was a double monastery founded by the Norbertines of the abbey of Septfontaines in 1147. In 1157, the men and women were housed separately, thanks to gifts by Olivier de Neufchâteau and Viard de Rebeuville, in the *département* of Vosges and the (then) diocese of Toul. Bar is on the border of Champagne and Lorraine. The advocate in 1157 was the lord of Bourlémont, which is also located on the Lotharingian border. After 1180 the kings of France became important patrons of the house. Its location on the border between France and Lorraine made for a stormy history: its buildings were frequently damaged and rebuilt.[1]

In 1106 Emperor Henry V of Germany gave the duchy of Lower Lorraine to Godfrey, count of Louvain. His descendants were called dukes of Brabant from 1190 until 1430, when the duchy was combined with that of Burgundy. Bar was a county of the duchy of Upper Lorraine, which included the dioceses of Metz, Toul, and Verdun, and was held by the descendants of Albert of Alsace from 1048 until 1431. Thibaut's father, Renaud, died at Acre, while his son was consolidating territory in Europe by repudiating his wife (1189) in order to marry the heir of Henry of Luxembourg. As a result Thibaut (1189-1214) was involved in a war over disputed territory which led to difficulties both with the bishop of Liége and with Philip Augustus of France. In 1201 the king formally pardoned the disputants, including Baldwin of Hainaut and Flanders, who left for the Fourth Crusade. Thibaut himself had been asked to lead the expedition but had refused. Here he confirms arrangements made for the journey by one of his men, Viard.

---

[1] Backmund, *Monasticon*, vol. 3: 89-92; Ardura, *Dictionnaire*, 397; Warlop, *Flemish Nobility*, index.

Finally Thibaut mended his fences with both king and church by taking the cross for the Albigensian crusade in 1211. He made a will before leaving, and was received with honor by the leader of the crusade forces, Simon de Montfort, at the siege of Carcassonne. Thibaut then fought for the obligatory forty days and left despite the protests of the main army. Later counts of Bar took the abbey of Mureaux under their protection, so there might have been a relationship of long standing between the family and the abbey.[2]

---

[2] M. Grosdidier de Matons, *Le comté de Bar des origines au traité de Bruges (vers 950–1301)* (Bar-le-Duc, 1922), 201–30, 610–11. See also the charters in Hugo, *Annales*, "probationes," clxxvii and following for Mureau and Pargny.

21
1202, BALDWIN, COUNT OF FLANDERS

W. Prevenier, ed., *De Oorkonden der Graven van Vlaanderen (1191-aanvang 1206)*, II. uitgave (Brussels, 1964), 422, no. 204. Cf. BN Collection de Picardie 267, fol. 216; and BN Collection Baluze 75, fol. 205.

Ego Balduinus, Flandrie et Hainonie comes, notum fieri volo tam futuris quam presentibus quod, Iherosolimam profecturus, volens memoriam mei relinquere ecclesiae Thenoliis pro salute anime mee et M[arie] comitisse, karissime consortis mee, et antecessorum meorum ac deinceps successorum, fratres ecclesiae predicte liberos penitus et quitos dimisi per totam terram meam eundo et transeundo quantum ad me pertinet, ab omni exactione theolonei, winagii et pedagii de vino suo et de omnibus rebus suis quas vendiderint vel emerint in terra mea, que pertinent ad proprios usus suos.

Ut autem hoc ratum et stabile maneat in perpetuum presentem super hoc ecclesie predicte contuli paginam sigilli mei appensione munitam.

Actum apud Haimmonis Quercetum anno dominice incarnationis M° CC° secundo, mense martio.

I, Baldwin, count of Flanders and Hainaut, wish to make it known to those both future and present that, about to set out for Jerusalem, and wishing to leave a memorial of myself to the church of Thenailles, for the salvation of my soul and that of Countess Marie, my dearest consort, and for the souls of my ancestors and descendants, declare that throughout my territory and insofar as it pertains to me, the brothers of the aforesaid church are free and quit in going and coming from every levy, whether customs or road toll, upon the wine and all those goods which they sell or buy in my territory and which pertain to their own use.

So that this may remain ratified and stable in perpetuity I confer upon this church this present document fortified with the impress of my seal.

Issued at Le Quesnoy in the year of the Lord's Incarnation, 1202, in the month of March.

SUMMARY OF THE CHARTER

Baldwin IX, count of Flanders and Hainaut, in preparation for the Fourth Crusade, released the Premonstratensian house of Thenailles from various taxes due to him, especially on wine consumed or sold by the canons. His wife Marie consented to the exemption.

NOTES ON THE CHARTER

Thenailles

Thenailles, in Laon, was the original site offered to St. Norbert by Bishop Barthélemy. Norbert preferred Prémontré, but Norbertine canons from Mont-Saint-Martin's, Laon, founded a house at Thenailles in 1130. Gobert (1191–1201) was abbot when this gift was made.[1] The Coucys and the lords of Guise were among the early patrons of this house. The women from the original double monastery were moved in the 1130s to Chaumont, in the canton of Marle. Thenailles held most of its property in the Coucy domains of Marle and Vervins, due to the liberality of Enguerran II and Raoul I.[2]

Baldwin

When count Philip of Flanders died in Acre in 1191, Baldwin V of Hainaut inherited Flanders, having married Philip's sister Margaret of Alsace. He inherited as Baldwin VIII of Flanders. Baldwin IX of Flanders married Marie, daughter of Count Henry of Champagne, in 1186. He inherited the county of Flanders in 1194 and Hainaut in 1195. His younger brother Philip inherited the county of Namur as his vassal, and their sister Elizabeth (Isabelle) married Philip Augustus, king of France. In 1200, Baldwin and Marie took the cross with a crowd of nobles at the cathedral of Bruges. He issued a number of charters for various monasteries including Prémontré and Thenailles before his departure, and left his brother Count Philip of Namur as regent.[3] Marie was pregnant when Baldwin left on crusade in the spring of 1202, so could not accompany him as she had planned. In 1204 the crusade was diverted from the original destination of Jerusalem. Baldwin was one of the leaders of a coalition of Europeans who managed to take the city of Constantinople, where he was elected first Latin emperor. He was crowned in the great church of Hagia Sophia, but shared power with the Venetian contingent as well as the followers of Boniface of

---

[1] Backmund, *Monasticon*, vol. 2: 400–2; Ardura, *Dictionnaire*, 525.

[2] Piette, *Thenailles*, 3–22, and see charters in his edition, 34, 37, for Radulf Canis and Enguerran III.

[3] LeGlay, *Flandre*, 287–93; and see charter 14, above.

Montferrat. In addition the crusaders had yet to conquer the bulk of the Byzantine empire, although the leaders had divided the territory and established the boundaries of feudal duchies. While Baldwin was defending his new kingdom, Marie left for the Holy Land, arriving in Acre in the summer of 1204, and only then finding out about the capture of Constantinople. When her husband's emissaries arrived in Acre to conduct her to Byzantium, they found she had died of the plague. They brought her corpse back to her husband, who was captured at Adrianople in 1205 by Bulgars taking advantage of the weak Latin kingdom. He presumably died in captivity. His brother Henry became regent and then emperor (1206–1216). The Europeans had lost their new empire by 1261.[4] Meanwhile, Flanders itself was threatened by Philip Augustus of France, who was uncle by marriage and guardian to Baldwin and Marie's daughter and heir Jeanne (see charter 26, below).

---

[4] Mayer, *Crusades*, 194–96. R. L. Wolff, "Baldwin of Flanders and Hainaut (1175–1205)," *Speculum* 27 (1952): 281–322. For the story of the Fourth Crusade, see Geoffroy de Villehardouin, *The Conquest of Constantinople*, translated and edited by Margaret Shaw, in *Chronicles of the Crusades* (London, 1963); and D. E. Queller, *The Fourth Crusade: The Conquest of Constantinople 1201–1204*, 2nd ed. (Philadelphia, 1997).

22
1202, SIMON DE MALESNES

Andre Du Chesne, *Histoire genéalogique de la maison de Béthune* **(Paris, 1639), "preuves", 53. Fragment:** 1202, Extr. fr. Archives abbey N.-D. de Chocques.

In nomine Patris, & c. Ego Balduinus de Bethunia Comes de Albemarle & dominus de Chokes. Omnibus tam futuris quam praesentibus notum fieri volo, quod Simon de Malesnes [sic] miles homo meus profecturus Hierusalem partam suam decimae de Maslenes [sic], quam de me in feodum cum reliqua possessione sua tenebat, ad opus Ecclesiae beati Iohannis de Chokes in manu mea resignavit, & c. Actum anno ab Incarnatione Domini M.CC.II. mense Aprili.

In the name of the Father, etc. I, Baldwin of Béthune, count of Aumale and lord of Chocques. To all, both future and present, I wish it to be known that Simon of Malesnes, a knight, my man, about to set out for Jerusalem, resigned into my hand for the work of the Church of St.-Jean of Chocques his part of the tithe of Malesnes, which he held from me in fief with the rest of his possessions. Done in the year of the Incarnation of the Lord 1202, in the month of April.

SUMMARY OF THE CHARTER

In this fragment of a charter, published by Duchesne, Baldwin de Béthune, count of Aumale and lord of Chocques, records the gift of his vassal Simon de Malesnes. The knight, Simon, before leaving for Jerusalem, gave the tithe of Malesnes to the church of St. Jean at Chocques.

Saint-Jean-Baptiste, a village between Béthune and Lillers, had become part of the Béthune family holdings under William I (1129-1144) by his marriage to Clemence d'Oisy. Clemence founded a chapel in the castle which was served by canons from St.-Jean. William's uncle Adam was lord of Bessan in Galilee, having accompanied Count Robert of Flanders to Palestine on the First Crusade. Robert V (1145-1191) of Béthune was with Count Thierry of Flanders in the Holy Land in 1157 and 1163, and then he accompanied Thierry's son Philip on the expedition of 1177. According to the historian of his house, this notable crusader died in the course of his fourth journey to Palestine, as a member of the Third Crusade of 1191.[1]

Baldwin of Béthune, who issued this charter, was the third of Robert V's six sons. His name appears in the sources for the first time in 1177 when he entered the service of Richard, duke of Aquitaine, later King Richard I of England (1189-1199). In 1191 he also was a member of the Third Crusade, a member of Richard's retinue, and he was captured with the king in 1194 by the duke of Austria. Richard was at war with Philip Augustus of France, who had used Richard's absence to seize England's holdings in Normandy. When Philip learned that Richard had been handed over to Henry VI of Germany, he offered the emperor a large sum to imprison his enemy. Richard's agents obtained his release with an even larger ransom. The king of England then rewarded Baldwin of Béthune for his loyalty during their captivity by marrying him to Countess Hawide of Aumale in Normandy. She was a ward of the king, and held land in Normandy (on the border of Picardy) and in Holderness, near York.[2] Baldwin's brother Jean became bishop of Cambrai in 1200, and died at Toulouse in 1219, as a member of the Albigensian crusade.

Besides their obvious connections to the counts of Flanders, the lords of Béthune were advocates of Arras (see charters 11 and 19) and intermarried with the Coucys in the late 1200s.

St.-Jean's was founded as a college of secular canons sometime before 1120, when it was converted to a regular house. By 1138, it was affiliated with the Augustinian order of Arrouaise. Simon I was abbot between 1202 and 1228.[3]

---

[1] Du Chesne, *Béthune*, 106-9 for St.-Jean, 94 for the First Crusade, and 123-29, 134, 149, for Robert V and his children.

[2] Du Chesne, *Béthune*, and see Tierney and Painter, *Western Europe in the Middle Ages*, 331-32; and charter 26.

[3] Gosse, *Arrouaise*, 355; GC, vol. 9, cols. 1125-28; and charter 11.

23
1204, THOMAS, SOLDIER OF LEEZ

[Joseph Barbier, ed.,] "Documents concernant Grand Leez et Sauvenière, extraits du cartulaire de l'abbaye de Floreffe," *Analectes pour servir à l'histoire ecclésiastique de la Belgique* 8 (1871): 236, no. 10; cf. 235, 237, nos. 9, 11.

Thomas, miles de Laiz, poenitens, quod querelas de quibus supra, movisset ecclesie Floreffiensi, dat in compensam terram integram curti de Leez.

Quoniam facile a memoria labitur, quod scripto non tenetur, ego Wericus, Dei gratia abbas Floreffiensis et conventus, tam presentibus quam futuris notum facimus, quod, cum Thomas miles de Laiz, homo liber, octo bonuaria terre, que pro compensatione damnorum nobis sepius illatorum legitime in eleemosinam contulerat, cupiditatis stimulo tactus repeteret, et nobis calumpniam faceret, tandem, quia cruce signatus erat, reatum suum recognoscens, predicte terre et fructibus eius integraliter abrenuntiavit coram multis testibus idoneis, werpivit et exfestucavit. Insuper etiam terram quandam, curti nostre de Laiz contiguam, quam ad dilatandam eandem curtem dudum nobis pro concambio donaverat, ab omni querela calumniatorum absolvere et legitimam warandam nobis inde exhibere compromisit. Ne igitur huius pactionis compositio ab aliquo deinceps valeat infirmari, et ecclesia nostra super hoc molestari, in assertionem veritatis virorumque prudentum sigilla huic scedule appendimus, scilicet abbatis Gemblacensis, abbatis Corneliensis, abbatis Leffiensis.

[Thomas, knight of Leez, repentant about his conflicts with the church of Floreffe mentioned above, gives in compensation the entire land of the estate of Leez.]

Because what is not retained in writing easily slips from the memory, I, Wéric, by God's grace abbot of Floreffe, and the community, make known to those present and future that when Thomas, knight of Leez, a free man, was struck by the goad of covetousness and took back the eight *bonuaria* of land which he had legitimately bestowed as alms in compensation for the damages often inflicted on us, and he made accusation against us, finally, because he was ready to go on crusade and recognized that he was guilty, completely gave up, renounced and abandoned that aforesaid land and its fruits before many suitable witnesses, especially a certain land, lying next to our estate of Leez, which to enlarge that same estate he had given us not long ago in an exchange, he promised to keep free of every dispute by plaintiffs and to offer us legitimate defense. Lest there be a possibility for someone to weaken the contents of this agreement and trouble our church in this matter, to verify its authenticity we append the seal of prudent men to this document, namely, the Abbots of Gembloux, Corneux (?), and Leffe.

SUMMARY OF THE CHARTER

Wéric, abbot of Floreffe (1203–1212), issued this charter to record a gift by Thomas, knight of Leez, made after the latter took the cross. In front of many witnesses, including the canons of the house, he gave land at Leez and confirmed previous gifts, which had been the subject of a quarrel between himself and the abbey.

NOTES ON THE CHARTER

Floreffe, Namus, and Leez

The charter represents the settlement of a quarrel, as do so many of the charters in this collection. Barbier, who wrote the history of Floreffe, refers to this as a grant made by Thomas, who wished to right wrongs on the eve of leaving on crusade. There is no more precise date than 1204 for this charter, but according to one version of the story told under charter 14 above, the relic of the cross of Christ owned by Floreffe was given to Wéric in 1204 by Count Philip of Namur, who had been left as regent by his brother during the Fourth Crusade. On the third of May in that year, the relic was displayed for the first time, as part of the celebration of the feast of the Holy Cross. The canons recorded a miracle on that occasion: many drops of blood flowed from the relic.[1] Like the other crusaders discussed here, Thomas's family had a relationship with the abbey, which apparently began before 1204, since the quarrel is ended then, and which certainly continued after his expedition. There would be further quarrels over land after this settlement. The story of the miracle as it is preserved by Barbier shows that the canons of Floreffe wanted to establish a connection between the crusades and their abbey, since it was important not only that they have a piece of the cross, but also that it was a gift of a famous crusader: the count of Flanders who became emperor in Constantinople. Whether the story is true or false is not important in this instance. What is important is what story the canons wanted to tell, and how others responded. The miracle, combined with the status of the relic, would make the abbey a pilgrimage center. The added emphasis on the crusade movement and the short-lived victory in Constantinople must have added to the appeal. Whether Thomas was swayed by the connection in settling his dispute and taking the cross is unknown. In fact the evidence for the identity of this man and the details of this transaction appears to be limited to several charters collected and published by Barbier in 1871.[2] Thomas's wife issued a charter making a gift to Floreffe in about 1204, in which she

---

[1] Barbier, *Floreffe*, vol. 1: 93–94.
[2] Barbier, "Grand Leez," 225–43.

refers to Thomas as a knight and "free man". She mentions his son and daughter. Thomas is first on the witness list, along with another free man, comital officials, and lesser men. In 1225 the abbey made a formal arrangement with "Thomas de Leez," dividing territory at Leez between them. The property was again the subject of a charter regulating its use by a Thomas of Leez and the abbey in 1255.[3]

There is no way of knowing how Thomas was influenced to take the cross, then, beyond his explicit connection in this charter between his settlement with the abbey and his vow. Penitence for attacking the possessions of the abbey is the motive Barbier emphasizes. What connection the abbey, which had been founded by the counts of Namur, had with the local war in the 1190s among Hainaut, Namur, Luxembourg, and Bar (see charter 20), is unknown. It may be significant that a number of the participants took vows for the Fourth Crusade and that the gift of the cross reportedly came out of that expedition. Thomas may have been a minor player in that sequence of events as well.

---

[3] Barbier, *Floreffe*, vol. 1: 93–94, 112, 138.

24
1209, GUY DE ARBLINCOURT
Bibliothèque nationale, Collection de Picardie 302, fol. 1.

Ego Guido dominus de Erblemcort. Omnibus ad quos presens scriptum pervenitur: Notum facio quod ego cruce signatus iter iherosolimitane peregrinationis arripiens excessus meos volens corrigere pro anima mea et antecessorum meorum ecclesie calniacensi jus suum quod habebat in curte de Bechencort et in appendicijs eius recognovi. Ita quod ipsam curtem in nullo michi vel successoribus meis obnoxiam. Sicut nec esse pro certo debebat. Omnino concessi et penitus quitavi et insuper terram ante portam ipsius curtis sitam. Quam Adam miles patruus meus eis in elemosinam contulerat eis in perpetuum concessi. Et preterea pasturagia de Erblemcort et de Bechencort, ipsis et hominibus suis communia esse in perpetuum statui ita quod ipsi et homines sui in pasturagia de Erblencort et de Bechencort animalia sua quantumque et quandocumque voluerint absque ulla contradictione ducere poterunt ad pascendum. Ego vero et homines mei de assensu abbatis et capituli in pasturagia de Marisel animalia nostra ad pascendum ducere poterimus. Nemus etiam quod habent in territorio predicte curtis eis imperpetuum quito ita quod nec ego nec homines mei aliqud iuris nec usagium nec aliud in ipso clamare poterim sed ad vendendum et ad secandum cum uoluerint ad faciendum uoluntatem suam in perpetuum concessimus. Et ut hoc ratum permaneat, presens scriptum meo feci sigillo communiri. Actum anno domini. m°.cc°.ix°.

I, Guy, lord of Arblincourt. To all whom the present document reaches: I make it known that when I was signed with the cross and eager to undertake the journey of the Jerusalem pilgrimage, I wished to correct my excesses. So for my soul and the souls of my ancestors I confirmed to the church of Chauny the right which it had in the estate of Bechencourt and what pertains to it. I did this in such a way that that estate would suffer nothing bad from me or my successors, as it certainly should not. All this I completely granted and freed from any claim, especially the land situated in front of the gate of that court, which Adam the knight, my maternal uncle, granted to them in alms, and which I granted to them in perpetuity. In addition, I established that the pasturages of Arblincourt and of Bechencourt were to be common to them and their men in perpetuity, so that they and their men can lead their animals to graze in the pasturages of Arblincourt and Bechencourt wherever, as much as, and whenever they wish without interference. I and my men, with the assent of the abbot and the chapter, will be able to lead our animals to graze in the pastures of Marisel. Also I grant quittance to them in perpetuity of the wood which they have in the territory of the above-mentioned court, so that neither I nor my men will be able to make a claim of law or usage or anything else against it; we grant to them the right to sell or mow it as they wish, in perpetuity. That this may remain ratified, I cause the present document to be fortified with my seal. Given in the year of our Lord 1209.

SUMMARY OF THE CHARTER

In this charter, dated 1209, Guy, lord of Arblincourt, makes a gift to the church at Chauny on the eve of his departure for Jerusalem. The charter says specifically that the issuer wishes to repent of his excesses, which seems to refer to his withholding of the property Bechencourt from the canons of Chauny.

NOTES ON THE CHARTER

Chauny and Coucy

Maximilien Melleville, in his *Histoire de la ville de Chauny*, published in 1851, identified *Calnacum* as the village of Chauny, on the right bank of the Oise River, near the city of Noyon. Charters of the tenth century mention a small fortress there, on the Roman road from Soissons to Saint-Quentin. It was Melleville's opinion that Chauny was originally royal domain, which was passed to the control of the counts of Vermandois in the ninth century. By 1167 the lordship belonged to Philip of Alsace, count of Flanders and of Vermandois. Philip laid claim to two Coucy holdings: Marle and Vervins, and to Chauny which was close to the Coucy castle of La Fère and the focal point of a dispute with Philip Augustus of France (1180–1223). By 1186 the king, allied with the Coucys, had forced the counts of Flanders to acknowledge him as overlord in Vermandois, which included Chauny.

The parish church there was founded in 1059 and had been transferred to a community of Augustinian canons in 1125. In 1139, the community retired to the forest retreat of Les Fontaines Saint-Eloi. The church at Chauny became a priory dependent on the new abbey.[1] Again, the connection to other charters in the collection is not only to repentance as motivation, but to new Augustinian houses and orders (especially Arrouaise and Prémontré), and to the network of relationships between the nobility of northern France, Flanders, and Hainaut, and so on. In this case, a charter of 1221 connects Guy to the Coucy family as a vassal.[2] Barthélemy, in the history of the Coucys, has summed up what can be known from these two charters and other scattered references. Guy II of

---

[1] Melleville, *Histoire ... Chauny* (Paris, 1851), 5–14. See also Charles Dereine, "Chauny," DHGE, where he says that the house adopted the Augustinian rule in 1130, and that it was affiliated with the order of Arrouaise.

[2] Bibliothèque nationale, Paris, *Collection de Picardie* 290, fol. 34. Also see Chesne, *Coucy*, "preuves," 351, where there is a charter issued by Raoul of Coucy to record a gift by "Robertus miles de Emblencourt" to Thenailles (O.Praem.) in 1188. The gift comes from a Coucy fief, according to the charter. See also Olivier Guyotjeannin, "Episcopus et comes ...," 224–25, on Guy's crusade.

Arblincourt died on crusade in 1192. Before leaving on crusade in 1209, Guy III acknowledged the claim of the abbey of Chauny to Bechencourt. In 1221 Guy's widow held a fief from Enguerrand III of Coucy, which was in turn held from her by Renaud de Sinceny.[3]

---

[3] Barthélemy, *Coucy*, 513–15. I have not seen Archives nationales, Paris, série S, no. 433 (6), "Titres de la prévoté du chapitre à Chauny."

25
1210, SIMON DE CHAVIGNY

Jean-Michel Lalanne, ed., *Le Cartulaire de Valpriez (1135–1250)*, Mémoires et Documents d'histoire médiévale et de philologie 4 (Paris, 1990), no. 16, p. 51.

Ego Haymardus, Dei gratia Suessionensis episcopus omnibus in perpetuum. Notum facimus universis tam presentibus quam futuris, quod Symon de Chavegni miles, in terram Albigensium profecturus, in nostra presentia recognovit, quod duos campos terre sitos in Monte de Biuci Premonstratensi ecclesie in elemosinam contulisset. In cuius elemosine recompensationem ipsa ecclesia ei ad prosequendam peregrinationem suam centum viginti libras laudunensis monete de sua caritate donavit. Nobilis autem mulier Emelina uxor eius, que similiter presens erat, elemosine facte assensit; et quia metuebat ecclesia, ne terra ipsa eidem Emeline assignata esset in dotem, dictus Symon, ac si de dote constaret, assignavit ei in recompensationem dotis culturam suam que dicitur Magnus Campus juxta boscum; et capit in semine triginta octo aissinos bladi ad mensuram suessionensem. Ipsa vero Emelina hanc assignationem gratanter recepit et, fide in manum nostram manualiter data, spopondit quod ecclesiam Premonstratensem super elemosina memorata nunquam in posterum molestabit. Nos igitur hec omnia coram nobis publice recitata et fideliter redacta in scriptis ad petitionem partium sigilli nostri fecimus impressione muniri. Actum mense julio, anno dominice Incarnationis M° CC° decimo.

I, Haimard, by the grace of God bishop of Soissons, to all in perpetuity. We make known to all here present and to come that Simon de Chavigny, knight, about to set off into the land of the Albigenses, confirmed in our presence that he had granted to the church of Prémontré two fields of land situated in Mont-de-Bieuxy. In return for these alms the same church gave to him of its charity, to aid the pilgimage he was undertaking, one hundred and twenty *libras* of money of Laon. The noble woman Emelina, his wife, who was likewise present, gave her assent to these alms. And because the church feared that the land had been assigned to the same Emelina as dowry, the same Simon, in case it should it be of her dowry, assigned to her in recompense for the dowry his field near the woods which is called the Great Field; it is sown with thirty-eight *esseins* of seed grain according to the measure of Soissons. Emelina accepted this arrangement gladly, confirmed it with her hand placed in ours, and promised that she would never trouble the church of Prémontré in the future. All these matters were declared publicly in our presence and faithfully put into writing. At the request of the parties involved we have caused them to be fortified with the impress of our seal. Issued in the month of July, the year of the Lord's Incarnation 1210.

SUMMARY OF THE CHARTER

Haimard de Provins, bishop of Soissons (1208-1219), issued this charter for Simon de Chavigny, a knight who was about to leave for the Albigensian crusade in July 1210. Simon gave two fields to Prémontré in exchange for one hundred and twenty *livres* in coin of Laon, which he intended to use for his expenses.[1] His wife, Emeline, gave her consent to the sale and received a rent in wheat as compensation for the alienation of part of her dowry. The transaction was made in the presence of the bishop, to ensure that the abbey would be free from any later claims.

NOTES ON THE CHARTER

Chavigny and Coucy

Chavigny was a fief of the Coucy family. The holders of it had previously been donors to Prémontré. One of Simon's sisters entered the order as a lay sister in 1173.[2] According to Barthélemy, Simon and his three brothers inherited the fief and shared the military duties attached to it. In this case, Simon apparently accompanied his lord, Enguerran III of Coucy, who was known to be on crusade in southern France in 1209-1210, and afterwards with the king of France in 1214, where he participated in the famous battle of Bouvines.[3]

The crusader of 1210 appears to be either the son or grandson of Boniface de Coucy, a frequent witness to charters issued between 1131 and 1147 by Enguerran II, lord of Coucy. Boniface is given the titles variously of *miles*, baron, and seneschal, among others. He and his wife and four sons made a gift to Prémontré of land in the forest of Rozières in 1142, when Melisende, Enguerran's mother, founded a convent there. One of the four, Simon de Coucy, was a frequent witness to Coucy charters between 1143 and 1184. In 1184, Simon bought land at Bieuxy, which he exchanged for property of similar value at Chavigny held by Prémontré. The connection between this Simon of 1184 and the crusader of 1210, who apparently still holds Bieuxy, is unclear.[4] It seems plausible that the crusader is Boniface's grandson, Simon II. If that were true, it then would be tempting to attribute this exchange not only to a desire to raise money for an expe-

---

[1] See the introduction to the charter in Lalanne, *Cartulaire*; and also Barthélemy, *Coucy*, 223.

[2] Archives départementales, Aisne, H777 (1142); H753, fols. 10, 18-19 (1173, 1184); Lalanne, *Cartulaire*, 43-44 (1173), no. 12; Barthélemy, *Coucy*, 186.

[3] Barthélemy, *Coucy*, 186, 420-21. Taiée, *Prémontré*, vol. 1: 21, 77, lists donations from Enguerran in 1210, and from an unidentified Gerard de Coucy, who could be one of Simon's relatives, in 1142, but I have not been able to locate these charters.

[4] Barthélemy, *Coucy*, 401-2, 472.

dition, but to the kind of effort at rapprochement with the church which was characteristic of the relationship between the Coucys and Prémontré. As a conjecture, this charter could be added to the list of so many in this collection which show an original gift to the order contested by an heir, who eventually decides to make his peace by taking a crusade vow and restoring the contested property. Without that conjecture, the exchange recorded in this charter points to a reciprocal relationship with the order, in which money was raised and the family holdings protected. The historian of the Coucy holdings has seen the motivation behind this exchange as clearly "economic" rather than pious. Yet the difficulty of that distinction is apparent. The years 1210 and 1211 are characterized by him as ones of unusual generosity by Enguerran just before his departure on crusade, in which he gave exemptions of wionage, especially, to neighboring churches.[5] In any case, the reader should look at this charter in the context of the Coucy relationship with Prémontré, and especially in light of the crusade letter of Abbot Gervase, issued in 1212 or 1213 (charter 26).

---

[5] Barthélemy, *Coucy*, 223, 420.

26
1212, GERVASE, ABBOT OF PRÉMONTRÉ

Charles Louis Hugo, ed., *Sacrae Antiquitatis Monumenta historica, dogmatica, diplomatica*, 2 vols. (Etival, 1725), vol. 1: 43, no. 43.

Universis Christi fidelibus ad quos litterae praesentes pervenerint Gervasius, Dei patientia Praemonstrati dictus Abbas, salutem in Domino.

Noverit Universitas vestra quod litteras Reverendi Patris A. Archiepiscopi Narbonensis, Sedis Apostolicae Legati suscepimus in haec verba: [*see below*]

Cum igitur propter occupationes domesticas (praeter negotia totius Ordinis, pro quo nos sollicitari oportet) non possimus personaliter circumquaque discurrere: et idem Archiepiscopus non nobis tantummodo, sed et aliis, quos ad hoc negotium duxerimus evocandos, officium commiserit praedicandi: et indulserit etiam (prout ex litterarum suarum potest tenore perpendi) ut iniectores manuum in Clericos seu in Religiosas personas, et incendiarios absolvamus, dummodo accingi velint ad iniurias fidei propulsandas in partibus Tholosanis: dilectum in Domino Guidonem Fratrem et Canonicum nostrum ad vos mittimus, Universitatem vestram rogantes attentius et exhortantes in Domino Jesu, quatenus illum ea curetis devotione suscipere, qua nos-ipsos: et attendentes quod, cum sola jam Tholosa refugium sit perversis, labor quem indicere vobis intendimus est non grandis, et remuneratio copiosa; tempus peregrinationis non multum, et ipsa peregrinatio non longinqua; et super haec omnia, fides in causa; in succursum fidei memoratae signum salutis nostrae (videlicet signum Crucis) assumere non tardetis: ut dum ipsa in pectoribus vestris assumitur, ita semper vobis prae oculis habeatur, ut et vobis sit iugiter ad munimen, et hostibus ad terrorem. Datum Praemonstrati mense Februario, Anno gratia millesimo ducentesimo duodecimo.

[The letter from the Archbishop of Narbonne immediately precedes Gervase's in Hugo's collection, *Monumenta*, 41–43, no. 42: "Venerabili Fratri et in Christo dilecto Gervasio Praemonstratensi Abbati F. A. Dei gratia Narbonensis archiepiscopus, Apostolicae Sedis Legatus, salutem in vero Salutarii."]

To all the faithful in Christ to whom the present document comes, Gervase, by the patience of God called abbot of Prémontré, wishes salvation in the Lord.

Let all of you know that we have received a document of the Reverend Father A., archbishop of Narbonne and legate of the Apostolic See, which reads [see below].

Since because of our conventual duties (besides the business of the whole order for which we must care) we cannot personally hurry about in every direction, so the same archbishop committed the duty of preaching not only to us but also to others whom we arranged to be called to this office. He also granted (as can be determined from the tenor of his document) that we may absolve those who lay hands on clerics or religious persons, and incendiaries, as long as they wish to be equipped to repulse the injuries to the faith in the territory of Toulouse. We send to you Guy, beloved in the Lord, our brother and canon, asking all of you insistently and exhorting you in the Lord Jesus, that you take care to receive him with the same devotion as you would us ourselves. Be aware that since Toulouse alone is a refuge for the wicked the work which we intend to enjoin on you is not great and the reward is abundant. The travel time is not great, nor is the pilgrimage long, and beyond all this, faith is in question. Do not hesitate to assume the sign of our salvation (that is, the sign of the cross) in aid of the same faith, so that when it is taken upon your breasts, you may always have it before your eyes, and it may be with you constantly as a source of protection and for the enemy a source of terror. Given at Prémontré, in the month of February, in the year of grace 1212.

[To the venerable brother and beloved in Christ, Gervase, abbot of Prémontré, A., by the Grace of God archbishop of Narbonne and legate of the Apostolic See wishes salvation in the true Savior.]

Olim Petri naviculae sapientissimus Gubernator ad extirpandam pestem Haereticorum, quae per Provinciam Narbonensem vicinasque partes multiformium dogmatum suorum urentissimum virus effuderat; ita quod *a planta pedis usque ad verticem vix ulla sanitas remansisset*, operarios destinavit *potentes in opere et sermone:* qui cum apud illud genus damnatissimum, quorum erat oculus obturatus et exorbitatus, *et insipiens cor eorum*, verbo praedicationis parum proficere potuissent: authoritate illius, qui eos miserat vocati sunt ad subsidium negotii huius *gens sancta, genus electum et populus acquisitionis* Regni Franciae, Principes et Barones, aliique fideles Catholicae fidei Zelatores.

Venientes itaque Christi exercitus, et miraculose incipientes caput conterere inimici; tandem consilio sibi divinitus inspirato praefecerunt huic negotio, tanquam specialiter ad hoc missum a Deo, nobilem virum Simonem, Dominum Montis-fortis, obedientiae quippe filium, atque *montem in quo beneplacitum est Deo habitare in eo;* fortem quidem in eo, qui est *fortis et potens in praelio:* per cuius Signatorum sudores virtus Dei altissimi, suae incomprehensibilis dispositionis clementia, tot et tanta est mirabiliter operata quod exclusis et destructis pro magna parte haereticis, et sautoribus, et defensoribus eorundem, maxima pars terrae, quam ipsorum spurcitia longo desoedaverat tempore, data est in manu fideli, et divino cultui restituta.

Cum autem de perditissma gente illa restent adhuc reliquiae, quae, sicut latens vipera serpit humo, per occulta et abdita incedentes insidiantur calcaneo huius negotii, et intendunt quod lassetur Catholicorum devotio, et zelus Cruce-signatorum tepescat, necesse est ut nos qui (aliis de sociis ad sollicitudinem istam nobiscum a Sede Apostolica deputatis iam coronatis martyrio, et aliis in sancta confessione vocatis) in onere Legationis soli remansimus, ad elidendam perversorum intentionem tota vigilantia intendamus.

Quocirca rogamus discretionem vestram in Domino, quatenus tam per vos personaliter, quam per alias personas idoneas sedulis exhortationibus Episcopos, et alios Clericos, Milites, et caeteros Christi Fideles, ut in subsidium praefati negotii contra haereticos et fautores eorum veniant, moneatis attentius, et inducere procuretis; exponentes eisdem in praedicationibus vestris, quod illis, qui se accinxerint ad opus huiusmodi pietatis, eadem remissio peccatorum a Deo, eiusque Vicario est indulta, quae transfretantibus in Terrae sanctae subsidium indulgetur. Personae quoque ipsorum et terrae, possessiones et homines, et caetera bona eorum, ex quo crucem susceperint in pectoribus, in subsidium praefati negotii donec de ipsorum reditu vel obitu certissime cognoscatur, sub protectione Sedis Apostolicae existant.

Not long ago, the wise captain of the bark of Peter appointed workers powerful in work and word to root out the plague of the heretics which had poured out throughout the province of Narbonne and neighboring areas the poison of their many-shaped and scorching doctrines, so that *"from the bottom of its feet to the top of its head there remained scarcely any health"* (Isaiah 1:6). Since they had been able to accomplish little by their words among that hellish race, *whose eye was closed and turned aside and whose heart was foolish* (Psalm 67:17 Vulgate), by the authority of him who had sent them there were called together to aid this enterprise *"a holy people, a chosen race"* (1 Peter 2:9), a people belonging to the Kingdom of France, princes, barons, and other faithful champions of the Catholic faith.

Hence, when the armies of Christ arrived and miraculously began to crush the head of the enemy, they finally, by divinely inspired counsel given them, put in command of this enterprise, as one specially sent for this by God, the noble man Simon, Lord Montfort, a son of obedience and *"a mountain on which God was pleased to dwell"* (Psalm 23:8 Vulgate). He was strong in *"him who is strong and powerful in battle"* (Psalm 73:13-14 Vulgate); by the sweat of his crusaders the power of the most high God, in the clemency of his incomprehensible providence, miraculously worked so many great things that, when the heretics and their defenders [*sautoribus*] had been for the most part driven out and destroyed, the majority of the land which for a long time had rested in their filth was given into the hands of the faithful and restored to divine worship.

Since, however, there still remain remnants of this most dissolute people who, like a viper which hides and creeps on the ground, hide and enter secret places to plot against the heel of this enterprise and who intend that the devotion of Catholics grow weak and the zeal of the crusaders grow lukewarm, it is necessary that we who (with other comrades deputed with us by the Apostolic See to take care of this who have already been crowned with martyrdom and still others called to this holy witness) have remained alone in the office of Legate aim with all vigilance at dashing the aims of the dissolute.

Therefore we ask your discernment in the Lord, whether through yourself personally or through other suitable persons, to admonish attentively and strive to induce with zealous exhortations bishops and other clerics, knights, and other faithful Christians, to come in support of this aforesaid undertaking against the heretics and their supporters. Tell them in your preachings that for those who gird themselves for this work of piety the same remission of sins by God has been granted by his Vicar as is granted to those sailing across the sea in support of the Holy Land. Their persons, lands, possessions, people, and other goods are under the protection of the Apostolic See from the time they take the cross on their breasts in support of the undertaking here under consideration until there is certain knowledge of their return or death.

Speramus autem in Domino Jesu Christo, cuius est ipsum opus, quod per eiusdem gratiam, et succursum Fidelium Signatorum, consummationem praedictum negotium sortietur in brevi: nam si caput draconis contritum fuerit, Tholosa videlicet civitas, in qua se fere totae vires inimicorum collegerunt (quae olim a Clodoveo Rege Francorum propter haeresim Arrianam legitur fuisse destructa; et nunc in angustia multa ob simile vitium esse dignoscitur constituta) tunc vel nihil, vel modicum de praedicto negotio supererit faciendum.

Ut autem plures tam libentius, quam liberius ad Dei servitium memoratum accedant, concedimus discretioni vestrae, ut tam per vos, quam per alios idoneos iniectoribus manuum in Ecclesiasticas seu Religiosas personas, (nisi eorum excessus extiterit difficilis et enormis, utpote si fuerit ad mutilationem membri, vel sanguinis effusionem processum, vel in Episcopum aut Abbatem violenta manus iniecta) necnon et incendiariis valeatis absolutionis beneficium secundum formam Ecclesiae impertiri, ut sic eos in succursum praedicti negotii transmittatis.

We hope in the Lord Jesus Christ, whose work this is, that through his grace and the aid of the faithful crusaders this undertaking will be completed quickly. For if the head of the dragon—namely the city of Toulouse in which practically all the forces of the enemy are gathered, and which formerly had been destroyed by Clovis, King of the Franks because of the Arian heresy, and now is known to be in much agony from a similar evil—is crushed, then little or nothing of this enterprise will remain to be accomplished.

So that many may advance to this service both gladly and willingly, we concede to your discretion that both personally and through other suitable persons you are empowered to grant the benefit of absolution according to the form of the church on those who have laid hands on ecclesiastical or religious persons (unless their waywardness was troublesome and outrageous, as for example, it led to mutilating a limb or spilling blood, or a violent hand was laid on a bishop or abbot) or started fires so that then you may send them on to aid in this undertaking.

SUMMARY OF THE LETTERS

In two undated letters, preaching and fund-raising are arranged for the Albigensian crusade. The Cistercian monk and papal legate Arnold Amalric was made Archbishop of Narbonne in 1212, and became the director of the fight against heresy in southern France. He wrote to the bishops and clergy of France, offering the same crusade indulgence available to those crusading in the Holy Land as an inducement to fight in the region around Toulouse instead. Those clergy who received his letter were to preach, or recruit others to do so. Prémontré was a powerful order, with a network of houses across Europe as well as property in Palestine. Gervase, abbot-general between 1209 and 1220, was later a papal procurator for the Fifth Crusade. Gervase did the same here, using his monastery as a local center for preaching and fund-raising for the Albigensian crusade. His letter includes the text of the archbishop's, and introduces a Premonstratensian canon, Guy, who is empowered to preach the crusade and register crusade vows. Presumably, Guy read Gervase's letter aloud when he visited churches on his preaching tour. The two letters offer a history of the fight against heresy and a summary of the church's attitude towards those involved. From the letters we learn that southern France has seen an outbreak of a dualistic heresy resembling Manichaeism, and that the violence of those infected with false belief is "dismembering" the body of Christ. The indulgence is offered with special urgency to those who have attacked church property or clergy—unless the priest held very high office, or the attack was particularly brutal, in which case more penance would apparently be needed to make satisfaction.

Gervase's letter is given here because of the relationship between the order and the crusaders whose charters make up this collection. It is noteworthy that the sin of attacking ecclesiastical persons is singled out as one that would appropriately lead to a crusade vow, since so many of the crusaders whose vows have been recorded here took them as part of an effort to be reconciled with their local churches. It is also worth pointing out that Enguerran III of Coucy and his vassals fought in the Albigensian crusade. Although there is no crusade charter for Enguerran's expedition, the charters for Chavigny, 1210, and Monceau, 1219, show Coucy vassals involved in the expeditions in southern France.

NOTES ON THE CHARTER

Gervase

Enguerran of Coucy fought in the Albigensian crusade, which started in 1209. He was also involved in Philip Augustus's attempt to encroach on Flanders, first through the regency for the young Jeanne of Constantinople, and then at the battle of Bouvines in 1214. He followed Prince

Louis, later Louis VIII, to England in 1216, earning excommunication as a member of that expedition. The abbot of Prémontré's letters show him as influential in all of these events.

Gervase of Prémontré, abbot-general of the order 1209-1220, is known to have been English, from his epitaph, but his career prior to 1209 is hazy. He was certainly a canon of St. Just, a Premonstratensian house in Beauvais. He served as abbot there, and then at the house of Thenailles, Laon.[1] In 1220 he was elected bishop of Séez, and he died in 1228. These few facts, and some dispute about them, have been investigated by C. R. Cheney in his analysis of the letter collection made by Gervase's secretary: "Gervase, Abbot of Prémontré: A Medieval Letter-Writer," in *Medieval Texts and Studies* (Oxford, 1973): 242-76. The letter collection is contained in Hugo, *Monumenta*, vol. 1, and includes the one here, along with eleven connected to the Fifth Crusade, and three more dealing with the Albigensian expeditions.[2] In 1216, Gervase wrote to Pope Honorius III to defend the conduct of one of his abbots, John of La Capelle, who had been excommunicated. La Capelle was in Toulouse, which had been placed under interdict because it was considered to be a center of heresy. The canons of La Capelle had assumed that the order had immunity from the interdict and had continued to celebrate the liturgy. Meanwhile, John, abbot from 1209 to 1213, preached the Albigensian crusade on a tour which lasted for two years through 1212 and 1213. He reported his situation to Gervase at the general chapter of 1214, and died in 1215. In an undated letter, Gervase requested the postponement of the vow of a crusader, identifying him only as "a servant of our church." The third Albigensian letter is addressed to Simon of Montfort's wife, Alice. Simon had been the leader of the crusade; he died in 1219. The text of Gervase's letter makes it clear that Alice wrote to him to pass along the circumstances of her husband's death, along with a request for "prayers, exhortations and preaching," as well as "counsel and help." Gervase's reply is revealing. Apparently he took her letter as a request for official action as a procurator, since he says that he can do nothing for her without "apostolic authority for this, or at least a letter from the cardinal who is with you ... so that I can have my brothers and fellow abbots preach about this business, and recite the apostolic indulgence."[3]

---

[1] Piette, *Cartulaire de Thenailles* (Soissons, 1878), 39-40, says that Gervase, as abbot 1205-1209, was involved in a dispute with the inhabitants of Vervins, which was judged by Enguerran III of Coucy. Chesne, *Coucy*, 354-58 lists three donations by Enguerran to Thenailles (1201-1205) and one to Prémontré (1207).

[2] Slack, "Premonstratensians and the Crusader Kingdoms," 76-110, 207-31.

[3] Hugo, *Monumenta*, vol. 1, nos. 97, 98. On the Albigensian crusade, see Walter Wakefield, *Heresy, Crusade and Inquisition in Southern France 1100-1250* (London, 1974); and

The four Albigensian letters, along with Gervase's involvement in the Fifth Crusade, make it clear that Prémontré was an important center for crusade recruitment and fund-raising. In the letter to Alice, Gervase said that the order prayed for Simon as for one of its own canons, that he himself had said masses on Simon's behalf, and that prayers had been said and alms collected, presumably for the expeditions Simon had led, in Norbertine churches in France and Germany.

Enguerran III of Coucy

At this point, Enguerran was the eldest of the three Coucy heirs, but his mother Alix de Dreux was still nominally in control of the lordship. She was related to the kings of France, and her influence cemented the Coucy ties to Philip Augustus. The Coucys were briefly chosen to play a pivotal role in the aggressive policy of Philip towards Flanders.

Enguerran was married three times. His second wife, the granddaughter of King Henry II of England, had died by 1210. Enguerran had been in southern France on the Albigensian crusade, when King Philip Augustus of France (1180–1223) offered him a marriage with Jeanne of Constantinople, heiress to the counts of Flanders. In terms of the past history of the two families, Flanders and Coucy, the marriage would have settled the long-standing quarrel which had flared up again in the 1180s.[4] The marriage never occurred. After negotiations lasting into 1211, the king opted for another bridegroom: Ferrand, the third son of King Sancho I of Portugal. The Coucys, with other loyal vassals, continued to play a role in the contest between France and Flanders. Philip had been encroaching on Flemish territory, and took advantage of the regency for Jeanne in 1206 to make demands the Flemish considered exhorbitant. Jeanne was five or six when her father died. He had joined the Fourth Crusade, and been made emperor of Constantinople when the city was taken. He died defending the new European kingdom there, and the regents who had been acting for his daughter handed her over to the king of France as a ward (see charter 21).

In 1212 Jeanne (now presumably aged 12) married Ferrand and was returning with her husband to Flanders. Prince Louis, heir to the French throne, captured the couple and took two of their cities, Aire and Saint Omer. To obtain their release they had to agree that France could keep the cities. When they were released, another major trading city, Ghent, insisted on negotiations before it would accept Ferrand as lord. Philip Augustus had manipulated the situation so that he could control Ferrand and

---

Thomas Bisson, *Cultures of Power. Lordship, Status, and Process in Twelfth-Century Europe* (Philadelphia, 1995).

[4] Chesne, *Coucy*, 222.

eventually take Flanders. Meanwhile, Philip was pursuing the war against the heretics of southern France and planning the invasion of England. Ferrand refused to serve his overlord. Instead, he made an alliance with King John of England (1199–1216) and the Emperor Otto IV (1208–1215).[5]

All three of the Coucy brothers were at Bouvines in France in 1214, when France defeated England, Flanders, and the Holy Roman Empire. The quarrel between England and France is a given in the history of the Middle Ages after the Norman invasion of England in 1066. Philip Augustus had tried to block John's accession to the English throne in 1199. By 1206, he had taken most of the English holdings on the continent. In 1213 he was ready to invade England, but was distracted by the conflict in southern France. King John allied with the Holy Roman Empire, and carried the battle back to the continent. At the crucial moment, John was forced to retreat, leaving Philip to rout the armies of the emperor at Bouvines on 27 July 1214. The legend of the battle has Enguerran of Coucy stepping forward to receive communion as one who was ready to die with the king of France.[6] He certainly followed the crown prince to England in 1216 in defiance of the pope, who excommunicated the army.[7] As a result of the expedition, the English crown passed to John's nine-year-old son, Henry, in September of 1217. Philip Augustus imprisoned Ferrand, leaving Jeanne to rule Flanders. Gervase wrote three letters concerning the English expedition, two to the papal legate and one to the archbishop of Canturbury. They covered not only the interests of Norbertine canons who had supported the rebels and therefore been excommunicated, but also the peace negotiations between France and England. The letters indicate that Gervase was reasonably well-informed and expected his opinion on the peace treaty to be heard.[8]

Enguerran was pardoned for his role in the English expedition in 1218. His original excommunication is complicated by evidence that he was excommunicated in 1216, for an attack on the canons of Laon. When this attack occurred is unclear. Enguerran was in charge of the French garrison at London in 1216–1217. Possibly before he left on crusade he was involved in a dispute with the cathedral canons at Laon, during which he

---

[5] Nicholas, *Flanders*, 150–53; Wolff, "Baldwin," 293 and ff.

[6] See Duby, *Bouvines*, for the story of this battle and the legend of Enguerran's participation at communion.

[7] Chesne, *Coucy*, 362–64, from a copy of the excommunication letter in the Cartulary of the church of Laon; and for the story of Enguerran in England and Laon, 423–26. Cf. BN Collection de Picardie 267, fol. 52, charter 8a, 94, 117, 186, 188; Potthast, *Regesta Pontificum Romanorum*, 2 vols. (Berlin, 1874–1878; repr. Graz, 1957), vol. 1: 471, no. 5348; Marlot, *Reims*, vol. 3: 544–45, 548, 785 no. 138.

[8] Cheney, "Gervase," 252–54; also see BN Collection de Picardie 267, fol. 1.

imprisoned one of them. In 1223 he attended the council at Paris which expelled the Jews from France, and in 1226 he and his brothers assisted at the consecration of Louis IX at Reims. According to Tardif, his daughter married into the Brienne family (charter 16).[9] Enguerran died in 1242 and was buried at Prémontré.

The relationship between Prémontré and the Coucys has been demonstrated by previous charters. Gervase and Enguerran are shown here to have known each other before Gervase became abbot, since Enguerran made several donations to Thenailles in the early 1200s (see n. 1 below). Both had been reasonably major players in the Albigensian crusade as well as the struggle between Philip Augustus and John of England. Enguerran's consistent support for the king fits his family's hard-won acceptance as members of the court, and Gervase's actions are equally consistent with his position as head of a widespread order dependent on the papacy. For the purposes of this collection the point is that their involvement in the crusade in particular is unremarkable, routine, to be expected given their positions. The overwhelming impression is of business as usual, the motivations are prosaic, and even the theme of this collection of charters, penance or reconciliation with the church, is missing.

---

[9] Tardif, "Enguerran," 426–30, 441. Cf. several references from n. 7: Collection de Picardie 267, fol. 52; Marlot, *Reims*, 785 no. 138; Chesne, *Coucy*, 362–64. I have not been able to see Nicholas Vincent, ed., *The Letters and Charters of Cardinal Guala Bicchieri, Papal Legate in England, 1216–1218* (Rochester, N.Y., 1996), which might shed more light on the excommunication of the French on the English expedition.

27
1216, GODESCALC DE MORIALMÉ

J. Barbier, ed., "Documents concernant Sautour et Aublain, extraits du cartulaire de l'abbaye de Floreffe," *Analectes pour servir à l'histoire ecclésiastique de la Belgique* 8 (1871): 364–66, nos. 1 and 2. The third of these charters was issued in 1216.

[1188] Radulfus, Dei gratia leodiensis episcopus, tam futuris quam praesentibus in perpetuum. Contra importunas saeculi levitates praesentis paginae veritatem necessarium duximus nostrae auctoritatis munire signaculo, et impugnantium falsitatem sub scripto refutare testimonio. Nobilis quaedam femina, Herlendis nomine, pio desiderio inflammata, a quibusdam militibus, Adam scilicet et Alberto, fratre eius, de Machange, quidquid juris habebant in ecclesia de Ablaen, ad quod quidem dominium eiusdem ecclesiae et patronatus spectabant libere acquisivit; sed et illud, quod ibidem Nicholaus praepositus de Vierve habebat, duos videlicet solidos, qui de eadem ecclesia annuatim ei solvebantur. Quae suam in ecclesia Floreffiensi memoriam assignare desiderans, eandem ecclesiam de Ablaen, quam, ut dictum est, libere acquisierat et legitime possidebat, et duos illos solidos ecclesiae Floreffiensi in remedium animae suae libere donavit. Qua rebus mundanis exempta, praedicti milites Adam et Albertus, cum pacem ecclesiae Floreffiensis inde turbarent, judicio consilii quieverunt, et ecclesia Floreffiensis eodem iudicio et libertatem eleemosynae suae retinuit, et possessionis pacem de cetero accepit. Illi autem poenitentia ducti, quod ecclesiam injuste vexaverant ecclesiae remiserunt, quidquid calumniae ibi habuerant, et successoris eorum habere poterant. Hoc factum in consilio de Coving sub praesentia multorum clericorum et militum, innovatum in capitulo majoris ecclessiae in Leodio, sub testimonio praepositi, decani, archidiaconorum et ceterorum fratrum, tandem a nobis est confirmatum. Testes sunt de majori ecclesia: Albertus praepositus, Simon decanus, archidiaconi Albertus, Everardus, Albertus, Henricus de Donglebert, Alardus cantor; et alii de Floreffiensi ecclesia: Hermannus abbas, Renerus decanus de Covin, Simon decanus de Giveil, Theodoricus sacerdos de Vierve, Gilbert sacerdos de Hieme, universum concilium; Waltherus dominus eiusdem patriae, Urius, Jacobus, Balduinus de Ablen, liberi homines; Waltherus, Johannes

[1188] Radulf, by the grace of God bishop of Liège, to those in the future and those present, in perpetuity. Against the distressing changeableness of the age we have deemed it necessary to confirm with the seal of our authority the truth of the present page and to refute with written evidence the falseness of those who question its authenticity. A certain noble woman, Herlend by name, enkindled by pious desire, freely acquired from certain knights, notably Adam and Albert his brother, of Machange, whatever was legally theirs in the church of Ablaen, to which the domain of that church and its patronage pertained, but also what Nicholas, the prevost of Vierve (Viers) had there, notably two *solidi*, which was paid to him annually from that same church. She wanted to assure remembrance of her in the church of Floreffe, so she freely gave to the church of Floreffe as a remedy for her soul the same church of Ablaen, which as was said, she had freely acquired and legally possessed. When she departed this life, the said knights Adam and Albert then disturbed the peace of Floreffe, but they were quieted by legal decision, and the church of Floreffe retained the liberty of its alms with the same security and moreover received its possessions in peace. They were moved by repentance for having unjustly disturbed the church, and they made restitution to the church for whatever false accusations they had made and that their successors could have made. This was done in the council of Coving in the presence of many clerics and knights, renewed in the chapter of the chief church in Liège and witnessed by the prevost, dean, archdeacons, and other brothers, and finally it has been confirmed by us. The witnesses from the chief church are Albert the provost, Simon the dean, the archdeacons Albert, Everard, Albert, Henry of Donglebert, Alard the cantor, and others from the church of Floreffe—Hermann the abbot, Rainer dean of Coving, Simon dean of Giveil, Thierry priest of Viereve, Gilbert priest of Hieme, the whole council; Walter, lord of this territory, Urius, Jacob, Baldwin de Ablaen, free men; Walter, John de Pel,

de Pel, Albertus, Adam et filius eius, Gerardus de Manchange, milites; Bovo villicus, Alardus, Walterus, burgensis de Covin, et plures alii.

Actum est hoc, anno incarnationis Domini M C LXXX VIII, indictione (VI), epacta (XX), regnante Friderico, Romanorum imperatore, Radulpho, episcopo Leodiensi.

[1188] Notum item facere tam presentibus quam futuris praesentis paginae indicio necessarium duximus, quod vir nobilis et probatae fidei, miles Godescalcus de Morealmeis, ligius homo noster, superno afflatus desiderio Iherosolimam proficiscendi cum coetu fidelium ad liberandam terram promissionis de manibus impiorum, ut eius peregrinatio gratior et peregrinationis fructus magis esset meritorius, religiosorum se orationibus commendare et meritorum ipsorum participium procurare, unde occasione, quod id opportune et honeste proficeret, pro voto reperta, patronatum ecclesiae de Sature, quem ab antecessoribus suis hereditaria successione ad se devolutum pacifice et inconcusse possidebat, cum omnibus ad eandem ecclesiam pertinentibus, ecclesiae beatae Mariae de Floreffia, pro salute animae suae et successorum et antecessorum suorum, legitima donatione ordine ecclesiastico, in perpetuae beneficium eleemosynae, per manum Hermanni, abbatis eiusdem ecclesiae, liberaliter et integraliter contradidit. Et, quia vir erat compatientis animi et sui admodum affectus, devote petijt a praedictis abbate scilicet et ecclesia Floreffiensi, ut duas partes fructuum, qui eis de praedicta ecclesia de Sature obvenire possent, sororibus de Herlamont, tertiam autem sororibus de Verofle, ad paupertatis ipsarum et ipsiusmet recordationem animis earum efficacius imprimendam, benigne concederent. Et quia haec omnia sicut legitime facta et rationabiliter consummata probavimus, ita etiam, ut illibata et intemerata conserventur, cautissime invigilare debemus, praesentem paginam, sicut in superiori scripto expressimus, auctoritatis nostrae signaculo, ad perpetui roboris firmitatem communimus, sub interminatione anthematis districte inhibentes, ne quis de cetero Floreffiensem ecclesiam super praedictis ausu temerario praesumat molestare.

Acta sunt haec sub eodem tempore, quo et superiora.

Edouard Poncelet, *Actes des princes-évêques de Liège: Hugues de Pierrepont, 1200–1229* (Brussels, 1941), no. 141, 141–42.

In nomine sancte et individue trinitatis, amen. Hugo Dei gratia Leodiensis ecclesie episcopus, omnibus presens scriptum inspecturis eternam in Christo salutem. Universitati vestre presentis scripti pagina notum facimus quod cum Godescalcus de Morialmeis, vir nobilis, Iherosolimam profecturus,

Albert, Adam and his son, Gerard de Machange, knights; Bovo villager, Alard, Walter citizen of Coving, and many others.

This was done in the year of the Lord's incarnation 1188, indiction 6, epact 20, during the reign of Frederick, Emperor of the Romans, and Ralph, bishop of Liège.

[1188] By the witness of the present page we have done what is necessary to make it known to persons present and future that the noble man of proven faith, the knight Godescalc of Morialmeis, our liege man, moved by a heavenly desire of traveling to Jerusalem with the great gathering of the faithful to free the land of promise from the hands of the unbelievers, so that his pilgrimage might be more grace-filled and the fruit of his pilgrimage more meritorious, to commend himself to the prayers of the religious and to secure a share in their merits, when the opportunity he hoped for occurred, he acted suitably and honorably, handing over freely and integrally the patronage of the church of Sautour, which he possessed peacefully and uncontestedly from his ancestors by hereditary succession devolved upon him, with all pertaining to the same church, to the church of Blessed Mary of Floreffe, for the salvation of his soul and the souls of his successors and ancestors, by a legal donation to the ecclesiastical order, as a benefit in the form of perpetual alms, by the hand of Hermann, abbot of the same church. And because he was a man of compassionate soul especially toward his relatives, he devoutly asked the said abbot and the church of Floreffe that they would kindly grant two parts of the fruits which they could obtain from the said church of Sautour to the sisters of Herlaimont, and a third part to the sisters of Verofle (Marienbourg) to [ease] their poverty and to more effectively impress his memory on their souls. And we have verified that all these things were legally done and reasonably completed, and so that they may be kept unimpaired and inviolate, we must very carefully pay attention that we fortify this present page, as we expressed it in the prior writing, with the firmness of perpetual strength by the sign of our authority, forbidding under the threat of strict anathema that anyone with reckless boldness presume to trouble the church of Floreffe regarding the above matters.

This was completed at the same time as the above.

In the name of the holy and undivided Trinity. Amen. Hugh, by the grace of God bishop of the church of Liège, to all who will look at the present document, eternal salvation in Christ. By this page of writing we make known to all of you that Godescalc de Morialmé, a noble man, about to

patronatum ecclesie de Sature cum dote integra et decima tota et omnibus ad ipsam pertinentibus, de consensu et favore bone memorie domini Radulphi Leodiensis episcopi, ecclesie Floreffiensi, tunc temporis in ea presidente Herimanno abbate, in perpetue beneficium elemosine contulisset, fructus ejusdem ecclesie de Sature usibus pauperum sororum de Hellamont predicti abbatis regimini subditarum petiit assignari, ut ex percepti gratia beneficii devotius et vigilantius pro ipso orarent, quod cum ei abbas et ecclesia Floreffiensis benigne concessisset, fructus eosdem diu et non solum usque ad tempora nostra, sed etiam temporibus nostris sine interruptione praedicte sorores perceperunt. Nos autem quorum est officium et intentio, non solum malis obviare, sed etiam bona firmare, propositum nobilis viri et beneficium ancillarum Dei inconcusse stabilire cupientes et omnem occasionem turbationis subtrahere volentes, ad preces Hillini abbatis et ecclesie Floreffiensis et instantiam Arnulphi nobilis viri filii prefati Godescalci, dispensatione discreta et stabilitate perpetua ordinavimus et jussione insolubili sancivimus ut quicumque a prememorata Floreffiensi ecclesia ad curam et regimen sepedicte ecclesie de Sature fuerit presentatus et ordine canonico investitus, mediam partem proventuum eiusdem ecclesie, tam in oblationibus quam decimis et ceteris omnibus in sumptus proprios percipiat; alia autem pars media fructuum usibus predictarum sororum deputetur, nullumque ius reclamandi in partem ipsarum eiusdem ecclesie investitus de cetero habeat, sed sine fraude et dolo inter partes equa particio fructuum fiat. Hoc etiam necessario exprimimus ut, sicut in fructibus dividendis pares sunt, in particione ita et in oneribus ecclesie, videlicet in cathedratico et ceteris aliis solvendis communes sint in expensis. Verum, quia scriptum est: *ante langorem adhibe medicinam* et item: *ante obitum operare justiciam*, quum non est apud inferos invenire cibum, ut nostri recordationem ancillarum Dei et votis et mentibus artius imprimamus, statuimus firmiter quatinus de fructibus ex proventibus predicte ecclesie eis assignatis refectionem communem et optimam quolibet anno semel habeant quamdiu advivimus die qua elegerint, et post obitum nostrum in die anniversaria transitus nostri in qua nostri specialem memoriam in sanctis et devotis orationibus suis facient, sicque nobis et vivo et defuncto earum refectio proficiet, vivo ad veniam, defuncto ad requiem. Ceterum ut hec nostra constitutio et necessaria dispensatio firma et immobilis permaneat, huic cartule autoritatis nostre sigillum appendimus, sub pena excommunicationis et suspensionis artius inhibentes ne quis ei refragari vel contra eam venire ausu temerario ullatenus presumat. Actum anno gratie M° CC° XVI°, pontificatus nostri anno XVII°.

set out to Jerusalem, had granted as a benefice of perpetual alms the patronage of the church of Satour with its entire endowment and all tithes and with everything pertaining to them, with the consent and favor of the Lord Radulph, Bishop of Liège of happy memory, to the church of Floreffe, at the time when Hermann was presiding as abbot in it. He asked that the fruits of the same church of Satour be assigned to the use of the poor sisters of Herlaimont who were subject to the regime of the said abbot, so that thanks to the reception of this benefice they might pray more devoutly and vigilantly for him. The abbot and church of Floreffe kindly granted this to him, and the aforesaid sisters have received those same fruits thereafter without interruption and not only up to our time but during our time as well. However, it is our duty and intention not only to turn aside evils but also to strengthen good things, and wishing that the arrangement of the noble man and the benefice of the handmaids of God stand unchallenged and wishing to remove every occasion for disturbance, at the request of Helin, abbot, and the church of Floreffe and the insistence of the noble man, Arnulph, son of the said Godescalc, we order by a discrete dispensation and with perpetual stability and sanction by an unshakable command that whoever is presented and invested in the canonical order by the aforementioned church of Floreffe for the care and rule of the said church, will receive half of the income of the same church, both in offerings and tithes and in other things for his own expenses. The other half part of the fruits is assigned to the uses of the said sisters. The church has no right to challenge the part given the sisters. Let each participate equally in their part of the fruits without fraud or deceit. We express this necessarily, so that as they are equal in dividing the fruits, so they may be equal in their participation in the burdens of the church; that is, they are to share equally in the annual cathedral levy and in certain other expenses. Indeed, as it is written: *"before sickness comes, apply medicine"* (Sirach 18:20); and *"before death, do justice"* (Sirach 14:17), for there is no food to be found in the underworld. That our memory may be impressed more sharply on the vows and minds of the handmaids of God, we establish firmly that once a year they may have a common and festive meal from the revenues assigned to them from the aforesaid church. As long as we live they may have it on any day they wish; after our death they will do this on the anniversary day of our passing, on which day they will make a special commemoration of us in their holy and devout prayers. Thus their eating will profit us both while we live and after we are dead; while we are living to gain us forgiveness, when we are dead to gain us rest. Moreover, so that this necessary arrangement of ours may remain firm and immobile, we append the seal of our authority to this charter, forbidding under pain of excommunication and strict suspension anyone who would presume in anyway, with foolhardy boldness, to renounce or contravene it. Issued in the year of our Lord 1216, the seventeenth year of our pontificate.

SUMMARY OF THE CHARTERS

There are three charters here recording gifts to the Premonstratensian abbey of Floreffe. The first two were issued on the same day, at a large assembly presided over by Radulf, bishop of Liège, in 1188. The third charter is a confirmation of the second, issued twenty-eight years later, in 1216.

The assembly witnessed the first charter, which was a pious donation by Herlend, a noble woman who was settling a quarrel between the abbey and two of her vassals. The two knights were brothers, Adam and Albert of Machange, who had withheld property at Ablaen from the canons of Floreffe, and were making a public acknowledgement of their repentance and the claim of the abbey to the property.

At this assembly, which included clergy from Liège and canons from Floreffe, as well as many lay people (see charters 14 and 15 for this assembly), Godescalc of Morialmé made his crusade vow. The charter recording his vow is also issued by Radulf, and styles Godescalc as a noble man of proven faith and a vassal of the bishop. He takes his vow to join the assembly of the faithful, having been inspired to free the promised land from the hands of the impious. In order for his pilgrimage to be pleasing and fruitful, he commends himself to the prayers of the clergy and wishes to procure participation in their merits. To that end, he offers the canons of Floreffe the church of Sautour and all that belongs to it, a property which belongs to him by inheritance, and which he gives to the canons for the salvation of his soul as well as those of his family, living and dead. The gift is given into the hands of the abbot, Hermann (1173–1193/4), as a perpetual fief, to be divided between the canons and the sisters of Herlaimont and Verofle [Mariembourg].

Hugh, bishop of Liège (1220–1229), issued the third charter to confirm the assets left to the Premonstratensian nuns of Herlaimont by Godescalc of Morialmé. Before leaving on crusade Godescalc, a "noble man," gave the church of Sautour, with its tithe and all that pertained to it, to the abbey of Floreffe, with the consent of previous bishop, Radulf. The date of the original gift is not given, but it happened while Hermann was abbot of Floreffe. The gift is confirmed after Godescalc's death, since the lord of Morialmé is now his son Arnulph, and the income is to be divided between the canonesses at Herlaimont and the abbey.

NOTES ON THE CHARTER

Liege and Morialmé

Morialmé, like Floreffe, is in the province and diocese of Namur. It was part of the principality of Liège, one of the major fiefs of the Holy Roman Empire. In 1021 the bishops of Liège were made princes of the empire as well. Durand, who was elected in that year, had been a serf belong-

ing to a Godescalc, lord of Morialmé. Godescalc's son, who was provost of the church of Saint-Lambert, had declined the election, and Durand was chosen instead. Herlaimont was a convent dependent on the Premonstratensian abbey of Floreffe. The village of Herlaimont was the site not only of the convent, but of the castle of the lords of Trazegnies, whose overlords were the counts of Namur. Sautour, also in the province and diocese of Namur, had been a Roman settlement, and was a walled town belonging to the castellans of Dinant.[1]

C. G. Roland, in his article on the family of Morialmé, dates its beginnings to 1087, when Arnoul was invested with the lordship by Bishop Henri of Liège (1075–1091). Since the evidence for the history of the lordship comes from charters, the details are sketchy. There was a castle belonging to the lordship, but also a tower in the village, which belonged to the counts of Namur. In 1113 an Arnoul of Morelmeis gave property to the church of St.-Niçaise at Reims. Godescalc I of Morialmé appears in charters of 1124–1140, and had a brother, Walter of Trognée, who founded the priory of Bertrée in 1124. There is an Arnoul of Morialmé who acted as advocate for Fosse in 1159–1161. The family was related to the counts of Chiny, and therefore to the Roucys, who were neighbors and relatives of the Coucys. Godescalc II, lord of Morialmé and Sautour, was also advocate of Fosse. He went on the Third Crusade in 1189 with Hugh of Florennes, and entered the order of the Hospitallers (St. John of Jerusalem). He had a brother, Alard, who died by 1189, and a wife, Halwide of Ham. His daughter Beatrice became a canoness at Nivelles. His son Arnoul, mentioned in the third charter, had a daughter who married into the family of Bethune (charter 22, above).[2]

Floreffe had been founded by the counts of Namur, and its patrons included other crusading families, notably the Joinvilles.[3] From no later than 1254 it was the site of an annual festival in honor of the cross but apparently possessed the relic as early as 1195 (see above on the relic and its feast). Charter 14 above records the assembly of crusaders at the

---

[1] Geographic location: *Dictionnaire encyclopédique de Géographie historique du Royaume de Belgique*, ed. Alf. Jourdain, 2 vols. (Brussels, 1896); and *Dictionnaire historique et géographique des communes Belges*, ed. Eugène de Seyn, 3rd ed., 2 vols. (Turnhout, no date).

[2] Morialmé: C. G. Roland, "Histoire généalogique de la maison de Rumigny-Florennes," *Annales de la Société archéologique de Namur* 19 (1891/2): 102–7, and also 109, for the connection to the crusader Simon of Thimèon, who is the subject of charter 15 above. Giles Constable briefly mentioned this charter in "Medieval Charters as a Source for the History of the Crusades," in *Crusade and Settlement*, ed. P. Edbury (Cardiff, 1985), 83 and n. 99.

[3] Barbier, *Floreffe*, vol. 1: 8, 59–60. See also L. Genicot, "L'évolution des dons aux abbayes dans le comté de Namur du Xe au XIe siècles," *Annales de la Fédération archéologique et historique de Belgique, XXXe congrés, Bruxelles, 1935* (Brussels, 1936), 146.

dedication of the church at Herlaimont in 1188. Among those present were the counts of Namur and Hainaut and the duke of Brabant, as well as Hermann abbot of Floreffe, and Radulf, bishop of Liège. Given the presence of the bishop and the abbot at both, and the involvement of Herlaimont, it is likely that this series of charters is related to the Trazegnies' group, and that Godescalc was another member of the expedition of 1188. These charters are placed here rather than with the 1188 group because the abbot mentioned in the confirmation of 1216 is Helin (1209–1219), who was commissioned by Gervase of Prémontré (see the previous charter, no. 26) to accompany the famous preacher Jacques de Vitry to Acre in 1216. Helin was commissioned to oversee the interests of the order in the Holy Land, but he died at the Premonstratensian abbey on Cyprus in 1219. This series connects the order to the crusade assembly of 1188, to Gervase's role as crusade procurator, and to the continuing concern to recover the canons' houses near Jerusalem. That concern by a religious organization to recover property is similar to the proprietary interest taken in the Holy Land by the canons of Thérouanne (charter no. 19).

The web of relationships among the Coucys, the Trazegnies, and the family of Morialmé is difficult to reconstruct, but it presents a powerful motive for crusading. What seems sketchy and distant to today's readers, because it is recorded only marginally in charter evidence, was of course very clear to people at the time: a web of intermarriages and patterns of church patronage in northern France which resulted in an identifiable crusade contingent in 1188. It is well known that people went on crusades in groups with relatives and neighbors. Here is just such a group, certainly in this case called together by the feudal overlords named in the charters. But surely part of what made the expedition possible was the patronage of the local church, combined with the "peer pressure" exerted on individuals as others decided to go. The crusade motivation here would appear to be a mixture of elements: the call of an overlord, the pressure to join a local expedition, the patronage and preaching of the bishop and the canons, plus another factor which has been seen in all the previous charters—the prestige which crusading offered to the "new" families—and possibly to the "new" orders and reformed chapters as well.

28
1218, GERARD, MERCHANT OF VEURNE

Ferdinand van de Putte and Charles Louis Carton, *Chronicon et cartularium abbatiae Sancti Nicolai Furnensis* (Bruges, 1849), 127, unnumbered charters. [I have not seen the original.]

De collatione unius mensure terre a Gerardo filio Ade Claikyn.

Ego Gheraerdus filius Ade Claichin, burgensis de Furnis, Iherosolimam profecturus, legavi ecclesie beati Nicolai Furnensis, unam mensuram terre in *Reilevalant* et in *Strinc*. Item ecclesie S. Walburgis Furnensis unam mensuram in eadem. Item ecclesie S. Marie de Dunis x solidos et v denarios super *Barouts werf*, ad anniversarium meum, si in peregrinatione decessero, singulis annis, in hiis tribus ecclesiis perpetuo faciendum. Item Mathildi, filie mee ex concubina, duas mensuras terre, in terra filiorum Prumbout. Hec autem que prescripta sunt, si in via decessero, etiam si heredes carnis mee reliquero, rata erunt; si autem heredem habuero, ea que subscripta sunt non tenebunt. Apud Heilsindam legavi unam mensuram terre, et quartam partem unius mensure in *Norder odolf Stic*. Item Margarete Gholias et sorori eius Clemme, unam mensuram et quartem partem unius mensure, in eadem terra. Item sorori mee Margarete Portige, duas mensuras terre, unam mensuram iuxta *sthiltleen*, Nicolai nepotis mei, et aliam mensuram juxta Baslins Stic, ab occidente. Item Brunekino nepoti meo dimidiam partem de *Baslins Stic*, hoc salvo quod mater eius in dimidietate ipsius partis dimidie, quamdiu vixerit habeat usumfructum. Item pauperibus parrochiarum S. Nicolai et S. Walburgis tres mensuras terre, et quantum heredes meos, preter partem uxoris mee, deberet contingere in *Thomas Stic* et in *Okebeles Diec*. Item in ecclesia beati Dionisii ad oleum lampadis ante crucifixum, duos solidos perpetuo super mansuram meam quam Stalin tenet. Item in ecclesia leprosorum, ad lumen, XVIII denarios perpetuo super mansuram quam tenet filius Bucs. Item domui S. Iohannis Noordtuut medietatem terre mee, juxta motam filiorum Simonis de Dunis, versus sud. Item capelle S. Iacobi in ecclesia S. Walburgis XXXII denarios perpetuo, super terram filiorum Papakins. Item in caritate sutorum, XX denarios per-

On the conveyance of one measure of land by Gerard son of Ade Claikyn.

I, Gerard, son of Ade Claichin, burgess of Veurne/Furnes, about to set out for Jerusalem, donate to the church of Blessed Nicholas of Veurne, one measure of land in Reilevalant and in Strinc. Likewise, to the church of St. Walburge of Veurne, one measure in the same. Likewise to the church of St.-Marie de Dune, 10 *solidi* and 5 *denarii* on Barouts Wharf for the anniversary of my death, to be made each year in perpetuity in these three churches if I should die while on pilgrimage. Likewise to Mathilde, my daughter by a concubine, two measures of land, in the territory of the sons of Prumbout. The preceding things which are prescribed if I should die on the road will be binding even if I leave heirs of my flesh. However, if I do have an heir, those which are written below will not bind. To Heilsindis I give one measure of land and a fourth part of one measure in Norder Odolf Stic. Likewise to Margarete Gholias and her sister Clemma, one measure and a quarter part of one measure, in the same area. To my sister Margarete Portige, two measures of land, one measure near Sthiltleen; to my nephew Nicholas another measure of land near Baslins Stic, from the west. Likewise to Brunekine, my nephew, a half part of Baslins Stic, except that his mother will have the usufruct of a half of a half part, as long as she lives. Likewise to the poor of the parishes of St. Nicholas and St. Walburge three measures of land, and like that of my heirs, aside from the part of my wife, it should fall in Thomas Stic and in Okebeles Diec. Likewise to the church of Blessed Dionysius for oil for the lamp in front of the crucifix, two *solidi* in perpetuity from my domain which Stalin holds. Likewise for the church of the lepers, for the light, eighteen *denarii* in perpetuity from the domain which the son of Bucs has. Likewise for the house of St.-Jean Noordtuut, a half of my land near the *mote* of the sons of Simon de Dunes, toward the south. Likewise for the chapter of St. James in the church of St. Walburgis, thirty-two *denarii* in perpetuity, from the land of the sons of Papakins. Likewise for the charity of the cobblers, twenty

petuo super mansuram meam, quam tenet Riclin filius Morkin. Item veteri capelle S. Marie Oostuut, XXVII denarios ad oleum lampadis, ante S. Mariam perpetuo, super mansuram meam quam Wilhelmus filius Lippini tenet. Item Mathildi filie mee ex concubina supradicte paratiori bono meo X lib. infra Furnensis villam. Ut autem hoc testamentum meum debitam habeat firmitatem, ipsum et abbatis S. Nicolai et H. prepositi S. Walburgis Furnensis, sigillis feci muniri, et hiis qui interfuerunt testibus idoneis annotatis. Actum anno Domini millesimo ducentesimo XVIII, mense iunio.

denarii in perpetuity from my domain which Riclin, son of Morkin, holds. Likewise to the old chapel of St.-Marie Oostuut, twenty-seven *denarii* for oil for the lamp before blessed Mary, in perpetuity, from my domain which William son of Pippin holds. Likewise for the aforesaid Mathilde, my daughter from a concubine, by my more ready goodwill, ten *libras* from the town of Veurne. Moreover, that this my testament might have due firmness, I fortify it with the seal of the abbot of St.-Nicholas, and H., provost of St. Walburge in Veurne, and by the names of suitable witnesses which are subscribed. Issued in the year of our Lord, 1218, in the month of June.

SUMMARY OF THE CHARTER

This is a charter issued by a non-noble crusader, a merchant from the town of Veurne (Furnes) in Flanders, who took a crusade vow in 1218, and before his departure made gifts to several abbeys. He identifies himself as Gerard, son of Ade Claichin, and the first gift, a measure of land, is to St.-Nicholas at Veurne (see charter 18). Other abbeys receive the same kinds of gifts, and members of Gerard's family are mentioned as recipients of other properties, making this more like the *ordinatio* of Raoul de Coucy (1190) than like the simple donations in the rest of this collection. Among the beneficiaries are: St. Walburge, Les Dunes, "Mathilde, my daughter by my concubine," and other heirs, including nephews, a wife, and a sister. Money for lamps to be kept lit in several churches follows the donations of rents and land. The document is issued after he took the vow to go to Jerusalem, and the arrangements are made in case he dies on crusade.

NOTES ON THE CHARTER

Furnes

Furnes, or St.-Nicolas at Veurne, was a Premonstratensian abbey, previously described in the notes to charter 18. St. Walburge was a chapter of secular canons at Veurne. Les Dunes was a Cistercian abbey founded by the counts of Flanders in 1107 and consecrated in 1128 by Jean de Warneton, bishop of Thérouanne, a notable patron of the new orders and regular canons.[1] In 1218 Mathilde of Portugal, the wife of Count Philip of Flanders, died at Veurne and was buried at Les Dunes before being moved to Clairvaux. So far, I have not come across any further information about Gerard and his family which would connect them to the counts or their court. The churches mentioned seem to be the institutions in and around Veurne, and the list of relatives appears to cover all possible claimants, so that there could be no later claims against the churches.

The canons of St. Nicholas were originally outside the city of Veurne, but by 1170 the suburbs had surrounded them, and they moved to the chapel mentioned in this charter, St. Mary of Oostuut. This new church was built by 1247 but destroyed by 1578, rebuilt, and finally again destroyed in 1798, when the records of the house were dispersed. Abbot Henry (1205–1233) was active as a witness and issuer of many charters in 1218/19, some of which mention "the old chapel" and a new canal, which had been built from Furnes to Nieuport.[2]

---

[1] Berlière, *Monasticon Belge*, vol. 3: 353 and ff; see also under the names of individual religious houses.

[2] Berlière, *Monasticon Belge*, vol. 3: 594–602.

In 1172, during the move to St. Mary's, the abbey split. Previously it had been a double abbey of men and women, but as we have mentioned the Premonstratensians discouraged such establishments after 1137. Thanks to the gift of a farm at Hem, the women moved to their own priory called Vrouwenhof. Count Philip of Flanders' sister Gertrude of Maurienne helped to establish this new priory in 1176/7. In 1218 the parish of Heewillemskapelle was created nearby, and the canonnesses reconfirmed their relationship to St. Nicholas. Almost no documentary sources remain for this house.[3]

---

[3] Berlière, *Monasticon Belge*, vol. 3: 653–54.

29
1219, GUY DE MONCEAU

Bibliothèque nationale, Collection de Picardie 290, fol. 33.

Ego Anselmus, divina miseratione Laudunensis Episcopus omnibus in perpetuum. Notum facimus tam presentibus quam futuris quia nunc Guido de Moncellis miles de novem portionibus minute decime veteris moncelli quasi hereditario iure quatuor reciperet portiones crucesignatus pro successu ecclesie Albigensis et cogitans de anime sue salute personaliter ad presentiam nostram accessit et decimam partem quam habebat in prefata decima in manum nostram intuitu dei et nomine elemosine resignavit ut premonstratensi ecclesie que habebat ius patronatus ibidem episcopali autoritate daretur. Nos autem recepimus resignationem ipsius et virum religiosum Gervasium Premonstratensem Abbatem nomine ecclesie sibi commisse investivimus de decima supradicta. Ut igitur tam resignatio quam investitura per nos facta perpetuam habeat firmitatem presens scriptum in memoriam rei geste sigilli nostri impressione duximus roborandum. Actum mense Aprilis Anno gratie millesimo ducentesimo nonodecimo is.[1]

Bibliothèque national, Nouvelles Acquisitions Latines 938, fol. 9.

Ego Anselmus dominus Moncelli noui. Notum facio universis tam presentibus quam futuris qui viderint istud scriptum quod Guido frater meus resignavit ecclesie premonstratensi nomine elemosine totam illam partem minute decime quam tenebat de me in feodo in minuta decima veteris Moncelli per manum domini Anselmi episcopi laudunensis. Ego autem elemosinam ipsam cui rationabiliter contradicere non poteram laudavi & presentes litteras in testimonium perpetuum sigilli mei appensione munivi. Actum mense maio Anno gratie MCC nonodecimo.

---

[1] Professor Hiestand has raised serious questions about my reading of this text, and especially with the identification with Albi. Please see the photograph of the manuscript original in the appendix.

I, Anselm, by divine mercy bishop of Laon, make it known in perpetuity to all both in the present and in the future, that Guy de Monceau, knight, held by hereditary right four of the nine portions of money from the old tithe of Monceau. He was signed with the cross for the crusade against the Albigensian church and, thinking of the salvation of his soul, he came personally into our presence. He gave over into our hand, in the sight of God, a tenth part of what he had in the aforesaid tithe, so that it would be given by episcopal authority to the church of Prémontré which had the right of patronage there. We received his resignation (of that part of the tithe) and we invested the faithful Gervase, abbot of Prémontré, in the name of the church committed to him, with the tithe. So that both the renunciation and investiture transacted through us might have solidity, we have caused the present text which memorializes the event to be fortified with the impression of our seal. Issued in the month of April, in the year of grace 1219.

I, Anselm, lord of new Monceau. I make it known to all, both present and future, who see this text, that Guido my brother resigned to the church of Prémontré in the name of alms that whole part of the money of the tithe which he held from me in fief, the money of the tithe of old Monceau, through the hand of Lord Anselm, bishop of Laon. I could not reasonably contradict this donation, and so I confirmed it and fortified the present letter in perpetual testimony of it with the impression of my seal. Issued in the month of May, in the year of grace 1219.

SUMMARY OF THE CHARTER

Anselm de Mauni, bishop of Laon 1215–1238, issued the first charter for Guy de Monceau, a knight who was about to leave for the Albigensian crusade. Concerned for his soul, Guy gave Prémontré, in the presence of the bishop, four-ninths of the tithe of Monceau-le-Vieux, which he had inherited.[2] Gervase, abbot of Prémontré (1209–1220), received the tithe from the bishop. In the second charter, Guy's brother Anselm confirms the gift, mentioning that Guy held the tithe in fief from him.

Bishop Anselm and Abbot Gervase were both involved in the excommunication and eventual absolution of Enguerran III of Coucy in February 1219 (see charter 26, above). The quarrel had concerned the chapter at Laon; Enguerran had briefly imprisoned the deacon. This charter was issued in April. Gervase had been active in preaching and raising funds for the war in southern France. Whether there is a connection between the Coucys and Guy is unknown, but there was presumably a connection between Gervase's procuration and Guy's crusade vow. Monceau-le-Vieux was a small village near Chevres, which had belonged in the eleventh century to the lords of Ribemont, and been given by them in 1083 to the abbey of St.-Nicolas-des-Prés. There is inconclusive information on the family of knights who were then enfeoffed with this village, but no Guy is mentioned until 1230.[3] At that time Guy held Monceau-le-Vieux, and his brother Anselm was lord of Monceau-le-Neuf ("old" and "new" settlements at Monceau). This fits with the two charters above. The second manuscript contains the original donation charter by Bishop Anselm of Laon, a confirmation of it by Conrad, who was abbot at Prémontré 1220 to 1233, and the charter issued by Guy's brother Anselm.

---

[2] Barthélemy, *Coucy*, 525, and see BM Soissons 7, fol. 51.
[3] Melleville, *Dictionnaire*, vol. 2: 35: 1169 Rohart de Monceau, 1178 Guillaume de Monceau, son of Eudes de l'Abbaye, 1205 Jean de Monceau (wife Ermengarde, brother Simon, sister Emmeline), 1230 Guy, knight, lord of Monceau-le-Viel, brother of Anselm, lord of Monceau-le-Neuf. Taiée, *Prémontré*, lists gifts by Guy and Anselm in the 1230s to Prémontré, 111, 113. On the other hand, Chesne, in *Coucy*, 214, mentions a document issued by the Coucys in 1188 in favor of St. Martin's of Cambrai, for which "Arnoul de Monceaux" is one of the witnesses. Then there is the Arnoul de Moncel who is sometimes credited with the founding of the Premonstratensian house of "Moncetz." See Ardura, *Dictionnaire*.

30
1232, JEAN DE VERNEUIL

Louis-Victor Pécheur, ed., "Cartulaire de Tinselve," *Bulletin de la Société historique, et archéologique [et scientifique] de Soissons*, 2nd series, 5 (1874): 235–37.

Karta Ingelranni, domini de Couciaco, super conventione habita inter Premonstratensem Ecclesiam et Johannem de Wernolio militem, supra terris et aliis minutis redditibus quos habebat dictus miles in domibus de Tinselve et de Luili.

Ingelrannus dominus Couciaci Universis tam presentibus quam futuris in Domino salutem. Noverint universi quod cum dominus Johannes de Vernolio miles quedam terragia et alios minutos redditus haberet in domibus Premonstratensis Ecclesia de Tinselva et de Luili, tandem, ipso Johanne ad peregrinandum in terram sanctam ex toto parato tam pro pace et liberatione ipsius ecclesie et dictorum domorum suarum quam pro utilitate etiam ejusdem militis et heredum suorum, taliter inter eamdem ecclesiam et ipsum Johanne convenit: quod idem Johannes et heredes sui quittaverunt dicte ecclesie in perpetuum totam quartam partem terragii quem accipiebant in terra ipsius ecclesie que dicitur sancti Remigii et quicquid ibidem habebant vel habere poterant tam in justitia quam in aliis proventibus, sive bonis. Quittaverunt etiam et dederunt eidem ecclesie omnes census qui debebantur eis apud Tinselvam et apud Luili, tam in ipsa domo dicte ecclesie de Luili quam in omnibus aliis locis eiusdem ville tempore hujus scripti, sicut eos tenebant, et quinque aissinos avene qui eis ibidem similiter debebantur. Dederunt preterea dicte ecclesie tres pichetos terre apud Luili, et decem et octo sextarios vinagii quos habebant in valle de Coches et omnia etiam alia vinagia que ibidem potuerunt provenire. Preterea quittaverunt et dederunt dicte ecclesie dictus Johannes et heredes sui in perpetuum, totam medietatem suam quam habebant et accipiebant cum eadem ecclesia in toto nemore de Creutis. Dicta vero Ecclesia Premonstratensis in recompensionem omnium predictorum tenetur, annis singulis in perpetuum, reddere predicto Johanni et heredibus suis tres modios bladi medietatis ad mensuram Suessionis currentem tempore hujus scripti, et triginta solidos parisienses; et tam dictos tres modios bladi quam prefatos triginta solidos recipere tenebuntur annis singulis dictus Johannes et heredes sui in domo

Charter of Enguerran, lord of Coucy, regarding an agreement between the church of Prémontré and Jean de Verneuil, knight, regarding lands and other rental money which the said knight had in the domains of Tinselve and Leuilly.

Enguerran, lord of Coucy, to all both present and future, salvation in the Lord. Let all know that Lord Jean de Verneuil, a knight, had certain land taxes and other money rents in the domains of the church of Prémontré, in Tinselve and in Leuilly. When Jean himself was finally ready to depart on crusade to the Holy Land, for the peace and liberation both of that church and of his domains and for the benefit of that knight and his heirs, an agreement was made between the same church and Jean to this effect: Jean and his heirs gave quittance to the church in perpetuity of the whole of one fourth part of the domain which they had held in the land of the church called St.-Remi, whatever they had there or could have, both in justice and in other revenues or goods. They also gave in quittance to the same church all taxes which were owed to them in Tinselve and Leuilly, both in the house of the said church at Leuilly, and in all other places of the same village at the time of this writing, as they had them, and five esseins of mill tax which were likewise due at the same place. They also gave to the said church three *picheti* of land at Leuilly, and eighteen *sectarii* of vineyard which they had in the valley of Coches, and all other vineyards that pertained to that place. Moreover, the said John and his heirs gave in quittance to the same church in perpetuity the whole of the half they had held of the wood of *Creutis*. The aforesaid church of Prémontré is bound in recompense for all the above to render to the abovementioned Jean and his heirs each year in perpetuity three *modii* of their half of the grain according to the measure current in Soissons at the time of this document, and thirty Parisian *solidi*; and both the said three *modii* of grain and the thirty Parisian *solidi* the said Jean and his heirs are required to receive annually at the house of the said church of Tinselve on

dicte ecclesie de Tinselva qua die erunt parata a festo sancti Andree usque ad Natalem Domini secuturam; ita quod si per negligentiam suam eadem ecclesia defecerit de solutione facienda modo predicto, idem Johannes vel heredes sui ipsi ecclesie aut magistro curie sue de Tinselva, defectum eorum ostendere tenebuntur; et si infra quindenam post ostensionem eorum eisdem solutio non fieret de promissis, ipse Johannes vel heredes ipsius ex tunc poterunt capere de rebus predicte domus de Tinselva sine foris facto, ubicunque eas invenerint extra domum, donec facta fuerit solutio tota sicut superius est expressum. Pro pace autem utriusque partis, de communi consensu ita provisum est: quod si intra ipsam ecclesiam fortassis et dictum Johannem vel heredes suos de ipso blado aliqua discordia moveretur, eisdem Johanne ne vel heredibus suis dicentibus forte bladum ipsum non esse tale quale debetur eisdem, dicta ecclesia pro voluntate sua accipiet unum burgensem de Couciaco quemcumque voluerint similiter accipient; et ipsi duo burgenses de predicto blado secundum tenorem kartarum fideliter judicabunt; et sine maiori audientia ratum habebitur ab utraque parte quicquid a duobus burgensibus predictis bona fide in hac parte fuerit judicatum. Preterea sciendum est quod idem Johannes, ob remedium anime sue, obtulit et dedit dicte ecclesie in puram et perpetuam elemosinam sex aissinos bladi ad mensuram Suessionensem accipiendos annis singulis super sex aissinos terre site super fontem sancti Remigii et unum denarium parisiensem censualem super eamdem terram solvendum eidem ecclesie annuatim in festo Beati Remigii, ita videlicet, quod quando dicta (terra) bladum portabit, bladum recipiet ecclesia, et quando portabit avenam, totidem recipiet aissinos avene. Quando autem vacua erit ipsa terra, nichil penitus recipiet in ea preter denarium supradictum. Quia autem prefatus Johannes et heredes sui tenebant a nobis in feodo ea que concesserunt et dederunt prefate Ecclesie Premonstratensi, sicut superius est expressum, et in recompensationem ipsius concessionis et donationis, reposuerit in feodum nostrum tres modios bladi predictos quos dicta ecclesia reddere debet eis, nos prefatam conventionem sive commutationem, prout est supra declaratum, laudamus et approbamus et ratam habemus. Et ut in perpetuum ab utroque parte firmiter teneatur, presentem kartam, ad petitionem partium, sigilli nostri munimine duximus roborandam. Actum mense Julio, anno gratie M.CC.XXX secundo.

a day chosen between the feast of St. Andrew and the following Christmas, so that if by their negligence the church will fail to discharge this debt in the said manner, the same Jean and his heirs must show their failure to the church itself or to the master of the court at Tinselve. And if within fifteen days of this disclosure they do not discharge their promised obligations, the same Jean or his heirs can then seize from the goods of the said house of Tinselve without forfeiture, wherever they will find them outside the house, until the whole debt is paid as spelled out above. However, for the sake of the peace of both parties, it is provided by common consent that if within the church the said Jean or his heirs are bothered by some complaint about the grain, or if Jean himself or his heirs say that the grain is not such as was owed them, the church will by its own choice select one citizen of Coucy, and let them select one, whomever they want. And these two citizens will judge faithfully regarding the said grain in accord with the tenor of this charter. Without appeal to higher authority, each party is to ratify whatever will have been decided by the two citizens in good faith. Moreover, it is to be known that the same Jean, for the salvation of his soul, offered and gave to the said church in pure and perpetual alms six esseins of grain measured according to the Soissons measure, to be received each year, above and beyond the six esseins of land situated over the spring of St.-Remi, and one Parisian *denarius* of tax on the same land to be paid to the same church annually of the feast of Blessed Remi; namely, in such a way that when the said land bears grain, the church will receive grain, and when it bears maslin it will receive the same number of esseins of maslin. However, when this land lies fallow, it will receive nothing at all except the above-mentioned *denarius*. However, because the aforesaid Jean and his heirs had in fief the things from which they would grant and give to the aforesaid church of Prémontré, as was declared above, and in recompense for this concession and donation, they put back into our fief the aforesaid three *modii* of grain which the said church must render them. We confirm and approve the aforesaid agreement and exchange, as it is declared above, and we consider it ratified. And so that it may be firmly held by each party in perpetuity, we have had the present charter fortified with the guard of our seal, at the request of both parties. Issued in the month of July, the year of grace 1232.

SUMMARY OF THE CHARTER

Enguerran III of Coucy (1197–1242) issued this charter on behalf of Jean de Verneuil, knight, who was about to depart on pilgrimage to the Holy Land. The document records an agreement made between Jean, his heirs, and the house of Prémontré over property the family held at Tinselve and Leuilly. The order was to have the property, in return for an annual rent of three *modii* of wheat and thirty Paris *solidi*. The charter records the history of a dispute between the canons and the family over an earlier gift, which John had given as alms, but then revoked.[1] Once again, a crusade vow is linked to the resolution of a quarrel with a local church. The persistence of that theme from 1138 through 1232 is striking, even in a small charter collection. Enguerran was involved as Jean's overlord and as patron of Prémontré.

Verneuil, Tinselve, and Leuilly were all small villages near Coucy.[2] Tinselve apparently had a small house of Premonstratensian canons. According to Martinet, in her study of Laon, Jean de Verneuil was the namesake and descendant of "un homme de corps" (a servant) who had been willed to the order in 1150, along with land and revenue, by a certain Bilhard, cantor of the cathedral.[3]

In the same year, 1232, Enguerran III of Coucy issued a charter for Prémontré. In honor of the dedication of a new church, he made a gift to the abbot, Conrad, of 100 *sous* of Paris. From 1225, the Coucys were granted the right to be buried at the abbey. Several sources list Jean of Verneuil among those who accompanied Raoul of Coucy and King Louis IX on crusade in 1248, but this seems to be an attempt to account for the charter above, since Jean was a vassal of the Coucys, and there does not appear to have been another expedition he could have joined. The charter itself gives no evidence other than the mention of his individual penitential pilgrimage.

This is the last in the series of charters for the Coucys and their vassals; the next charter is the last for those of the Flanders connections.

---

[1] Barthélemy, *Coucy*, 223 and note 235.

[2] Barthélemy, *Coucy*, 394, index; Hugo, *Annales*, vol. 1: xi–xix; Janvier, *Boves*, 23, says Enguerran I received Verneuil as part of negotiations with the abbey of Corbie; Melleville, *Dictionnaire*, s.v. "Verneuil," says Jean's wife was Ade and that he went on crusade in 1243; Taiée, *Prémontré*, lists this donation, 112; and Vernier, *Coucy*, 383, describes Verneuil as being three kilometers from Coucy and thirty-one from Laon.

[3] Martinet, *Montloon*, 109.

31
1270, EUSTACE DE TRAZEGNIES

Joseph Barbier, *Histoire de l'abbaye de Floreffe de l'ordre de Prémontré*, 2 vols. (Namur, 1880), vol. 2: 135-36, no. 302, 8 June 1270.

A tous cias ki ces presens lettres veront et oront jou Eustasses, sires de Trasignies et oirs dou Rouls, et Agnes, se femme, salut en Deu et connoistre veriteit. Por ce ke li memoire des hommes est petite et tost trespasse, si est il drois et raisons con metle en escrit les choses ki puelent mueir avec les tens et avec les persones, et por ce faisons nous savoir a tos cias ki sunt et ki seront, ke com le glise de Floreffe, de sa debonnaire volenteit, por ce ke nous Eustasses devant dis deviens alleir en le sainte terre doutre meir, nouse ewist fait honorable courtoisie et avenant don decent livres alle subvention de nostre voie; nos por lour bonne volenteit, lour debonnaireteit, aussi ke fait nos avoent, lour vosimes en contre faire cortoisie. Por tant si lor avons rendut, doneit, otsiet et quilte clammet, et nous et nostre femme Agnes, en nostre plaine vie, en nostre plain sens, tos les droes ke nos aviens et avoir porriens, ne nous oirs, ens es terres censaus ki sunt entre le Mort Pienthon et le Chaucie, et volons et otrios ke ces devant dites terres et li droit ki enasteront et naistre porront, soent it revoisent as us et a constumes de lour court delle Chapelle des or mais, save nostre droite avowerie. Apres nos volens et otrions ki li abbes et li glise devant ditte soent en bon paisicule usaige et maniement den droite de lor court delle Chaucie, dont nos le debatiens et disiens kelle se stendroit, plus avant kelle ne duist, par deviers le voe delle Chaucie; et des arbres ausi ki sunt et furent de hors le court pres dou chemin, nous en quitons tous les debas, et disons et recognissons ke nous ne nos oirs ni poons ne ni devos jamais rein demandeir par nul droit, fors tant ke nous iretenons nostre avowerie, ensi com nos lavos es autres; et des arbres et dou fosseit et dou siege delle court, ke nos kalengiens par deviers le voe delle Chaucie, nous enquitons tous les clains et tous les debas, save la vowerie deseur ditte. Et volons encor et otrions ke tout li bien ki viennent alle devant dite glise de Floreffe de par Jehan Dyron, nostre homme, et Liegart, se femme, soit en terre arable et en autre

To all who will see or hear this present document, I, Eustace, lord of Trazegnies and heir of Roeulx, and Agnes, his wife, send greetings in God and wish knowledge of the truth. Because the memory of human beings is short and soon fails, it is right and reasonable to place in writing that which can change with time and persons. We, therefore, make known to all those who are and who will be that the church of Floreffe, by its great good will, because we, the aforementioned Eustace, are to go across the sea to the Holy Land, having shown us honorable courtesy by making us a fitting gift of one hundred pounds to support our journey, we, for our part, in response to their good will and the great kindness they have done us, wish likewise to show them courtesy. And so we, both ourselves and our wife Agnes, in the fullness of our life and good sense, have given, donated, granted, and quit-claimed all the rights that we or our heirs had or could have had in the taxable lands which are between the Pieton and the Chaussée. We wish and grant that these lands and the rights which they will bring or could bring should be under and return to the uses and customs of their court of the Chapel from now henceforward, save only our rightful advowson. We also wish and grant that the abbot and the aforesaid church have the peaceful enjoyment and possession of their court of the Chaussée about which we fought with them and said that it extended further than it should towards the road of the Chaussée. We also end the quarrel concerning the trees which were and are outside the court near the road, and say and recognize that neither we nor our heirs can or should ever claim anything by any right except that we retain in that area our advowson, as we have done for the rest. Concerning the trees, the ditch and the seat of the court which we contested with respect to the road of the Chaussée, we end all quarrels and claims, save the aforesaid advowson. We further wish and grant that all the wealth which comes to the aforesaid church of Floreffe from John Dyron, our vassal, and Liegard,

chose, li demeurent perpetueiment en iretaige, et en puist aireteir li glise devant nommee cui Kelle vorra, soit dordene sout dou siecle. A ces devant ditte choses otreir furent present Watiers, abbes de Floreffe; Gerars, abbes de Leffle; Jehans dell Rayommee, baillius de Trasingies; Jehans de Tuing, baillus de Morlanweis, Watiers de Liebrecheis, prevos de Floreffe; Watiers de Lees, maistre de Hellamont; Godefrois de Trasingies, Jehans de Nivelle, Jehans de Dinant, Lambiers de Liege, Jehans de Huy, frere de Floreffe, et mount dautre bonne gent. Et por tant que ce soit ferme, el tens que nous aviens oirs loas de no cors, avons nous saellees ces presentes lettres de nos saias.

Ceste ordenance fu faite et otriie el an del Incarnational Nostre Signeur M CC LXX, le jour de sainte Triniteit.

his wife, whether in arable lands or other things, remain to it as a perpetual inheritance. The aforesaid church may grant them to whomever it wishes whether lay or in orders.

To these aforesaid arrangements the following were witnesses: Walter, abbot of Floreffe; Gérard, abbot of Leffe; John of Rayome, bailiff of Trazegnies; John of Tuing, bailiff of Morlanwies [Morialmeis? see charter 27]; Walter of Leibrecht, provost of Floreffe; Walter de Leez, master of Herlaimont; Godfrey of Trazegnies; John of Nivelles; John of Dinant; Lambert of Liège; John of Huy, a brother of Floreffe, and many other good men. And so that these arrangements may remain firm when we have legitimate heirs begotten of our flesh, we have sealed this document with our seal.

This ordinance is made and confirmed in the year of the Incarnation of our Lord 1270, on the day of the Holy Trinity.

SUMMARY OF THE CHARTER

Before leaving on crusade, Eustace, lord of Trazegnies and of Roeulx, gave to Floreffe, with the consent of his wife Agnes, all his rights over property situated between the Pieton and the Chaussée, in recognition of what they advanced him, 100 livres, for his journey to the Holy Land. Several long-standing quarrels over property are resolved in this agreement between the abbey and the family. Among the witnesses were: Walter d'Obaix, who became abbot in 1270, resigned in 1280, and died in 1288; and Gérard, abbot of the Premonstratensian house of Leffe, at Dinant.[1] Also listed are the provost of Floreffe, Watiers de Liebrecheis, and the master of Herlaimont (see charter 14, above), Watiers de Lees, who became abbot of Floreffe in 1281.

---

[1] Berlière, *Monasticon Belge*, vol. 1: 117, 126: Piéton, prov. Henegouwen, arr.Charleroi, can. Fontaine-l'Évêque.

Charter 1: 1138, Enguerran II de Coucy.
Archives de la Société archéologique, historique
et scientifique de Soissons 1, pièce 5.
By permission of the Société archéologique, historique
et scientifique de Soissons.

Charter 2: 1142, Radulph Canis.
Collection de Picardie 290: Originaux de Prémontré, folio 3.
By permission of the Bibliothèque nationale de France, Paris.

Charter 6: 1147, Burchard de Guise.
Archives départementales de l'Aisne, H. 797.
Be permission of the Archives départementales de l'Aisne, Laon.

Charter 10: 1178, Raoul I de Coucy.
Archives de la Société archéologique, historique
et scientifique de Soissons 1, pièce 13.
By permission of the Société archéologique, historique
et scientifique de Soissons.

Charter 12: 1178, Henry, Count of Troyes.
Collection de Picardie 290: Originaux de Prémontré, folio 13.
By permission of the Bibliothèque nationale de France, Paris.

Charter 24: 1209, Guy de Arblincourt.
Collection de Picardie 302, folio 1.
By permission of the Bibliothèque nationale de France, Paris.

Ego Anselm's dina miseratione Laudunens Eps. omnibus t presentib; t futuris. qz t Guido de Moncell' miles. de Souay precomb; mnre dcrne uestis comely. gr be- redicatio nre. Eccle megnet peccos. crucesignat' p suscepti ecclie Alb[...]es. t cesegnan' de die sue salutiz. pfomult ad pretentay may accesset. t Sctay pariety gnā hebat i prefata Scti maī t maīū mean. Iuuti S. t noīe elemosine resignauit. uv Premonstantes ecclie que hebat uī patumar ībidem. Quali auctoritate Sauez. Itez aut uecepm i resignanoem Ipus. t uttri religiosum. Certuasti Premonstrates Abbem. noīe ecclie sibi cōmisse. iuestiuim? de Seruna. Sguerā. Ut i tay resignano. g iuestitia. g uos fca. ppetuay habeat firmitate. presens scriptu t memoriay rez geste. sigillis nris īpressione duprig roboranum. Actum [...] [...] Apud. Anno grae Willesimo Sucentesimo nonodemo.

BIBLIOGRAPHY

MANUSCRIPT AND EDITED PRIMARY SOURCES

(Note: the English translations of Latin chronicles are under Secondary Sources.)

Archives départementales de l'Aisne (at Laon):
H 797, donation of Burchard of Guise to Prémontré
Archives de la Société archéologique, historique et scientifique de Soissons

Bibliothèque municipale de Soissons:
7, *Cartulaire de Prémontré*

Bibliothèque nationale, Paris:
Collection de Picardie
    7 (*Notices généalogiques et extraits relatifs à la maison de Coucy*)
    185–187 (Dom. Varoqueaux, *Essai sur l'histoire ecclésiastique et civile de Laon et du pays Laonnois*, 3 vols., 18th cen.)
    257 (*Copies de documents ... concernant la Picardie*)
    267, 268 (*Variarum tabularum ... excerpta ad ... Historiam Laudunensem*)
    290 (*Chartes de l'abbaye de Prémontré ...*)
    302 (*Chartes du Diocèse de Noyon*)
Fonds latin
    11004 (*Cartulaire de Saint-Jean-de-Vignes, de Soissons, XIII s.*)
    17141 (*Collection de 62 chartes relatives à Picardie du milieu du XII s. à l'an 1481*)
Latin 5478 (*Cartulaire de Mont-Saint-Martin*)
    17141, no. 15 (*Original d'Enguerran III*)
Nouvelles Acquisitions Latines 938 (*Cartulaire de l'abbaye des Prémontrés. Manuscrit du XIIIe siècle*)
    3064 (*Cartulaire de St.-Léger de Soissons*)

British Library, London:
Add. ms. 15604, cartulaire no. 21: *Cartulaire de St. Acheul.*

Albert of Aix. *Historia Hierosolymitania*, in RHC, vol. 4.

Albon, le Marquis d'. *Cartulaire de l'ordre général du Temple, de l'origine à 1150*. Paris, n.d.

Albricus monachus Trium Fontium/Aubry de Trois-fontaines, *Chronique*, ed. Paul Scheffer-Boichorst in MGH SS 23.

Andrea Marchianensis, *Historia regum Francorum*, ed. O. Holder-Egger in MGH SS 26.

Balduinus Avennensis, *Chronicon Hanoniense*, ed. I. Heller in MGH SS 25.

Balduinus Ninovensis, *Chronicon*, ed. O. Holder-Egger in MGH SS 25.

Baluze, S., ed. *Miscellaneorum libri vii*. 7 vols. Paris, 1678–1715.

Barbier, J. and V., eds. "Cartulaire de l'abbaye de Floreffe." *Analectes pour servir à l'histoire ecclésiastique de la Belgique*, 2nd series, 1 (1881). This is a register, not a cartulary.

Barbier, Joseph, ed. "Chronique des abbés de Floreffe." *Analectes pour servir à l'histoire ecclésiastique de la Belgique* 8 (1871).

———. "Documents concernant Grand Leez et Sauvenière, extraits du cartulaire de l'abbaye de Floreffe, Namur." *Analectes pour servir à l'histoire ecclésiastique de la Belgique* 8 (1871).

———. "Documents concernant la Paroisse de Thiméon, extraits du cartulaire de l'abbaye de Floreffe." *Analectes pour servir à l'histoire ecclésiastique de la Belgique* 9 (1872).

———. "Documents concernant Sautour et Aublain, extraits du cartulaire de l'abbaye de Floreffe." *Analectes pour servir à l'histoire ecclésiastique de la Belgique* 8 (1871).

———. "Documents concernant Trazegnies, extraits du cartulaire de l'abbaye de Floreffe." *Analectes pour servir à l'histoire ecclésiastique de la Belgique* 7 (1870).

———. *Histoire de l'abbaye de Floreffe, de l'ordre de Prémontré*. 2 vols. Namur, 1880.

———. "Nécrologe de l'abbaye de Floreffe de l'ordre de Prémontré, au diocèse de Namur." *Analectes pour servir à l'histoire ecclésiastique de la Belgique* 18 (1876).

Barthélemy de Joux. *Epistola*, in Migne, *PL* 182, col. 696. See also *PL* 70, cols. 1359–1364.

Benton, John F., ed. *Recueil des actes des comtes de Champagne, 1152–1197*. Princeton, 1988.

Bresc-Bautier, Geneviève, ed. *Le Cartulaire du chapitre du Saint-Sépulcre de Jérusalem*. Paris, 1984.

Brouette, E. "Actes inconnus de Thierry et de Philippe d'Alsace en faveur de Braine." *Revue du Nord* 37 (1955).

———. "Documents relatifs au temporel de Saint-Augustin de Thérouanne ignorés du cartulaire abbatial." *Analecta Praemonstratensia* 44 (1968).

Chronique française des Rois de France par un anonyme de Béthune, in RHGF, vol. 24, pt. 2.

De Hemptinne, Thérèse, and Adriaan Verhulst, eds. *De Ooorkonden der Graven van Vlaanderen (Juli 1128–September 1191)*, II. Uitgave/Band I: *Regering van Diederik van de Elzas (Juli 1128–12 Januari 1168)*. Brussels, 1988.
Duchet, Th., and A. Giry. *Cartulaires de l'église de Térouane*. St. Omer, 1881.
Du Pré, Maurice, ed. and trans. Auguste Janvier and Charles Bréard. *Annales de l'abbaye de Saint-Jean-d'Amiens*. Amiens, 1899.
Feys, E., and Alois Nélis, eds. *Les Cartulaires de la Prévôté de Saint-Martin à Ypres*. 4 vols. Bruges, 1884–1887.
Flodoard, *Annales*, ed. Ph. Lauer. MGH SS 13.
GC. See *Gallia Christiana* under Secondary Sources.
Galterus abbas. *Fundatio Arroasiensis*. MGH SS 15.
Galterus archdiaconus. *Vita Johannis Episcopi Teruanensis*. MGH SS 15.
Gesta Senonensis Ecclesiae. MGH SS 25.
Gilbert de Mons, ed. Léon V. Vanderkinder. *Gilbert de Mons. La Chronique*. Brussels, 1904.
Guibert, abbot of Nogent, ed. and trans. Edmond-Rene Labande. *Autobiographie. Les classiques de l'histoire de France au Moyen Âge*, 34. Paris, 1981.
Herman de Tournai. *De miraculis Beatae Mariae Laudunensis*. Migne, *PL* 156; also ed. R. Wilmans in MGH SS 12.
———. *De restauratione monasterii sancti Martini Tornacensis*, in Migne, *PL* 180; also ed. G. Waitz in MGH SS 14.
Hugo, Charles Louis. *Sacrae Antiquitatis Monumenta historica, dogmatica, diplomatica*, 2 vols. Etival, 1725.
———. *Sacri et Canonici Ordinis Praemonstratensis Annales*. 2 vols. Nancy, 1734–1735.
Jean de Joinville, *Mémoires*, ed. Natalis de Wailly. Bar-le-Duc, 1879.
Johannes Longus, *Chronica monasterii Sancti Bertini*, ed. O. Holder-Egger in MGH SS 25.
Lalanne, J.-M., ed. *Le Cartulaire de Valpriez (1135–1250 [a.st.])*. Mémoires et Documents d'histoire médiévale et de philologie 4. Paris, 1990.
Lalore, Charles, ed. *Collection des principaux cartulaires du diocèse de Troyes*. 6 vols. Paris, 1875–90.
Lambert Ardensis ecclesiae presbyteri chronicon Ghisnense et Ardense, ed. D. C. de Godefroy Menilglaise. Paris, 1855.
Lohrmann, Dietrich, ed. *Papsturkunden im Frankreich. Neue Folge. 7. Nördliche Ile de France und Vermandois*. Göttingen, 1976.
Mansi, G. D., ed. *Sacrorum Conciliorum Nova et Amplissima Collectio*. Ed. novissima. Continued by L. Petit and J. B. Martin. 53 vols. Florence et alibi, 1759–1962.
Martène, E. and U. Durand, eds. *Veterum scriptorum et monumentorum amplissima collectio*. 2nd ed. 9 vols. Paris, 1724–1733.

Mémoires de la Société des Antiquaires de Picardie. Documents inédits concernant la province, vols. 14, 18: *Cartulaire du Chapitre Cathédrale d'Amiens.* 2 vols, eds. J. Roux and E. Soyez. Amiens, 1905, 1912.

Mennesson, E. *Les Chartes de Vervins, XIIe, XIIIe et XVIe siècles.* Extrait du *Bulletin de la Société archéologique de Vervins* 13 (1889). Vervins, 1889.

———. "Partage testamentaire de Raoul Ier de Coucy et Vervins." *La Thiérache. Bulletin de la Société archéologique de Vervins (Aisne)* 14 (1890).

Newman, William Mendel. *Charters of Saint-Fursy of Péronne.* Cambridge, Mass., 1977.

———. *Les seigneurs de Nesle en Picardie (XIIe–XIIIe siècles): leurs chartes et leur histoire.* 2 vols. Philadelphia-Paris, 1971.

Obituaire de l'abbaye de Prémontré. There are two parts, both under the same title: R. van Waefelghem, pt. 1, in *Analectes de l'Ordre de Prémontré* 5/8 (1909/1912); and J. Evers, pt. 2, in *Analecta Praemonstratensia* 1 (1952).

Pécheur, Louis-Victor, ed. *Cartulaire de l'abbaye de Saint-Léger de Soissons.* Soissons, 1870.

———. "Cartulaire de Tinselve." *Bulletin de la Société historique, archéologique [et scientifique] de Soissons,* 2nd series, 5 (1874).

Peter of Vaux-Cernay. *Petri Vallium Sarnaii Monachi Historia Albigensis.* Eds. P. Guébin and E. Lyon. 3 vols. *Société de l'histoire de France,* 412, 422, 442. Paris, 1926, 1930, 1938.

Piette, Amedée. *Histoire et Cartulaire de l'abbaye de Thenailles, ordre de Prémontré.* (Extract from the *Bulletin de la Société historique, archéologique et scientifique de Soissons*). Soissons, 1878.

Piot, Charles. *Cartulaire de l'abbaye d'Eename.* Bruges, 1881.

Poncelet, Edouard. *Actes des princes-évêques de Liège: Hugues de Pierrepont, 1200–1229.* Brussels, 1941.

Potthast, A., ed. *Regesta Pontificum Romanorum,* 2 vols. Berlin, 1874–1878; repr. Graz, 1957.

Pressutti, Pietro, ed. *Regesta Honorii Papae III.* 2 vol. Rome, 1888.

Prevenier, W., ed. *De Oorkonden der Graven van Vlaanderen (1191–1206).* II. Uitgave. Brussels, 1964.

Récits d'un ménestrel de Reims au XIIIe siècle. Ed. O. Holder-Egger in MGH SS 26; and by Natalis de Wailly, Paris, 1876.

Richer, ed. G. Waitz. *Gesta Senonensis Ecclesiae,* in MGH SS 25.

Richard the Pilgrim, *La Chanson d'Antioche,* ed. S. Duparc-Quioc. Paris, 1977–1978.

———, *La Conquête de Jerusalem,* ed. C. Hippeau. Paris, 1868.

Röhricht, Reinhold. *Regesta Regni Hierosolymitani, MXCVII–MCCXCI.* Innsbruck, 1893; and *Additamentum,* Innsbruck, 1904.

Roux, Joseph, and E. Soyez, eds. *Cartulaire du Chapitre Cathédrale d'Amiens.* 2 vols. Mémoires de la Société des Antiquaires de Picardie.

Documents inédits concernant la province, vols. 14, 18. Amiens, 1905, 1912.
Sigebert of Gembloux, *Sigeberti Gemblacensis Chronica cum Continuationibus*, ed. D. L. C. Bethmann, MGH SS 6.
Smet, J.-J. de. *Corpus chronicorum Flandriae*. 4 vols. Brussels, 1837–1865.
Suger, abbot of Saint-Denis, *Historia Gloriosi Regis Ludovici VII*, in RHGF, vol. 12; also ed. A. Molinier, *Vie de Louis le Gros . . . suivie de l'Histoire du Roi Louis VII*. Paris, 1887.
Tailliar, Eugène-François Joseph, ed. *La féodalité en Picardie. Fragment d'un cartulaire de Philippe-Auguste*. Amiens, 1868.
Tardif, Jules, ed. *Monuments historiques*. Archives de l'Empire. Inventaires et Documents, 122. Paris, 1866; repr., Nendeln, Liechtenstein, 1977.
Van de Putte, Ferdinand, and Charles-Louis Carton, eds. *Chronicon et cartularium abbatiae Sancti Nicolai Furnensis, ordinis Premonstratensis, et Chronicon Bethaniae seu domus S. Joseph Furnensis. (Recueil de Chroniques, Chartes et autres Documents concernant l'Histoire et les Antiquités de la Flandre-Occidentale. 1er séries: Chroniques des monastères de Flandres*, IX). Bruges, 1949.
Vercauteren, Fernand, ed. *Actes des comtes de Flandre, 1071–1128*. Brussels, 1938.
Vita Johannis episcopi Teruanensis, auct. Waltero. Ed. O. Holder-Egger in MGH SS 15, pt. 2.
Vita Norberti archiepiscopi Magdeburgensis; and *Additamenta fratrum Cappen-bergensium*. Ed. R. Wilmans in MGH SS 12.
William of Tyre. *Chronique*. Ed. R. B. C. Huygens et al. 2 vols. *Corpus Christianorum, Continuatio Mediaevalis*, 63, 63A. Turnhout, 1986.

SECONDARY SOURCES

Ambroise, ed. and trans. J. Hubert and J. La Monte. *The Crusade of Richard the Lion Heart*. New York, 1941.
Annales Gandenses, ed. and trans. Hilda Johnstone. London and New York, 1951.
Arbois de Jubainville, Henri d'. *Histoire de Bar-sur-Aube sous les comtes de Champagne, 1077–1284*. Paris, 1859.
———. *Histoire des ducs et des comtes de Champagne (VIe–XIe fin)*. 8 vols. Paris, 1859–1869.
Ardura, Bernard. *Abbayes, prieurés et monastères de l'ordre de Prémontré en France des origines à nos jours. Dictionnaire historique et bibliographique*. Nancy, 1993.
Aubert, R. "Fontenelles"; "Henri de Troyes," DHGE.
Avril, J. "Observance monastique et spiritualité dans les préambules des actes (X^e–XIIIe s.)." *Revue d'Histoire Ecclésiastique* 85 (1990): 5–29.

Backmund, Norbert. *Die Mittelalterlichen Geschichtsschreiber des Prämonstratenserordens*. Bibliotheca Analectorum Praemonstratensium 10. Averbode, 1972.

——. *Monasticon praemonstratense*. 3 vols. Straubing, 1949–1956; 2nd ed., 1 vol. in 2 pts., Berlin, 1983.

Baix, F. "Baudouin V, comte de Hainaut." DHGE.

Barber, Malcolm. "The Order of Saint Lazarus and the Crusades." *Catholic Historical Review* 80 (1994).

——. *The New Knighthood. A History of the Order of the Temple*. Cambridge and New York, 1994.

Barthélemy, A. de. "Les pèlerins champenois en Palestine, 1097–1249." *Revue de l'Orient latin* 1 (1893).

Barthélemy, Dominique. "Aux origines du 'Laonnois féodal': Peuplement et fondations de seigneuries aux XIe et XIIe siècles." *Mémoires de la Fédération des Sociétés d'histoire et d'archéologie de l'Aisne* 26 (1981).

——. *Les deux âges de la seigneurie banale. Pouvoir et société dans la terre des sires de Coucy (mil. XIe–XIIIe siècle)*. Paris, 1984.

——. "Monachisme et aristocratie aux XIIe et XIIIe siècles. Les Bénédictins de Nogent-sous-Coucy face à la concurrence et à l'exemple de Prémontré." In *Sous la Régle de Saint-Benoît*, Colloque de Saint-Marie de Paris, 23–25 octobre 1980 (Geneva, 1982), 185–98.

——. *L'ordre seigneurial, XIe–XIIe siècle*. Paris, 1990.

——. "Raoul de Coucy et Vervins." *Mémoires de la Fédération des Sociétés d'histoire et d'archéologie de l'Aisne* 27 (1982).

——. "Les Sires Fondateurs: Enjeux impliqués dans les traditions et les recours au passé en seigneurie de Coucy." In *Actes du XIIIe Congrès des Médiévistes de l'Enseignement supérieur public*, 1982 (Paris, 1983).

——. *La société dans le comté de Vendôme de l'an mil au XIVe siècle*. Paris, 1993.

Bavel, T. J., and R. Canning, ed., trans. *The Rule of St. Augustine*. London, 1984.

Beaunier, Besse, Becquet, eds. *Abbayes et prieurés de l'ancienne France . . .*, 16 vols. Paris, 1905–1981.

Bellenger, Yvonne, and Danielle Quéruel, eds. *Les Champenois et la Croisade*. Paris, 1989.

Benson, Robert, and Giles Constable, eds. *Renaissance and Renewal in the Twelfth Century*. Cambridge, Mass., 1982.

Benton, John F., ed. *Self and Society in Medieval France: The Memoirs of Abbot Guibert of Nogent*. Toronto, 1984.

Béraud, J.-B. de l'Allier. *Histoire des comtes de Champagne et de Brie*. 2 vols. Paris, 1839–1842.

Berlière, Ursmer. See *Monasticon Belge*, below.

Berman, Constance Hoffman. *Medieval Agriculture, the Southern French*

Countryside, and the Early Cistercians: A Study of Forty-three Monasteries. Philadelphia, 1986.
Bisson, T. N. *Cultures of Power. Lordship, Status, and Process in Twelfth-Century Europe.* Philadelphia, 1995.
———. "Medieval Lordship." *Speculum* 70 (1995): 743-59.
———. "The Organized Peace in Southern France and Catalonia, ca. 1140-ca. 1233." *American Historical Review* 82 (1977): 290-311.
Blumenthal, Uta-Renate. *The Investiture Controversy. The Church and Monarchy from the Ninth to the Twelfth Century.* Philadelphia, 1988.
Bolton, Brenda. *The Medieval Reformation.* London, 1983.
Bouchard, Constance Brittain. *Holy Entrepreneurs. Cistercians, Knights, and Economic Exchange in Twelfth-Century Burgundy.* Ithaca, N.Y., and London, 1991.
Bourgeois, M. *Histoire des comtes de Brienne.* Paris, n.d.
Boyle, Leonard E. *Medieval Latin Palaeography: A Bibliographical Introduction.* Toronto, 1984.
Braud, Charles M. *Byzantium Confronts the West, 1180-1204.* Cambridge, Mass., 1968.
Bréhier, Louis. "Brienne." DHGE.
Brouette, E. "La date de décès de Milon Ier, évêque de Thérouanne." *Bulletin trimestriel de la Société académique des Antiquaires de la Morinie* 21 (1970): 335-40.
Brundage, James A. "'Cruce Signari': The Rite for Taking the Cross in England." *Traditio* 22 (1966): 289-310.
———. *Medieval Canon Law and the Crusader.* Madison, Wisc., 1969.
———. "A Note on the Attestation of Crusaders' Vows." *Catholic Historical Review* 52 (1966).
———. "The Votive Obligations of Crusaders: The Development of a Canonistic Doctrine." *Traditio* 24 (1968): 77-118.
Brunel, Ghislain. "Les activités économiques des Prémontrées en Soissonnais aux XIIe et XIIIe siècles: politique originale ou adaptation au milieu?" In *Actes officiels du 14ème colloque du CERP.* Amiens, 1989.
———, with D. Defente. *Soissons et des villages.* Soissons, 1986.
Bull, Marcus. *Knightly Piety and the Lay Response to the First Crusade: The Limousin and Gascony, c. 970-c.1130.* Oxford, 1993.
Bur, Michel. *La formation du comté de Champagne, v.950-v.1150.* Nancy, 1977.
———. *Histoire de Laon et du Laonnois.* Toulouse, 1987.
———. *Vestiges d'habitat seigneurial fortifié en Champagne centrale.* Reims, 1987.
Bynum, Caroline Walker. *Docere verbo et exemplo. An Aspect of Twelfth-Century Spirituality.* Missoula, Mont., 1979.
———. *Holy Feast and Holy Fast: The Religious Significance of Food to Medieval Women.* Berkeley and Los Angeles, 1987.
———. *Jesus as Mother.* Berkeley and Los Angeles, 1982.

———. "The Spirituality of Regular Canons in the Twelfth Century: A New Approach." *Medievalia et Humanistica* n.s. 4 (1973): 3–24.

Calonne, Alberic de. *Histoire des abbayes de Dommartin et de Saint-André-aux-Bois.* Arras, 1875.

———. *Histoire de la ville d'Amiens.* 3 vols. Amiens, 1899–1906.

Canivez, J. M. "Barthélemy de Jura." DHGE

Carrière, Victor. *Histoire et cartulaire des Templiers de Provins.* Paris, 1919.

[no author]. *Le château de Coucy.* Coucy, 1989.

Châtillon, Jean. *Le mouvement canonial au moyen âge: Réforme de l'Eglise, spiritualité et culture.* Paris and Turnhout, 1992.

Chaurand, Jacques. *Thomas de Marle, Sire de Coucy.* Marle, 1963.

Chazan, Robert. *European Jewry and the First Crusade.* Berkeley, Los Angeles, and London, 1987.

Cheney, C. R. "Gervase, Abbot of Prémontré: A Medieval Letter-Writer." In *Medieval Texts and Studies* (Oxford, 1973), 242–76.

———, ed. "Epistolae Gervasii Abbatis Generalis (1216–1219)." *Bulletin of the John Rylands Library* 33 (1950).

Chesne, André du. *Histoire genéalogique de la maison de Béthune.* Paris, 1639.

———. *Histoire généalogique des maisons de Guines, d'Ardres, de Gand et de Coucy ....* Paris, 1631.

Choux, J. *Recherches sur le diocése de Toul au temps de la réforme grégorienne: l'épiscopat de Pibon (1069–1107).* Nancy, 1952.

Coët, Emile, and Charles Lefèbvre. *Histoire de la ville de Marle et des environs.* Compiègne, 1897.

Cole, Penny Jane. "Christians, Muslims, and the 'Liberation' of the Holy Land." *Catholic Historical Review* 84 (1998): 1–10.

———. *The Preaching of the Crusades to the Holy Land, 1095–1270.* Cambridge, Mass., 1991.

Colliette, Louis-Paul. *Mémoires pour servir à l'histoire ecclésiastique, civile, et militaire de la province du Vermandois.* 3 vols. Cambrai, 1771–1772.

Constable, Giles. "The Financing of the Crusades in the Twelfth Century." In *Outremer: Studies in the History of the Crusading Kingdom of Jerusalem Presented to Joshua Prawer* (Jerusalem, 1982), 64–88.

———. "Medieval Charters as a Source for the History of the Crusades." In *Crusade and Settlement*, ed. Peter Edbury (Cardiff, 1985), 73–89.

———. *Monks, Hermits and Crusaders in Medieval Europe.* London, 1988.

———. *The Reformation of the Twelfth Century.* Cambridge, 1997.

———. *Religious Life and Thought (11th–12th Centuries).* London, 1979.

Constant, Jean-Marie. *Les Guise.* Paris, 1984.

Coolen, Georges. "Le Chapitre de Licques et la Croisade." *Bulletin trimestriel de la Société Académique des Antiquaires de la Morinée* 21 (1968).

Cowdrey, H.E.J. "The Papacy and the Origins of Crusading." *Medieval History* 1 (1991).

———. "Pope Urban II and the Idea of the Crusade." In *Festschrift für Bernhard Töpler* (Weimar and Böhlau, 1994).
———. *Popes, Monks and Crusaders*. London, 1984.
———. "The Reform Papacy and the Origin of the Crusades," paper given at an international colloquium in Clermont-Ferrand, June 1995: "Le concile de Clermont de 1095, et l'appel à la croisade."
Courtoy, F. "Les reliques de la passion dans le comté de Namur, au XIIIe siècle." In *Mélanges Félix Rousseau* (Brussels, 1958).
Daire, Louis-François. *Histoire civile, ecclésiastique et littéraire du doyenné de Picquigny*. Amiens, 1860.
———. *Histoire de la ville d'Amiens*. 2 vols. Paris, 1857.
———, and Alcius Ledieu. *Histoire des doyennés du diocèse d'Amiens*. 2 vols. Abbeville, 1912.
Darsy, F.-Irénée. *Picquigny et ses seigneurs, vidames d'Amiens*. Abbeville, 1860; reproduction in facsimile, Saint-Pierre-de-Salerne, 1981.
Dauphin, Jean-Luc. *Notre-Dame de Dilo. Une abbaye au coeur du pays d'Othe*. Villeneuve, 1992.
Delaforge, E. *Diocèse de Meaux; Dignitaires des abbayes, chapitres et prieurés*. Meaux, 1885. Delaporte, Y. "Chartres." DHGE.
Dereine, Charles. "Chanoines"; "Chauny"; "Conon de Préneste." DHGE.
———. "L'élaboration du statut canonique des chanoines réguliers, spécialement sous Urbain II." *Revue d'histoire ecclésiastique* 46 (1951).
———. "Enquête sur la règle de Saint Augustin." *Scriptorium* 2 (1947/8).
———. "Les origines de Prémontré." *Revue d'histoire ecclésiastique* 42 (1947).
———. "Les prédicateurs 'apostoliques' dans les diocèses de Thérouanne, Tournai et Cambrai-Arras durant les années 1075–1125." *Analecta Praemonstratensia* 59 (1983).
De Sars, Maxime. *Le Laonnois féodal*. 5 vols. Paris, 1924–1934.
Devillers, Léopold. "Trazegnies, son château, ses seigneurs et son église." *Annales de l'Académie [royale] d'archéologie de Belgique* 39 (1883).
Dictionnaire historique et archéologique de la Picardie. Ed. the Société des Antiquaires de Picardie. 5 vols. Paris and Amiens, 1909–1929.
Dictionnaire historique et géographique des communes Belges. Ed. Eugène de Seyn. 3rd ed., 2 vols. Turnhout, n. d.
Dictionnaire encyclopédique de Géographie historique du Royaume de Belgique. Ed. Alf. Jourdain et al. 2 vols. Brussels, 1896.
Dictionary of the Middle Ages, see Strayer, below.
Dhondt, J. *Les Origines de la Flandre et de l'Artois*. Arras, 1944.
Doehaerd, R. "Féodalité et commerce. Remarques sur le conduit des marchands (XIe–XIIIe siècles)." In *La noblesse dans la France médiévale*, ed. Ph. Contamine (Paris, 1976).
Dubrelle, A. "Anselme, moine de St.-Médard de Soissons." DHGE.

Duby, Georges. *Le dimanche de Bouvines. 27 juillet 1214*. Paris, 1973; repr., 1985.

———. *France in the Middle Ages 987–1460: From Hugh Capet to Joan of Arc*. Trans. Juliet Vale. Oxford and Cambridge, Mass., 1991.

Du Cange, Charles. *Histoire de l'état de la ville d'Amiens et de ses comtes*. Amiens, 1840.

DuChesne. See Chesne, above.

Dunbabin, Jean. *France in the Making 843–1180*. Oxford, 1985.

Du Plessis, Dom Toussaint. *Histoire de la ville et des seigneurs de Coucy*. Paris, 1728.

Durvin, Pierre. *Histoire de la préfecture de l'Oise, ancienne abbaye Saint Quentin de Beauvais*. Beauvais, 1978.

Edbury, Peter, ed. *Crusade and Settlement*. Cardiff, 1985.

Enlart, C. *Monuments religieux de l'architecture romane et de transition dans les anciens diocèses d'Amiens et de Boulogne*. Amiens, 1895.

Estienne, Joseph. "Usage du style de l'Annonciation à Arras et à Amiens au début du XIIIe siècle." *Bibliothèque de l'Ecole des Chartes* 98 (1937).

Evergates, Theodore. *Feudal Society in the Bailliage of Troyes Under the Counts of Champagne, 1152–1284*. Baltimore, 1975.

———. *Feudal Society in Medieval France. Documents from the County of Champagne*. Philadelphia, 1993.

———. "Louis VII and the Counts of Champagne." In *The Second Crusade and the Cistercians*, ed. Michael Gervers (New York, 1992), 109–17.

Expilly, J. J. de. *Dictionnaire géographique, historique et politique des Gaules et de la France*. 6 vols. Paris, 1768–1770; repr. Liechtenstein, 1978.

Floreffe, 850 ans d'histoire. See Jacquet, below.

Florival, Adrien Maurice Derousen de. *Etude historique sur le XII siècle: Barthélemy de Vir, évêque de Laon*. Paris, 1877.

Folda, Jaroslav. *The Nazareth Capitals and the Crusader Shrine of the Annunciation*. University Park, Pa., and London, 1986.

Fossier, R. *Chartes de coutume en Picardie*. Paris, 1974.

———. "Chatillon-sur-Seine, N.D." DHGE.

———. *La terre et les hommes en Picardie jusqu'à la fin du XIIIe siècle*. 2 vols. Paris and Louvain, 1968; new edition, without maps or bibliography, Amiens, 1987.

Gallia Christiana, ed. Congregation of St. Maur. 16 vols. Paris, 1751; repr., Farnborough, Hants, 1970.

Ganshof, François-L. *La Flandre sous les premiers comtes*. 2nd ed. Brussels, 1944.

Garel, Jean. *Les fondations monastiques et les abbayes du département de l'Aisne. Histoire et architecture*. Paris, 1970.

Geary, Patrick J. *Living with the Dead in the Middle Ages*. Ithaca and London, 1994.

———. *Phantoms of Remembrance. Memory and Oblivion at the End of the First Millennium*. Princeton, 1994.

Genicot, Léopold. *L'économie rurale Namuroise au Bas Moyen Age*. 3 vols. Brussels, 1982.

———. "L'évolution des dons aux abbayes dans le comté de Namur du Xe au XIe siècles." *Annales de la Fédération archéologique et historique de Belgique, 30e congrès* (Brussels, 1936).

Geoffroy de Villdhardouin. See M.R.B. Shaw, below.

Gerits, T. J. "Les actes de confraternité de 1142 et de 1153 entre Cîteaux et Prémontré." *Analecta Praemonstratensia* 40 (1964): 192–205.

Gervers, Michael, ed. *The Second Crusade and the Cistercians*. New York, 1992.

Gheldolf, A.-E. *Histoire administrative et constitutionnelle des villes et chatellenies d'Ypres, Cassel, Bailleul et Warneton jusqu'à l'an 1305*. Paris, 1864; originally published as vol. 5 of L.A. Warnkönig, *Histoire de la Flandre et ses institutions civiles et politiques*. Brussels, 1835–1864.

Giry, A. *Histoire de la ville de Saint-Omer et de ses institutions jusqu'au XIVe s*. Paris, 1877.

———. *Manuel de diplomatique*. Paris, 1894; repr., New York, 1925.

Godet, M. "Amiens." DHGE.

Gosse, M. *Histoire de l'abbaye d'Arrouaise*. Lille, 1786.

Grauwen, W. "Norbert et les débuts de l'abbaye de Floreffe." *Analecta Praemonstratensia* 5 (1975).

Greetham, D. C. *Textual Scholarship. An Introduction*. Rev. ed. New York, 1994.

Grosdidier de Matons, M. *Le comté de Bar des origines au traité de Bruges (vers 950–1301)*. Bar-le-Duc, 1922.

Guibert of Nogent, see Benton, above.

Guyotjeannin, Olivier. *Episcopus et comes. Affirmation et déclin de la seigneurie épiscopale au Nord du royaume de France (Beauvais-Noyon Xe-début XIIIe siècle)*. Société de l'école des chartes, Mémoires et documents, 30. Paris, 1987.

Hamilton, Bernard. "The Impact of Crusader Jerusalem on Western Christendom." *Catholic Historical Review* 80 (1994).

———. *The Latin Church in the Crusader States. The Secular Church*. London, 1980.

———. *Religion in the Medieval West*. Baltimore, Md., 1986.

———. "Women in the Crusader States." *Studies in Church History, Subsidia* 1 (1978).

Head, Thomas, and Richard Landes, eds. *The Peace of God, Social Violence and Religious Response in France around the Year 1000*. Ithaca, N.Y., 1992.

Hehl, E.-D. *Kirche und Krieg im 12. Jahrhundert: Studien zu kanonischem Recht und politischer Wirklichkeit*. Stuttgart, 1980.

Hiestand, Rudolf. "Kardinalbischof Matthäus von Albano, das Konzil von Troyes und die Entstehung des Templerordens." *Zeitschrift für Kirchengeschichte* 99 (1988): 295–325.

———. "Königin Melisendis von Jerusalem und Prémontré. Einige Nachträge zum Thema: Die Prämonstratenser und das Hl. Land." *Analecta Praemonstratensia* 71 (1995): 77–95.

———. "Saint-Ruf d'Avignon, Raymond de Saint-Gilles et l'église latin du Comte de Tripoli." *Annales du Midi* 98 (1986).

Huyghebaert, N. "Furnes." DHGE.

Jacquemin, L. *Annales de la vie de Joscelin de Vierzi, 57e évêque de Soissons (1126–1152)*. Paris, 1905.

Jacquet, Ph. et al. *Floreffe, 850 ans d'histoire. Vie et destin d'une abbaye de prémontrés*. Ed. the Ministère de la Culture française. Floreffe, 1973.

James, B. S. *The Letters of Bernard of Clairvaux*. London, 1953.

Janvier, Auguste. *Boves et ses seigneurs*. Amiens, 1877.

———. "Canton de Boves." *La Picardie historique et monumentale. I: Amiens* (Amiens, 1898–1899).

———. *Petite Histoire de Picardie. Dictionnaire historique et archéologique*. Amiens, 1884.

Johnson, Paul. *A History of the Jews*. New York, 1987.

Joinville and Villehardouin, trans. and ed. Margaret Shaw. *Chronicles of the Crusades*. London, 1963.

Jotischky, Andrew. *The Perfection of Solitude: Hermits and Monks in the Crusader States*. University Park, Pa., 1995.

Kaiser, R. Review: "Laon aux XIIe et XIIIe siècles." *Revue du Nord* 56 (1974).

Kedar, B. Z., et al, eds. *Montjoie: Studies in Crusade History in Honour of Hans Eberhard Mayer*. Aldershot, 1997.

———. *Outremer: Studies in the History of the Crusading Kingdom of Jerusalem*. Jerusalem, 1982.

Keen, Maurice. *Nobles, Knights and Men-at-Arms in the Middle Ages*. London and Rio Grande, Ohio, 1996.

Koziol, Geoffrey G. "Monks, Feuds, and the Making of Peace in Eleventh-Century Flanders." *Historical Reflections* 14 (1987) [revised in Head and Landes, above].

Labrusse, L. de. "Ascendance maternelle et paternelle du 'bienheureux' Barthélemy, évêque de Laon de 1113 à 1150." *Bulletin de la Société historique et académique de Haut-Picardie* 18 (1950–1952).

L'Alouëte, François de. *Traité des nobles et des vertus dont ils sont formés ... avec une histoire ... de la maison de Coucy*. Paris, 1577.

Lambert, Malcolm. *Medieval Heresy: Popular Movements from the Gregorian Reform to the Reformation*. 2nd ed. Oxford, 1992.

La Meyre, Alain. *Guide de la France templière*. Poitiers, 1975.

Lamy, Hugues. "Vie du Bienheureux Hugues de Fosses." Extract from vol. 13 of *La Terre Wallonne*. Charleroi, 1925.
Lawless, George. *Augustine of Hippo and His Monastic Rule*. Oxford, 1987.
Lecomte, M. "Baudouin III." DHGE.
Ledieu, A. "Ache et Acheul." DHGE.
Le Glay, Edward. *Histoire des Comtes de Flandre et des Flamands au moyen âge*. 2 vols. Lille, 1886.
Le Long, Nicholas. *Histoire ecclésiastique et civile du diocèse de Laon et de tout le pays contenu entre l'Oise et la Meuse, l'Aisne et la Sambre*. Châlons, 1783; repr., Brussels, 1980.
Léonard, E.-G. *Introduction au Cartulaire manuscrit du Temple (1150–1317)*. Paris, 1930.
Letts, Malcolm. *Bruges and Its Past*. Bruges, 1926.
Leyser, Henrietta. *Hermits and the New Monasticism*. New York, 1984.
Leyser, Karl. "The Crisis of Medieval Germany." *Proceedings of the British Academy* 69 (1983): 409–43.
———. *Medieval Germany and Its Neighbors, 900–1250*. London, 1982.
Lillich, Meredith. "Gifts of the Lords of Brienne: The Abbey of Basse-Fontaine (Aube) and its Gothic Windows." Paper given at the third annual meeting of the Society for the Study of the Crusades and the Latin East, July, 1991.
Lohrmann, Dietrich. *Kirchengut im nördlichen Frankreich: Besitz, Verfassung und Wirtschaft im Spiegel der Papstprivilegien des 11.–12. Jahrhunderts*. Bonn, 1983.
———. "Répartition et création de nouveaux domaines monastiques au XIIe siècle: Beauvaisis-Soissonnais-Vermandois." In *Villa, curtis, grangia: Landwirtschaft zwischen Loire und Rhein von der Römerzeit zum Hochmittelalter*. Proceedings of the Colloque historique franco-allemand 16, 1980, ed. Lohrmann (Zurich, 1983).
Longnon, Auguste, ed. *Documents relatifs au comté de Champagne et de Brie, 1172–1361*. 3 vols. Paris, 1901–1914.
Louvet, Pierre. *Histoire de la ville et cité de Beauvais*. 2nd ed. Beauvais, 1635.
Luchaire, Achille. *Étude sur les actes de Louis VII*. Paris, 1885.
———. *Louis VI le Gros. Annales de sa Vie et de son Règne (1081–1137)*. Paris, 1890; repr. Brussels, 1964.
———. *Louis VII, Philippe Auguste, Louis VIII (1137–1226)*. Paris, 1902.
Lusse, Jackie. *Laon et le Laonnois: du Ve au Xe siècle: naissance d'une cité*. Nancy, 1992.
Luttrell, Anthony. *The Hospitallers of Rhodes and their Mediterranean World*. Andershot, 1992.
Maison d'Amiens. Généalogie des Princes châtelains d'Amiens. St. Pol-sur-Ternoise, 1934.

Marchegay, P. "Cartulaires français en Angleterre." *Bibliothèque d'École des Chartes* 4th série 16. 1, (1885).
Marlot, Guillaume. *Histoire de la ville ... de Reims*, ed. Jean Lacourt. 4 vols. Reims, 1843–1846.
Martin, G. A. *Essai historique sur Rozoy-sur-Serre*. 2 vols. Laon, 1863–1864.
Martinet, S. *Montloon reflet fidèle de la montagne et des environs de Laon de 1100 à 1300*. Laon, 1972.
Marville, Martin. *Trosly-Loire ... ses châteaux, ses villas, ses fiefs . . . .* Noyon, 1869.
Massiet Du Biest, Jean. *La Carte et le plan considérés come instruments de recherche historique. Études sur les fiefs et censives et sur la condition des tenures urbaines à Amiens (XIe–XVIIe siècle) avec atlas de 10 cartes*. Tours, 1954.
Matton, Auguste. *Dictionnaire topographique du département de l'Aisne*. Paris, 1871.
———. *Histoire de la ville et des environs de Guise*. Laon, 1897–1898.
———. *Inventaire sommaire des Archives départementales antérieures à 1790: Aisne*. 3 vols. Laon, 1878–1899.
———. *Notice historique sur la formation du département de l'Aisne et ses arrondissements*. Laon, 1865.
———. *Notice sur le balliage de Marle*. Laon, 1857.
Mayer, Hans Eberhard. *Bistümer, Klöster und Stifte im Königreich Jerusalem*. Monumenta Germaniae Historica, Schriften 26. Stuttgart, 1977.
———. *The Crusades*. 1st ed., trans. John Gillingham. Oxford, 1972 (2nd ed., 1988).
———. "Die Gründung des Doppelklosters St. Lazarus in Bethanien." In *Bistümer, Klöster und Stifte im Köinigreich Jerusalem*, 372–402.
Melleville, Maximilien. *Dictionnaire historique, généalogique, biographique et agricole du département de l'Aisne*. 2 vols. Laon, 1857.
———. *Histoire de Coucy le Château*. Laon, 1848.
———. *Histoire de la ville de Chauny*. Laon, 1851.
———. *Notice historique et généalogique sur les châtelains de Coucy*. Laon, n.d.
———. *Notice historique sur l'ancien diocèse de Laon et les évêques de cette ville*. Paris, 1844.
———. *Notice historique sur Quierzy*. Paris, no date.
Melville, Marion. "Les débuts de l'Ordre du Temple." In *Die Geistlichen Ritterorden Europas*, ed. Josef Fleckenstein and Manfred Hellmann (Sigmaringen, 1980).
Milis, L. *L'ordre des chanoines réguliers d'Arrouaise*. 2 vols. Bruges, 1969.
Moeller, C. "Les Flamands du Ternois au Royaume latin de Jérusalem." In *Melanges Paul Fredericq* (Brussels, 1904).
Molinier, A. *Catalogue générale des manuscrits des Bibliothèques publiques de France, III: Soissons*. Paris, 1885.

Monasticon belge. Centre national de recherches d'histoire religieuse. Liège, 1890-. Vol. 3: *Province de Flandre Occidentale*, ed. N. Huyghebaert, L. Dahieux, P. Favorel et al. Liège, 1960-1966.

Morard, N. "L'abbaye d'Humilimont et les comtes de Champagne." *Zeitschrift für schweizerische Kirchengeschichte* 82 (1988).

Moreau, É. de. "Belgique." DHGE.

——. *Histoire de l'église en Belgique*. 2nd ed. 5 vols. Brussels, 1945.

Morris, Colin. *The Papal Monarchy: The Western Church from 1050 to 1250*. Oxford and New York, 1989.

——. "Propaganda for War. The Dissemination of the Crusading Ideal in the Twelfth Century." In *Studies in Church History* 20 (1983): 79-101.

Morris, Rosemary. *Monks and Laymen in Byzantium, 843-1118*. Cambridge and New York, 1995.

Murray, A. V. "The Origins of the Frankish Nobility of the Kingdom of Jerusalem, 1100-1118." *Mediterranean Historical Review* 4 (1989): 281-300.

——. "Questions of Nationality in the First Crusade." *Medieval History* 1 (1991).

Newman, William Mendel. *Le domaine royal sous les premiers Capétiens (987-1180)*. Paris, 1937.

——. *Le personnel de la cathédrale d'Amiens (1066-1306). Avec une note sur la famille des seigneurs de Heilly*. Paris, 1972.

Nicholas, David. *Medieval Flanders*. New York and London, 1992.

Noble, Thomas F.X. "Morbidity and Vitality in the History of the Early Medieval Papacy." *Catholic Historical Review* 81 (1995).

Pacaut, Marcel. *Louis VII et les élections épiscopales dans le Royaume de France*. Paris, 1957.

Parisse, Michel, ed. *A propos des actes d'évêques: Hommage à Lucie Fossier*. Nancy, 1991.

Pennington, K. "The Rite for Taking the Cross in the Twelfth Century." *Traditio* 30 (1974): 429-35.

Perrichet, Lucien. *La grande chancellerie de France, des origines à 1328*. Paris, 1912.

Peters, Edward, ed. *The First Crusade*. 2nd. ed. Philadelphia, 1998.

Petit, François. "Milon de Sélincourt, évêque de Thérouanne." *Analecta Praemonstratensia* 48 (1972): 73-93.

——. *Norbert et l'origin des Prémontrés*. Paris, 1981.

——. *La Spiritualité des Prémontrés aux XIIe et XIIIe siècles*. Paris, 1947.

——. "L'Ordre de Prémontré de Saint Norbert à Anselme de Havelberg." See *La vita comune*, below.

Phillips, Jonathan. *Defenders of the Holy Land: Relations between the Latin East and the West 1119-1187*. Oxford, 1996.

——. "St. Bernard of Clairvaux, the Low Countries and the Lisbon Letter

of the Second Crusade." *Journal of Ecclesiastical History* 48 (1997): 485–97.

Picquigny, le château-fort, la collegiale, la ville. Société des antiquaires de Picquigny, Amiens, 1987.

Pirenne, Henri. *Histoire de Belgique.* 6 vols. 5th ed. Brussels, 1929.

Pierrard, Pierre, ed. *Les diocèses de Cambrai et de Lille.* (*Histoire des diocèses de France,* vol. 8.) Paris, 1978.

Plouvier, Martine. "Les soeurs de l'abbaye de Prémontré." In *Actes officiels du 17e colloque du* CERP (Amiens, 1991).

Poncelet, Edouard. "Trazegnies." *Biographie Nationale de Belgique.* Brussels, 1868– .

Porges, W. "The Clergy, the Poor, and the Non-Combatants on the First Crusade." *Speculum* 21 (1946): 1–23.

Powell, James M. *Anatomy of a Crusade, 1213–1221.* Philadelphia, 1986.

———., ed. *Innocent III: Vicar of Christ or Lord of the World?* 2nd ed. Washington, 1994.

———. *Medieval Studies: An Introduction.* 2nd ed. Syracuse, 1992.

Prawer, Joshua. *The History of Jerusalem. The Crusader and Ajubid Periods (1099–1291).* Jerusalem, 1991.

Prestwich, Michael. *Armies and Warfare in the Middle Ages. The English Experience.* New Haven, 1996.

Queller, Donald E. *The Fourth Crusade: The Conquest of Constantinople 1201–1204.* 2nd ed. Philadelphia, 1997.

Radiquès, H. de. "Les seigneuries et terres féodales du comté de Namur." *Annales de la Société archéologique de Namur* 22 (1895).

Raedts, Peter. "St. Bernard of Clairvaux and Jerusalem." *Studies in Church History, Subsidia* 10 (1994): 169–82.

Remensnyder, Amy G. *Remembering Kings Past: Monastic Foundation Legends in Medieval Southern France.* London and Ithaca, N.Y., 1995.

Reuter, Timothy, ed. *Warriors and Churchmen in the High Middle Ages: Essays Presented to Karl Leyser.* London, 1992.

Richard, Jean. "Départs de pèlerins et de croisés bourguignons au XIe s. A propos d'une charte de Cluny." *Annales de Bourgogne* 60 (1988).

Riley-Smith, Jonathan Simon. *The Crusades. A Short History.* New Haven and London, 1987.

———. "Family Traditions and Participation in the Second Crusade," in *The Second Crusade and the Cistercians,* ed. Michael Gervers (New York, 1992), 101–8.

———. "The First Crusade and the Persecution of the Jews." In *Studies in Church History* 21 (1984): 51–72.

———. *The First Crusaders, 1095–1131.* Cambridge, 1997.

———, ed. *The Oxford Illustrated History of the Crusades.* Oxford and New York, 1995.

———, and Louise Riley Smith. *The Crusades, Idea and Reality, 1095–1274*. London, 1981.
Robinson, I. S. *The Papacy, 1073–1198. Continuity and Innovation*. Cambridge, 1990.
Roland, C. G. "Histoire généalogique de la maison de Rumigny-Florennes." *Annales de la Société archéologique de Namur* 19 (1891–1892).
Rondeau, A. *Chansons attribuées au chastelain de Coucy*. Paris, 1964.
Roux, Joseph. *Histoire de l'abbaye de Saint-Acheul-lez-Amiens, étude de son temporel au point de vue économique*. Amiens, 1890.
Russo, F. "Pénitence et excommuication. Etude historique sur les rapports entre la théologie et droit canonique dans le domaine pénitentiel du IXe au XIIIe siècle." *Recherches de science religieuse* 33 (1946).
Ryan, Christopher, ed. *The Religious Roles of the Papacy: Ideals and Realities, 1150–1300*. Toronto, 1989.
Sabatier, A. "L'abbaye de Marcheroux de l'ordre de Prémontré et de la filiation de St.-Josse-au-Bois ou de Dommartin." *Mémoires de la Société académique d'archéologie, sciences et arts du département de l'Oise* 6 (1865–1867): 614–23.
Sabbe, E. "La réforme clunisienne dans le comté de Flandre au début du XIIe s." *Revue Belge de philologie et d'histoire* 9 (1930).
Saint-Denis, Alain. "Les Débuts du Temporel de Saint-Martin-de-Laon, 1124–1155." In *Actes officiels du 14ème colloque du CERP* (Amiens, 1989).
Salch, Charles-Laurent, ed. *L'Atlas des châteaux forts en France*. Strasbourg, 1977.
Sanders, Antonio. *Flandria Illustrata*. 2 vols. Cologne, 1641–1644.
Sassier, Yves. *Louis VII*. Paris, 1991.
Sayers, Jane. *Innocent III: Leader of Europe, 1198–1216*. London and New York, 1994.
Schneider, Reinhard. *Vom Klosterhaushalt zum Stadt- und Staatshaushalt: Der Zisterziensische Beitrag*. Stuttgart, 1994.
Schein, Sylvia. "Between Mount Moriah and the Holy Sepulchre: The Changing Traditions of the Temple Mount in the Central Middle Ages." *Traditio* 40 (1984): 181–86.
———. *Fideles Crucis. The Papacy, the West, and the Recovery of the Holy Land 1274–1314*. Oxford, 1991.
Setton, Kenneth, gen. ed. *A History of the Crusades*. 2nd ed. 6 vols. Madison, Wis., 1969–1989.
Shaw, M.R.B., trans., ed., Geoffroy de Villehardouin. *The Conquest of Constantinople*. London and New York, 1963.
Slack, Corliss Konwiser. "The Premonstratensians in the Crusader Kingdoms in the Twelfth and Thirteenth Centuries." *Analecta Praemonstratensia* 67/68 (1991/1992).

——. "Royal Familiares in the Latin Kingdom of Jerusalem, 1100–1187." *Viator* 22 (1991): 15–67.

Souchon, Cécile. "Le temporel des abbayes prémontrées dans les diocèses de Laon et Soissons." In *Actes officiels du 14ème colloque du* CERP (Amiens, 1989).

Southern, R. W. *Western Society and the Church in the Middle Ages*. Baltimore, 1970.

Strayer, Joseph R. *The Albigensian Crusades*. Ann Arbor, Mich., 1992.

——, ed. *Dictionary of the Middle Ages*. 13 vols. New York, 1982–1989.

Studies in Church History. The Ecclesiastical History Society, Oxford, in two series: 1– , (1964); and *Subsidia*, 1– , (1978–).

Suger. *The Deeds of Louis the Fat*, transl., ed., notes, by Richard C. Cusimano and John Moorhead. Washington, D.C., 1992.

Taiée, Charles. *Prémontré. Étude sur l'abbaye de ce nom, sur l'ordre qui y a pris naissance, ses progrès, ses épreuves et sa décadence*. 2 vols. Laon, 1872–1873.

Tardif, J. "Le procès d'Enguerran de Coucy." *Bibliothèque de l'École des Chartes* 79 (1918).

Tellenbach, Gerd. *The Church in Western Europe From the Tenth to the Early Twelfth Century.*, trans. Timothy Reuter. Cambridge, 1993.

Tierney, Brian, and Sidney Painter. *Western Europe in the Middle Ages, 300–1475*. 5th ed. New York, 1992.

Tock, B. M. *Les chartes des Évêques d'Arras (1093–1203)*. (Collection des Documents inédits sur l'Histoire de France. Section d'Histoire médiévale et de Philologie, 20). Paris, 1991.

——. "Les élections épiscopales à Arras de Lambert à Pierre 1er (1093–1203)." *Revue belge de philologie et d'histoire* 65 (1987): 709–21.

Toffin, René. *L'Église Notre-Dame de Coucy*. Marle, 1963.

Toussaint, Françoise. *L'abbaye de Floreffe, de l'ordre des Prémontré, histoire et description*. 3rd ed. Namur, 1879.

Tuchman, Barbara. *A Distant Mirror. The Calamitous 14th Century*. New York, 1978.

Tyerman, C. J. "Were There Any Crusades in the Twelfth Century?" *English Historical Review* 110 (1995): 553–77.

Van Dijck, L. C. "Herlaimont." DHGE.

Vauchez, André. *The Laity in the Middle Ages. Religious Beliefs and Devotional Practices*, trans. Margery J. Schneider. Notre Dame, 1993.

——. *La Spiritualité du Moyen Age occidental, VIIIe–XIIe siècles*. Paris, 1975.

Vernier, Arthur. *Histoire du canton de Coucy-le-Château*. Paris, 1876.

Versteylen, A. "Basse-Fontaine"; "Beaumont-les-Nonains." DHGE.

Vicaire, M.-H. *L'imitation des apôtres: moines, chanoines et mendiants IVe–XIIIe siècles*. Paris, 1963.

Vion, Michel. *Pierre l'Hermite et les croisades*. Amiens, 1853.

Vodola, Elisabeth. *Excommunication in the Middle Ages*. Berkeley, 1986.

Waghenaere, Pierre de. *Sancti Norberti ... vita lyrica* .... Douai, 1639.
Wakefield, Walter L. *Heresy, Crusade and Inquisition in Southern France 1100-1250.* London, 1974.
Warlop, Ernest. *The Flemish Nobility before 1300.* Trans. J. B. Ross and H. Vandermoere. 4 vols. Kortrijk, 1975-1976.
Warnkönig, Leopold August. *Histoire de Flandre.* Ed., trans., continued by A. E. Gheldorf. 5 vols. Brussels, 1835-1846.
Wauters, A., ed. *Table chronologique des chartes et diplômes imprimés concernant l'histoire de la Belgique.* 11 vols. Brussels, 1866-1912.
Werner, K. F. "La rôle de l'aristocratie dans la christianisation du Nord de la France." *Revue d'histoire de l'Eglise de France* 62 (1975).
Werveke, Hans van. "La contribution de la Flandre et du Hainaut à la troisième croisade." *Le Moyen Age* 78 (1972): 55-90.
White, Stephen D. *Custom, Kinship, and Gifts to Saints: The "Laudatio parentum" in Western France, 1050-1150.* Chapel Hill and London, 1988.
Wolff, R. L. "Baldwin of Flanders and Hainaut, First Latin Emperor of Constantinople: His Life, Death, and Resurrection 1172-1225." *Speculum* 27 (1952): 281-322.
Wyss, Alfred, and Daniel de Raemy. *L'ancienne abbaye de Belley, Moutier.* Intervalles, 1992.

INDEX

(Numerals refer to page and note numbers.)

Arnulf III (1170–1207), advocate of Thérouanne, 7, 126–31
Augustinian (or "regular") canons, xvi, xviii, xix
    at Amiens, 84–87
    at Arrouaise, 74–75, 130, 140–42, 148–51
    at St. Acheul, 26, 27
    at St.-Jean, Amiens, 38
    at St.-Marie, Voormezele, 52
    at St. Martin, Épernay, 81n. 2
    at St. Martin, Ypres, 48–52
    at Thérouanne, 130
    Augustinian reform movement, xx–xxi, 83
    Augustinian rule, xvii
    in the Holy Land, 63
    See also the Templars as an Augustinian order, xxv
Barthélemy de Joux, bishop of Laon (1113–1151), xix–xxiv, xxv, 62, 71, 112
    and Floreffe, 94–95
    and the Guise family, 46
    and Radulf Canis, 12–16
    bishopric ravaged by local lords, 8
    issues charters for the Coucys, 2, 3, 4, 5
    related to Vermandois, 6
Benedictine monks, rule of St. Benedict of Nursia, xvi–xvii
    at St. Vincent, Laon, 8n. 8

    See also Nogent.
Bernard, St., abbot of Clairvaux (1116–1153) O. Cist., preacher of the Second Crusade, xx, xxi, 18, 19, 20, 23, 51, 57, 75n. 7, 81–82
    and the Holy Cross, 97
    patron of Prémontré, 112–14
Brabant, dukes of, 97, 134
Enguerran II (Coucy 1130–1147), xxiv–xxvi, 2–11, 32, 66–71, 120
    and Chavigny, 154
    and Radulf Canis, 12–14
    buried at Nazareth, 60–64
    on the Second Crusade, 20
Enguerran III (Coucy 1197–1242), xxviii, 186, 188–92
    and Chauny, 148–51
    and Chavigny, 152–55
    and the Albigensian Crusade, 156–62
    baptized at Prémontré, 14
Enguerran de Boves, 31n. 4, cf. 7
Flanders, chancellor of (Gerard), 122–25
    counts of, xxix, xxx, 86, 162–66
    Arnulf I (918–965), 124
    Baldwin IV (988–1035), 20
    Robert I, the Frisian (1071–1093), 20, 124
    Robert II (1093–1111), 20, 124, 140–42
    Thierry of Alsace (1128–1167), 18–

23, 48–52, 76, 82, 124, 142
Philip of Alsace (1167–1191), 20, 32, 48–52, 104–5, 125, 142
  and Chauny, 148–51
  and Furne, 182–3
Baldwin IX (1195–1206), first Latin Emperor of Constantinople, xxviii, xxix, 134, 136–39, 146
See also Premonstratensians, at Floreffe, at Furnes.
Furnes (Veurne), city and Premonstratensian abbey, 51, 122–25, 178–83
Gerard l'Oreille, Coucy vassal, 2, 3, 4, 7, 10
Guyencourt, Hugh, Odo (crusaders), 27, 30; Peter, 28–29
Hainaut, xxviii, xxx, 21, 51, 76n. 8, 134–39, 147, 150
  and Floreffe, 176
    Baldwin V, count of (1150–1195), 88–98
Holy Cross (relic and festival of the), 96–97, 124, 144–(46)47, 175–76
See also Premonstratensians, at Floreffe.
I/Yves de Nesle, count of Soissons (1171–1178), 7, 72–76
Jean de Warneton, bishop of Thérouanne (1099–1130), xxxn. 40, 20, 51, 130, 182
Laon, cathedral city, xix, 121, 165–66
  and the Holy Cross, xxvi
    bishop of, 78–80, 184–86. See also Barthélemy de Joux.
    canons of Nazareth hold a hospital at Chambry, 63
    crusade memorials in, xxvi
    dispute over tolls, 8, 9n. 10
    Templar chapel in, xxv, 60–64
    Thenailles, 136–39
    Verneuil, 192
    visited by Pope Innocent II, 6
See also Prémontré.

Louis VII, king of France (1137–1180), xxv, xxvi, 7, 8n. 8, 36, 37, 38, 60–62, 70, 81
  and Robert I (Boves), 31
  charter issued by, 54–59
  Second Crusade, 18–23, 75
Melisende of Crécy, founder of Rozières, third wife of Thomas de Marle, xxiii–xxiv, 2, 3, 4, 6, 7, 62, 70, 154
  mother of Enguerran II (Coucy) and Robert I (Boves), 27–30, 40n. 6
Milo, bishop of Thérouanne (1131–1158), xxxn. 40, 18, 19, 20, 22, 23, 48–52, 75n. 7, 124
Namur, xxviii, 21, 104, 147
  and Morialmé, 174–77
  and Thimèon, Trazegnies, 175n. 2
  Erme(n)sende, countess of, 95
  Henry II, count of (1139–1194), 88–98, 101–5
  Philip, count of, 97, 146
See also Premonstratensians, at Floreffe.
Nazareth (Palestine), Augustinian canons at, xxvi, 60–65
  hospital at Chambry, Laon, 63
Nogent, St.-Marie de, Benedictine abbey, xviii, xxiii, xxiv, 7n. 4, 66–68
Norbert of Xanten, St., founder of Prémontré, ix, xx–xxiii, xxv, 58, 71
  and Floreffe, 94
  and Radulf Canis, 12–16
See also Prémontré.
Philip II Augustus, king of France (1180–1223), xxviii, 32, 82, 121, 134
  and Flanders, 138–39, 148–51, 156–61
  at war with England, 142
Picardy, region of northern France, xix, 63, 80, 142
Picquigny, lordship and family, 33n. *, 63
  Gerard of, 39nn. 4, 5
  patrons of St.-Jean, Amiens, 38, 38n. 3

INDEX

"Pigneium," 111
Prémontré, Premonstratensians (Norbertines, see also Norbert of Xanten), order of canons regular, ix, x, xviii, xviiin. 15, 2, 3, 4, 7, 31
   and Burchard de Guise, 42–47
   and Henri de Troyes, 78–83
   and Radulf Canis, 12–16
   Coucy, founders, xix, xxiv–xxvii, 66–71, 116–21, 192
   Gervase, abbot of, 156–66, 176, 184–86
   Holy Land, property in, xxvii, 95, 176
   Laon, Premonstratensian bishop of, xxv–xxvi
   wine production, 9
   women:
      Chaumont, 138
      Furnes, 183
      Herlaimont/Verofle, 171, 196–97
   See also Rozières.
Premonstratensian houses at
   Basse-Fontaine, 106–7
   Braine, 130
   Chavigny, 152–55
   Floreffe, 88–105, 144–47, 168–77, 194–98
   Furnes (Veurne), 51, 122–25, 178–83
   Leffe, 198
   Marcheroux, 54–59
   Monceau, 184–86
   Mureau, 132–35
   Septfontaines, 134
   St.-Jean of Amiens, 38

Thenailles, 136–39, 150n. 2, 163n. 1, 166
Verneuil (Leuilly, Tinselve), 188–92
Radulf Canis, 12–16, 40n. 6, 66–71
   See Eustace Canis, 60–64
Raoul I (Coucy 1147–1190), xxvi–xxvii, 182
   charters issued by, 60–71, 116–121
Robert I (Boves), xxiv, 2, 3, 4, 5
   count of Amiens, 24–33, 86
   uncle of Alelmus de Flichecourt, 37–40
Rozières, Premonstratensian house for women, hospital (Fontenille, Bonneuil), xxiii, xxvii, 7, 7n.7, 40n. 6, 66–68
   See also Melisende of Crécy.
Templars, military order under the Augustinian rule, xxv, 125
   at Laon, xxvi, 60–64, 80–81, 116–21
Temple (of Solomon, of the Lord, Templum Domini), Jerusalem, xxi
   priory of canons at, 74, 130
   See also Augustinians at Arrouaise.
Thierry, bishop of Amiens (1145–1169),
   and Boves, 24–33
   and Flichecourt, 36–40
Thomas de Marle (Coucy), crusader and possible founder of Prémontré, xviii–xxiv, 2, 3, 8, 62, 66–71
   and Boves, 24–31
   deseizes Gautier de la Tournelle and Radulf Canis, 14
Veurne. See Furnes.
Yves. See Ives.

The *Crusade Charters*, a collection of thirty-one charters from northern France, records gifts to Premonstratensian abbeys founded throughout Europe between 1121 and 1150. The donors are predominantly lower nobility whose families accumulated wealth and prestige during the twelfth century due to the crusades. The theme of the book is imminent departure on crusade, and its primary importance lies in offering material evidence of the lay response to preaching and promotion of the crusades by the Premonstratensians. About a third of these charters are edited from manuscript, and the rest are from various printed, but inaccessible sources.

Corliss Konwiser Slack is associate professor of history at Whitworth College, Washington.